THE MARKET AND THE STATE

The Market and the State

Studies in Interdependence

Edited by

Michael Moran
Professor of Government
University of Manchester

and

Maurice Wright
Professor of Government
University of Manchester

St. Martin's Press   New York

First published in the United States of America in 1991

Printed in Great Britain

ISBN 0–312–06802–6

Library of Congress Cataloging-in-Publication Data
The Market and the State : studies in interdependence / edited by
Michael Moran and Maurice Wright.
p. cm.
Includes index.
ISBN 0–312–06802–6
1. Free enterprise—Congresses.   2. Trade regulation—Congresses.
3. Commercial policy—Congresses.   4. Economic policy—Congresses.
I. Moran, Michael.   II. Wright, Maurice, 1933–   .
HB95.M35   1991
330.12'2—dc20   91–24192
                                                                        CIP

Contents

List of Tables

Preface

The contributors to this volume are all members of the Department of Government at the University of Manchester. There is a simple explanation for this exclusiveness. In October 1949 the Department achieved a separate existence under its first Professor of Government, W. J. M. Mackenzie. The celebration of the fortieth anniversary of that event provided the occasion for a series of seminars. Our theme was chosen partly to reflect the diversity of interests represented in the Department. We wished also to acknowledge its historical and evolutionary association with issues of political economy: the Department of Government (and Administration) evolved from the Department of Political Economy created three years after the founding of the original Owens College in 1851.

No records exist of the papers given at the first Government Department seminars in 1949–50. It is safe to assume that some of them addressed the relations between the state and the market. They could scarcely have avoided doing so: while revolutions in Eastern Europe and East Asia were creating new states dedicated to the suppression of market forces, West Germany and Japan were taking the first steps in the design of new models of liberal democratic economy. At home a Labour government was laying the foundations of a mixed economy, and across the channel Marshall Aid had helped launch the French upon the road to the *économie concertée*. Forty years later the agenda of issues discussed in our papers is an almost perfect mirror-image of those which confronted Mackenzie and his colleagues.

The papers collected here were first given in 1989–90, and revised in the light of the critical but constructive working-over they received at the hands of our colleagues. The concluding chapter alone escaped such bruising. We therefore absolve both the contributors and our colleagues from a direct responsibility for the argument we present there. We are grateful to them all for their encouragement and support throughout the seminar-series, and to our contributors for their help in the preparation of this book.

Michael Moran
Maurice Wright
October, 1990

Notes on the Contributors

Paul Cammack is Senior Lecturer in Government at the University of Manchester. He is the joint author of *Third World Politics: A Comparative Introduction* (1988) and of numerous articles in Latin American politics and comparative political theory.

Michael Evans is Senior Lecturer in Government at the University of Manchester, author of *Karl Marx* (1975) and of articles on Marx and on political economy in the nineteenth century. He is steadily inching towards an intellectual biography of Marx.

Norman Geras is Reader in Government at the University of Manchester. He is the author of *The Legacy of Rosa Luxemburg* (1976); *Marx and Human Nature* (1983); *Literature of Revolution* (1986); *Discourses of Extremity* (1990). He is on the editorial committee of *New Left Review*.

Peter Humphreys is Lecturer in Government and a Fellow of the European Institute of the Media at the University of Manchester. He has published a number of books and articles in the field of telecommunications and media policy, most recently, *Media and Media Policy in Western Germany* (1990) and (with K. Dyson) *Broadcasting and New Media Policies in Western Europe* (1988).

Peter Mair was a member of the Department of Government in Manchester until 1990. He is now a member of the Department of Political Science in the University of Leiden in the Netherlands. He is author or co-author of *The Changing Irish Party System* (1987), *Identity Competition and Electoral Availability* (1990), and *Representative Government in Western Europe* (1991). He has edited or co-edited a number of books including *Western European Party Systems* (1983), *Party Politics in Contemporary Europe* (1984), *How Ireland Voted* (1987), *Understanding Party System Change in Western Europe* (1990), and *The West European Party System* (1990).

Michael Moran is Professor of Government at the University of Manchester. His publications include *Politics and Society in Britain* (1989) and *The Politics of the Financial Services Revolution* (1990).

George Moyser, formerly in the Department of Government at the University of Manchester, is now Professor of Political Science at the University of Vermont. He has written extensively on religion and politics and on political participation. His publications include *Church and Politics in a Secular Age* (1988), *Church and Politics Today* (1985), *Local Politics and Participation in France and Britain* (1989), and *Political Participation in Britain* (in press).

Geraint Parry is W. J. M. Mackenzie Professor of Government at the University of Manchester. His major interests are in the history of political thought, and democratic theory and practice. He is author of *Political Elites* (1969) of *John Locke* (1978) and, jointly, of *Local Politics and Participation in France and Britain* (1989). He is also joint author of *Political Participation in Britain* (in press).

Martin Rhodes is Lecturer in Government at the University of Manchester. He has published numerous articles on the regulation of labour markets, on Italian politics and on the political economy of steel. He is completing a monograph on *Steel and the State in France*.

Hillel Steiner is Senior Lecturer in Government at the University of Manchester. He has published articles on rights, liberty and moral reasoning in various collections and journals of philosophy and politics. A member of the editorial boards of *Ethics* and *Social Philosophy and Policy*, he is author of the forthcoming books *An Essay on Rights*, *Socialism and the Market* (with Ian Steedman) and *Utilitarianism*.

Ursula Vogel is Lecturer in Government at the University of Manchester. Her publications include *Konservativ Kritik an der bürgerlichen Revolution* (1972) and *Feminism and Political Theory* (1986). She is currently writing a book on the patriarchal foundations of modern civil law.

Michael Waller is Senior Lecturer in Government at the University of Manchester. He read Greats at Oxford before taking up his studies of the communist movement through an analysis of its rhetoric (in *The Language of Communism*, 1972), and of its organisational principles (in *Democratic Centralism: An Historical Commentary*, 1981). Work on the crisis in Western European communism led to his editing (with Meindert Fennema) *Communist Parties in Western*

Europe (1988) and (with Stephane Courtois and Marc Lazar) *Communist Parties and Trade Unions in Europe East and West* (1991).

Roger Williams is Professor of Government and Science Policy at the University of Manchester. He trained in physics and operational research before becoming a political scientist. He is a specialist adviser to the House of Lords Select Committee on Science and Technology. His publications include *The Nuclear Power Decisions* (1980) and *Public Acceptability of New Technologies* (1986).

Maurice Wright is Professor of Government at the University of Manchester. His most recent books are *Comparative Government-Industry Relations* (with Stephen Wilks, 1987), and *The Promotion and Regulation of Japanese Industrial Policy* (with Stephen Wilks, 1990).

Ralph Young is Lecturer in Government at the University of Manchester. His chief research interests lie in the field of political development, notably the study of African politics.

Introduction: Markets Against the State?

Michael Moran and Maurice Wright

The most famous modern attempt to suppress the market in favour of command by the state happened under Soviet Communism: it was, to use Williams' words in this volume, 'the world's greatest social science experiment' (p. 188). One of the first efforts to understand this extraordinary and tragic episode was Sidney and Beatrice Webb's study of the early years of the Soviet experience, first published in 1935. When the Webbs revised their work they made one notorious change: their first edition had been called *Soviet Communism: a new civilization?*; in the second edition the question mark was omitted.[1]

The preparation of this volume underwent a change of similar magnitude, though in a different direction. The original working title of the collection was called, baldly, *Markets Against the State*. As the seminar series on which these essays are based progressed, we were forced to adopt a more complex position on the relationship between market and state – a position reflected both in the neutrality of the volume's final title and in the question mark placed, Webb-fashion, against our introduction. The reasons for this shift in position have to do with some of the important themes that emerged during the seminars – themes that, consequently, are repeated in this book.

The notion that 'the market' and 'the state' are two diametrically opposed systems of social organisation is embedded in both the rhetoric of political actors and in the thinking of scholars. In recent years, for instance, the language of both Thatcherism in Britain and of Reaganism in the United States has suggested that there is a stark choice to be made in political life between reliance on the state and resort to the market – and that the choice should favour the latter. Indeed, the notion that such an alternative exists has deep historical roots. As Gilpin has remarked, since the sixteenth century nation state and market have been the two key organising principles of social life – 'two opposed forms of social organization', to use his words.[2] And as Evans shows in his opening contribution to this volume, modern arguments that oppose the market and state are echoes of disputes from the dawn of political economy.

Scholarship in political science is, perhaps more than in any other discipline, sensitive to the wider social setting in which it is carried on. The agenda of political science is substantially influenced by the course of political events; and the course of political events during the time when these essays were prepared might almost have been deliberately designed to reinforce the notion that political life is a kind of Manichaean struggle between state and market. The papers here revised were originally given in Manchester in the autumn and winter of 1989–90. The duration of the seminar series thus coincided with the most extraordinary events witnessed in Europe since the end of the Second World War: the collapse of Soviet power; the disintegration of the regimes underwritten by that power; the full revelation of the depths of degradation to which those regimes had dragged their unfortunate citizens; and the revulsion against state control over economic life that swept through large parts of those impoverished populations. For a brief moment 'state' and 'market' seemed to confront each other – and the state, at least insofar as it embodied command economics, was apparently swept to one side.

The events of 1989–90 looked like the most dramatic sign of tendencies already well established in the Anglo-Saxon democracies. These tendencies included the growing influence of pro-market theories among economists and among other social scientists; the rise of political coalitions advocating the displacement of the state by the market; and a series of institutional reforms, ranging from privatisation of whole industries to the piecemeal relaxation of regulatory controls, designed to put into practice the newly prestigious pro-market theories.

It is undeniable that momentous changes have taken place in the economic organisation of many nations; and equally undeniable that these changes have often given a newly important role to private property and to the mechanism of the price system. The changes are well represented in the range of contributions collected here: both Steiner and Geras, though arguing from different positions, testify to the renewed vitality of theoretical advocacy of markets as systems of allocation; Vogel and Evans to the reborn interest in the historical roots of the newly influential theories; Rhodes, Humphreys and Williams to their effect on key economic sectors; Waller, Cammack and Young to their impact well beyond Anglo-Saxon political arenas;

Mair, and Parry and Moyser, to how far the language of the market has penetrated established discourses about political competition and political participation.

The language used by politicians (and not a few academics) to explain and exploit these changes employs a false antithesis in the relationship between the state and the market. They are not opposed. The divorce of the market from the state is as demonstrably absurd as the now discredited concept of states without markets. Political scientists must bear some of the responsibility. While they have long struggled to clarify the meaning and use of the word 'state', they have given less attention to what is meant by 'the market'. During the Manchester seminars it became apparent that it could be used legitimately in a wide variety of different senses. Four of them are employed at different points in the chapters which follow. First, market can be used as a metaphor for competition, in either the economic or the political sphere. Thus Mair's chapter is primarily about the market for votes and about the changing extent to which that market is regulated. Secondly, market can be defined as a distinctive mechanism of social choice and expression. This meaning is best exemplified in Parry and Moyser's chapter, where the market as a machinery for signalling preferences – through the exercise of choice in economic exchange – is explored against the mechanism of 'voice', which citizens can employ through participation in the political arena. In political rhetoric and ideological confrontation the mechanism of market is often identified with individual choice and with liberty, against mechanisms of collective provision which are associated with constraints on freedom.

Thirdly, market can be used as a synonym for capitalism – in other words for economic systems, embodying varying degrees of free competition, whose main features are private ownership of productive property underwritten by state power, and the exchange of goods and services through contracts similarly guaranteed by law. Most of what Cammack, for instance, talks about in his chapter construes the market in this sense. Finally, it can also be used as a synonym for minimally regulated economic exchanges. In this conception, well illustrated in Humphreys' chapter, 'deregulation' is identified with the extension of the market's domain, and reregulation with its restriction.

The most elementary ground for denying that there is straightforward opposition between market and state is now clear: 'market' offers a series of very different images of a range of social processes which, inevitably, stand in complex and varying relationships with state structures and political processes. But the Manchester seminars soon made clear that there were other, more substantive, grounds for denial. Three emerge with particular clarity in the following chapters: the most important actors in the markets of advanced capitalism, the large firms, turn out to be political institutions just as certainly as the state is a political institution; states themselves, far from standing in opposition to these giant firms, are commonly joined to them in complex networks of policy making; and the state is a vital institution in managing, legitimating and enforcing the results of competition in markets.

But this is to anticipate the substance of our separate contributions. We return to these matters in the proper place – the conclusion to this volume.

NOTES

1. Sidney and Beatrice Webb, *Soviet Communism: A New Civilisation?* (London: Longmans Green, 1935, 2 vols); Webb and Webb, *Soviet Communism: A New Civilisation* (London: Victor Gollancz, 2nd ed., 1937).
2. Robert Gilpin, *The Political Economy of International Relations* (Princeton: Princeton University Press, 1987) p. 4.

1 The Classical Economists, Laissez-Faire and the State

Michael Evans

INTRODUCTION

The period of classical political economy has often been seen as an age dominated by the principles and policies of *laissez-faire*, where the role of the state is limited to little more than 'the protection of person and property against force and fraud' both internally and externally.[1] Carlyle inveighed against 'that self-cancelling Dono-thingism and *Laissez-faire*' which he contrived to associate with political economy and identify as the source of all the miseries of the poor.[2] Dicey named the years 1825–75 as 'the period of Benthamism or Individualism'. In more recent historiography another view has been taken. For Brebner, Bentham and J. S. Mill are 'the formulator of state intervention for collectivist ends and his devout disciple'.[3] The two are seen as having a decisive influence on the undeniable rise in the level of state activity throughout the nineteenth century, despite the prevalence of anti-paternalist sentiments, the fear of state power, and (more importantly) the fear of new corruption and jobbery with each new creation of administrative machinery. Roberts has argued that between 1833 and 1854, albeit in a cumulative and unplanned fashion, 'a centralised, paternalistic state' had been created.[4] Watson writes of 'the myth of *laissez-faire*' so far as the history of the Victorian period is concerned.[5]

In fact, a *laissez-faire* ideology existed in Britain throughout most of the nineteenth century, finding expression through the great quarterlies, in weeklies like *The Economist*, in accounts of political economy by popularisers like Harriet Martineau, and in the work of social theorists like Herbert Spencer. In 1830 Macaulay urged that statesmen should confine themselves

1

to their own legitimate duties, by leaving capital to find its most lucrative course, commodities their fair price, industry and intelligence their natural reward, idleness and folly their natural punishment, by maintaining peace, by defending property, by diminishing the price of law, and by observing strict economy in every department of the state.[6]

Scott Gordon has shown how Martineau's *Illustrations of Political Economy* (1832–4) in fact showed 'the perfection of the competitive system; the harmony of interests . . . the illegitimate and perverse consequences of governmental interference'; and how in *The Economist* of James Wilson there was developed a *laissez-faire* ideology which was consistently applied to issues of policy.[7] It was no wonder that Spencer wrote *Social Statics* during his period as a sub-editor on *The Economist*.[8]

Thus *laissez-faire* was by no means a myth. But while a free-trade ideology undoubtedly dominated public policy in mid-Victorian England, the *laissez-faire* ideology did not. This is the whole point of Spencer's *Social Statics* (1851) and his later reiteration of the same themes in *The Man Versus the State* (1884).[9] Spencer assailed the utilitarian or 'expediency-philosophy' which he felt lay behind the interventions of government, whether Liberal or Tory. In opposition he stated his law of equal freedom: 'as liberty to exercise the faculties is the first condition of individual life, the liberty of each, limited only by the equal liberty of all, must be the first condition of social life'. The state consists of 'men voluntarily associated for mutual protection'. Its duty is to enforce the law of equal freedom. This involves the protection of each individual against force and fraud, the enforcement of voluntary contracts and the securing of external defence. And that is *all*: 'whilst the state ought to protect, it ought to do nothing more than protect'.[10] For Spencer's rights-based philosophy, the test of expediency is no test at all: there is nothing a government cannot convince itself to be expedient. In a series of chapters a number of specific state activities are prohibited: one, trade preferences and restraints; two, the use of taxation to support any creed; three, state aid to the indigent; four, a state education system; five, the financing and administration of colonies; six, the promotion of public health, including sewage, water, housing standards, street paving and lighting, and vaccination; seven, control of the currency and banking systems; eight, public works, including infrastructural items like lighthouses and harbours.[11] In justification of these views three arguments are advanced: the argument that any state activity requires taxation and often involves taking more of a person's property than is necessary for the maintenance of rights and to that extent an unwarranted interference; the practical argument that much intervention is counter-productive; and third, the economic argument that if there is a want, then the market will provide.[12]

If there is a theorist of *laissez-faire*, then Spencer is his name. In the rest of this chapter, we shall first compare Spencer's absolutist position with the wholly pragmatic attitude of the classical school, in order to emphasise the distance that separates the utilitarianism of the English classical economists from the natural rights views of the *laissez-faire* school. We shall then go on to utilise some important recent historical research in order to show that the theological doctrines of moderate evangelicalism had as much, if not more, to do with the *laissez-faire* bias of particular thinkers as classical political economy itself.

SMITH AND MILL ON THE STATE

By classical political economy is meant the period of economic thought from the publication of Smith's *Wealth of Nations* in 1776 to the death of J. S. Mill in 1873. Jevons' *The Theory of Political Economy* (1871) is generally regarded as this tradition to an end. It encompasses the high theory of Malthus, Bentham, Ricardo, McCulloch, Torrens, Senior, James and J. S. Mill, and J. E. Cairnes, whose lecture 'Political Economy and *Laissez-faire*' was given in 1870. Not one of these theorists supported Spencer's position. Of his eight prohibited areas, only the first received general support, and even here, it was not unequivocal. Furthermore, rights-based arguments play little part in their discussion. Even the practical and economic arguments are deployed with a good deal more circumspection. There is no general belief that the market will provide. We shall develop this point by looking more closely at Smith and J. S. Mill.

In *The Wealth of Nations* (hereafter WN),[13] Smith argued that the annual product of a society bears a greater or smaller proportion to the population according to two circumstances, the skills of the labour that produces it, and the proportion of productive to unproductive labour. The first of these is of the greater importance, and depends upon the development of the division of labour. Behind this development lies the human propensity 'to truck, barter and exchange one thing for another' (WN.I.ii.1). We engage in exchange through self-love rather than benevolence, hoping thereby to better our condition, 'a desire which . . . comes with us from the womb, and never leaves us till we go into the grave' (WN.II.iii.28). It is this desire which prompts us to save and to accumulate, to the extent that we are 'protected by law and allowed by liberty' (WN.II.iii.36). Smith's main theme is that a society would progress in a balanced manner towards 'real wealth and greatness' through 'the simple and obvious system of natural liberty' (hereafter SNL). The optimal allocation of resources between alternative uses would be produced, not by the interventions (whether of preference or restraint) of a wise statesman, but through each individual, knowing his own interest best (or at least better than anyone else) being 'left perfectly free to pursue his own interest his own way, and to bring his industry and capital into competition with those of any other man, or order of men' (WN.IV.ix.51). The SNL must operate 'within the bounds of justice' (minimally defined as protection of the individual against violence, theft and fraud) and is always subject to the needs of defence, which takes precedence over opulence (WN.IV.ii.30). The SNL will lead to an economic growth balanced between the agricultural, manufacturing and trading sectors. Smith envisaged such growth to reflect his conceptions of the sectoral hierarchy (WN.II.v) and of the natural progress of opulence (WN.III.i), which together constitute the cashing out of the way in which he believed the SNL would behave if allowed to operate undisturbed by preference or restraint with respect to any individual, group or social order. Both conceptions place great weight on the 'natural' centrality of agriculture in providing both materials and subsistence to the manufacturing sector.[14]

In this perspective the role of the state is confined to defence, the administration of justice, and 'the duty of erecting and maintaining certain public works' because the market is limited in what it can deliver to those goods and services from which individuals could realistically expect to profit; and in addition, the state must correct certain negative effects of the SNL itself: 'Man is by nature directed to correct, in some measure, that distribution of things which she herself would otherwise have made.'[15] Thus infrastructure, maintenance of the church, public relief of the indigent (locally administered) and basic education in an effort to ameliorate the negative effects of the division of labour, are all seen as legitimate public functions. In addition, the SNL is not a spontaneous affair: it can only work within a system of laws which regulate the market (enforcing competition rather than monopoly) and provide a stable monetary framework.[16]

Beyond this, however, Smith considered state intervention to be at best ineffective, and at worse counterproductive or positively harmful to the economy. His distinction between productive and unproductive labour placed the state firmly in the unproductive camp, living off the revenues created by the productive labourers. Bureaucrats (whether state or corporate, as in the East India Company) were largely negligent and corrupt, unmotivated to seek profit other than their own. State attempts to control wages or prices could never be successful. Statistics were too unreliable to allow of viable administrative decisions. More importantly, there could be no correct wage or price level independently of what in a free market a buyer is willing to give or a seller to take. In particular, the state is incapable of regulating the economy so as to produce extra employment or a greater product.

> No regulation of commerce can increase the quantity of industry in any society beyond what its capital can maintain. It can only direct a part of it into a direction into which it might not otherwise have gone; and it is by no means certain that this artificial direction is likely to be more advantageous to the society than that into which it would have gone of its own accord (WN.IV.ii.3).

As we have seen, Smith made several exceptions to this latter claim: but all the exceptions are charged against a total revenue which the state itself cannot increase. This argument became a basic assumption in the position of classical economics on the issue of the economic effects of state expenditure, and was re-stated in the 'Treasury View' of 1929.[17] The individual seeks the most profitable use for his capital: yet 'the study of his own advantage naturally, or rather necessarily leads him to prefer that employment which is most advantageous to the society' (WN.IV.ii.4). Hence, in expectation of equal profit, a merchant will prefer the home to the foreign trade, and the foreign to the carrying trade. The home trade has greater security and a quicker rate of return than foreign trade, while the carrying trade is the most insecure and complicated. Thus self-interest dictates the use of capital at home, which will maximise employment, and also its use in producing commodities that are in the highest demand. Each individual, looking only to his own security and his own gain, necessarily works to render the national product as great as he can, 'and he is in this, as in many other cases, led by an invisible hand to promote an end which was no part of his intention' (WN.IV.ii.9). If too much capital is invested in what appears to be the most advantageous sector, then competition will force a fall of profits in this sector and a rise in all others, thus causing individuals to transfer their capital.

> Without any intervention of law, therefore, the private interests and passions of men naturally lead them to divide and distribute the stock of every society among all the different employments carried on in it, as nearly as possible in the proportion which is most agreeable to the interests of the whole society (WN.IV.vii.88).

The individual in his local situation can judge these things much more effectively than the statesman; it is in any case dangerous to entrust any state with the power to make such judgments; and in many cases state intervention will be an unjustifiable invasion of natural liberty.

J. S. Mill's *Principles* was an avowed attempt to update Adam Smith by assimilating into one structure of argument the advances made in political economy, in particular the Malthusian population thesis and the Ricardian theory of rent. Mill also gave the first systematic expression of the classical view on public policy. Having listed a number of objections to state intervention, Mill urged that the presumption should always be against interference: '*Laissez-faire*, in short, should be the general practice: every departure from it, unless required by some great good, is a certain evil.'[18] But he goes on to list a range of cases where 'some great good' may well be obtained by state intervention: where the consumer is an incompetent judge, or where persons (for instance, children) cannot be presumed to be the best judge of their own interests; where a measure would not profit a private person but is one in which 'the general interests of mankind' are involved; and even where private agency might be viable but cannot be induced to perform.[19] On this basis Mill was prepared to advocate state intervention in the provision of basic education and funds for the sciences and the universities; relief of the indigent; the protection of children, juveniles, and the lower animals; the regulation of joint-stock companies and of natural monopolies; funds for low-cost housing, and aid to workers displaced by machinery; state schemes of emigration and colonial settlement; and restrictions on inheritance and a proportional income tax. Equally, however, Mill does not mention many policies familiar today: he has no positive views concerning the duty of government to maintain full employment, maximise output or ensure high growth rates, nor does he advocate a progressive income tax system to pay for such policies.[20] Senior fully approved of Mill's account in his review of the *Principles*, commenting that 'it is the duty of a government to do whatever is conducive to the welfare of the governed. The only limit to this duty is its *power*'.[21] In general, then, the classical school considered that their economic analysis had established certain pragmatic limits to the power of the state to intervene beneficially in the economy.

NATURAL THEOLOGY AND THE MARKET

The incompatibility of the classical positions with Spencer's views should now be clear. And in fact, just as *Social Statics* as a whole opposes utilitarianism, so the chapters on the functions of the state (chapters 21–9) attack the views put forward by Mill in his chapter on the *laissez-faire* principle.[22] This itself indicates the wide gulf that separates the classical economists from the *laissez-faire* ideology. How, then, should we characterise this gulf? In his influential account of classical views on policy, Lord Robbins urged that whereas the French tradition of political economy from Mercier de la Rivière to Bastiat had been one of *Naturharmonie*, the English tradition had been based on utilitarian values, though in a Humean rather than Benthamite sense. True, Smith sometimes 'clothes his results in the language of Deistic philosophy' but this is irrelevant to the economic validity of his arguments. 'A theory of economic policy . . . must take its ultimate criterion from outside economics': and the classical school found their criterion in 'the principle that the test of policy is to be its effects on human happiness'. Smith might appear to be an exception, in that he opposes Hume's utilitarian version of how we come to have moral sentiments, but throughout the *Wealth of Nations* Smith's policy test is consistently utilitarian.[23]

Recently this view has been challenged by E. F. Paul.[24] She assumes that during the period of classical economics, there was a change from an early acceptance of *laissez-faire* to an acceptance among political economists of the need for state intervention. Paul asks whether this change reflected changes in the substantive or

methodological claims of economic theory, or rather in a fundamental change in moral perspective. This presentation, of course, rules
out the possibility of other alternatives: we have the choice of *either*
theory change *or* moral change. Paul chooses the second: *contra*
Robbins, she argues that the classical school was not originally
utilitarian. In the late eighteenth century both the natural rights
tradition and the utilitarian school supported *laissez-faire*, but for
different reasons. Subsequently, the two diverged on the issue of
state intervention in the market. The utilitarians saw intervention as
counterproductive: wealth would be re-directed, not increased, and
the allocative mechanism would be disrupted. The rights school
accepted this, but rather emphasised the violation of individual
liberty and property rights implied by intervention, as we saw in the
case of Spencer. Paul claims this is also true of Smith, who had
opposed Hume's utilitarian moral philosophy and had invoked natural rights at critical points in his rejection of specific acts of state
intervention. His belief in a natural harmony in the universe led
logically to the view that each individual, in pursuing his own
interest,would be led to that course most beneficial to society.
Clearly *laissez-faire* cannot be deduced from the utility principle in
the same way. Paul equates the end of *laissez-faire* with the victory
of utilitarian values.

There are many problems with Paul's account of the matter. The
interpretation of Smith is badly flawed, and even within the terms of
Paul's discussion it is clear that changes in method and substantive
theory did affect policy advice quite independently of moral values.
And if we refuse to accept the dichotomous choice between morality
and theory, it is clear that there are other alternatives.

Natural harmony, we are told, dominates Smith's economics.
Thus, when he goes beyond defence and justice and argues that the
state should engage in certain public works, a utilitarian standard has
been smuggled in.[25] Yet nowhere in the *Wealth of Nations* is a natural
harmony mentioned. The whole point of the book is that a natural
harmony does not prevail, that the pursuit of individual self-interest
has not led to the public good, but on the contrary to a mercantile
system which benefits narrow sectional interests. Paul suggests that
Smith was wrong to portray a clash of interests between landlords
and labourers on the one hand and merchants and master manufacturers on the other. But the claim is a clear deduction from his
theory.[26] Only if the SNL is present could there be an approach to a
harmony, but established by state regulation, not by nature. In his

attack on Quesnay, Smith explicitly states that 'the exact regimen of perfect liberty and perfect justice' cannot exist. To believe that a full SNL could exist in Britain 'is as absurd as to expect that an Oceana or Utopia should ever be established in it'. Why? Because 'the private interests of many individuals irresistibly oppose it'.[27]

No doubt, as Paul shows, a natural rights defence of economic freedom can be drawn out of Smith. Thus property in one's own labour is 'sacred and inviolable'; 'violations of natural liberty' are 'therefore unjust'. Only in cases of 'the most urgent necessity' should we sacrifice 'the ordinary laws of justice to an idea of publick utility'. To prohibit an individual from using his capital and labour in any way he deems advantageous is a 'manifest violation of the most sacred rights of mankind'.[28] But Smith makes clear that natural liberty can be overridden by social utility: 'those exertions of the natural liberty of a few individuals which might endanger the security of the whole society, are, and ought to be, restrained by the laws of all governments; of the most free, as of the most despotical.'[29] Indeed, 'governments are valued only in proportion as they tend to promote the happiness of those living under them'. Campbell and Ross have provided a mass of evidence to show that Smith's policy advice was consistently utilitarian.[30] True, Smith controverts Hume's utilitarian account of the *origins* of moral rules, but he evaluates policies and systems by reference to their utility in maximising human happiness.

This is not to deny that there are elements of natural harmony ideas in Smith, most notably in the *Theory of the Moral Sentiments* (hereafter TMS). In the eighteenth century it was widely supposed that Newton, through his use of the 'experimental method', had discovered the basic laws governing the physical universe, and in so doing had revealed a major part of God's Design. Why, then, could there not be a Newton of the moral sciences, using the experimental method to discover the laws of the social world, and thus another part of God's Design? It is against this background that we should understand Smith's work in ethics, jurisprudence and political economy. In TMS there is an explicit natural theology which informs all Smith's work.[31] Indeed, the 'invisible hand' passage in WN is parallelled by one in TMS. Despite the natural rapacity of the rich,

They are led by an invisible hand to make nearly the same distribution of the necessaries of life, which would have been made had the earth been divided with equal portions among all its inhabitants, and thus, without intending it, without knowing it, advance the interest of society . . . When Providence divided the earth among a few lordly masters, it neither forgot nor abandoned those who seemed to have been left out in the partition.[32]

In TMS Smith argues that general rules of morality are formed by induction from experience and used as standards of moral judgment. The rules so prescribed suit our human nature and are to be seen 'as the commands and laws of the Deity'. All rules are commonly known as laws: thus the laws of motion. Moral rules are even more like laws, laid down by the divine sovereign 'to direct the free actions of men'. If we follow the dictates of our moral faculties,

> We necessarily pursue the most effectual means for promoting the happiness of mankind, and . . . co-operate with the Deity, and to advance as far as in our power the plan of Providence.

Indeed, virtue has its natural reward. Thus the reward for 'industry, prudence and circumspection' is 'success in every sort of business', which means wealth and honour.[33] In a passage Smith added to the 1790 edition, he reaffirmed that

> the belief of the wise and virtuous man must be that all the inhabitants of the universe . . . are under the immediate care and protection of that great, benevolent and all wise Being, who directs all the movements of nature; and who is determined . . . to maintain in it, at all times, the greatest possible quantity of happiness . . . [who] . . . can admit into the system of his government, no partial evil which is not necessary for the universal good.[34]

How far this theology is specifically Christian is disputable. Raphael discerns a trend towards natural religion, shown by the way in which Smith re-arranged and expanded the Stoic passages of TMS. Within Christian theology we should align Smith with the theological utilitarianism of William Paley. As we shall see, it is significant that a major passage on the Christian Atonement is omitted from the 1790 edition.[35]

But despite the presence of these notions, even in TMS it is clear that human free-will often impedes the Divine Plan. Natural jurisprudence may tell us the rules of natural justice, but positive law only imperfectly reflects these rules, and can be warped both by state interests, and by the interests of particular orders of men 'from what natural justice would prescribe'. All independent states comprise 'many different orders . . . each of which has its own particular powers, privileges and immunities'. Individuals define their interests in relation to that order to which they are attached. The delicate balance between orders gets upset if one order gets the ear of government to the disadvantage of the others.[36] And this is precisely the picture we are given in WN. The unhindered working of the SNL has been constantly thwarted by the mistaken policies of the· European states, suborned by the actual or perceived interests of individuals, groups and classes to pursue courses inimical to the public good. And so 'the sneaking arts of underling tradesmen . . . the mean rapacity, the monopolising spirit of merchants and manufacturers' have dominated the policy of a great empire.[37]

We must conclude that the natural harmony doctrine had little effect on classical economics. It plays an insignificant role even in Smith's economics, Malthus was to throw grave doubt on the whole idea, and it was denied by Bentham, Ricardo, James Mill and J. S. Mill. As a 'classical principle' it is a non-starter. Further, the role of utility in some sense is constant. For this very reason the supposed rise of utility as the dominant value cannot be a reason for the 'decline' of the *laissez-faire* principle.

We should also note that on Paul's own account, shifts in method and substantive theory did, contrary to her central claim, remove the connection between political economy and *laissez-faire*. First, Mill distinguished science (a collection of truths) and art (a body of rules for conduct). As Senior emphasised, an economist does not recommend or dissuade, but merely states general principles 'which it is fatal to neglect, but neither advisable, nor perhaps practicable, to use as the sole, or even the principal, guides in the actual conduct of affairs'.[38] Second, Senior distinguished between laws of production, which are universally true, and laws of the distribution of wealth, which are liable to be effected by particular institutions. Mill used this distinction to back reform arguments. The first distinction broke any direct link between theory and policy; the second widened the field within which policy recommendations could be made.

Paul admits that important theory changes had led to policy advice advocating state intervention. Malthus was led 'to propose an expanded role for governmental activity in the market as a direct result of a change he had wrought in pure economic theory'. Ricardo's rent theory suggested that the interests of landlords were unreconcilably opposed to the other classes of the community. J. S. Mill drew the interventionist conclusion to which Ricardo could logically have arrived, and used the rent theory to justify a tax on the unearned increment of landlord income. Here we have 'a clear case of a change in pure economic theory . . . which finally had its effect on the theory of government policy'.[39] Paul seeks to avoid inconsistency by claiming that it was Mill's values which led to his conclusion. But this is to miss the point. The rent theory made the policy a plausible one to adopt. It is not that theory ever leads unambiguously to certain policy conclusions, but that some changes in theory and method make it more plausible to claim that the state can effectively intervene to bring about desirable change. Mill used theory to suggest that what he wanted on grounds of social utility was not ruled out by theory.

Paul finds it 'truly remarkable' that the marginal revolution in economic theory had no effect on the question of state intervention in the economy.[40] Yet Jevons was not only a moral utilitarian, which would make it remarkable if he had been in principle against state intervention, but in addition he introduced elements of utilitarian thought into economic theory itself. His 'final utility' theory of value used the pain-pleasure calculus, and Bentham's point that increments of income have a progressively decreasing significance for persons of high income was central to the construction of the concept of marginal utility.[41] This became important for policy issues, as it gave weight to the claim that greater equality of income would increase the greatest happiness via the distribution of increments of money from the rich to the poor to whom it represented a greater marginal utility. Paul notes this but misses the significance: once again a theoretical point gives substance to a policy recommendation.

For all these reasons, Paul's revision of Robbins seems wholly misplaced. But there are further limits to the approaches of both Paul and Robbins. First, they stick to *texts*. That the environment to which the classical school responded changed radically during the period is only glancingly noticed. By 1850, despite attempts to massage the statistical evidence, even the most extreme agrarian had to admit the dominance of manufacture. This involved all the problems of rapid urbanisation with which we are familiar: slum housing, poor sanitation, overcrowding. It was clear to nearly all that *laissez-faire* was no guide: hence the Factory Acts, sanitary provision, basic public education and all the other measures to which Spencer was so opposed. Tory paternalists like Fielden and Oastler; cultural critics like Coleridge, Carlyle and Ruskin; and socialist writers who argued that the free market neither optimised resource allocation nor led to distributive justice: all these could argue for state intervention without being suspected of utilitarianism. How far any of these views weighed with the classical school is a matter for debate. What is clear is that values other than Benthamite ones could lead to demands for state intervention. It is clearly a case of tunnel vision to concentrate only upon the traditions of natural rights and secular utilitarianism. In the next part of this paper we shall seek to sketch some ways in which particular forms of theological belief could lead to demands for, or resistance to, state intervention in the economy.

EVANGELICAL THEOLOGY AND THE MARKET

Throughout the period of classical economics, religion pervaded all areas of thought. Historians of science have conclusively demonstrated the major impact of theological convictions on the development of natural science, whether in astronomy or physics, geology or biology. Political economy did not escape: 'religious belief was important in shaping as well as rationalising the economic philosophy of the period'.[42] Smith's natural theology assumes that physical laws of nature and moral rules are two aspects of the Divine Plan of a Creator who had 'confirmed and conducted the immense machine of the universe'.[43] In the *Wealth of Nations*, Smith speaks the language of causal generalisation. But the market model of Book I, where the market price is said to oscillate around the 'natural price' and would equal it in conditions of perfect liberty, could be understood as indicating that the natural price is the 'just price'.[44] Hence the market could be said to reflect rules of justice and be a part of the Divine Plan. Smith does not make this connexion, but others, notoriously Burke, were to do so. Even in famine conditions we must resist the idea

> that it is within the competence of government . . . to supply to the poor, those needs which it has pleased the Divine Providence for a while to withhold from them. We . . . ought to be made sensible, that it is not in breaking the laws of commerce, which are the laws of nature, and consequently the laws of God, that we are to place our hope of softening the Divine displeasure . . .[45]

Waterman has suggested that in the early nineteenth century, clerical divines did far more than merely respond to a science of political economy created by others. Chalmers, Copleston, Malthus, Paley, Sumner and Whately made technical contributions to political economy and at the same time interpreted it within a theological framework.[46] In this way, we have a possible solution to a paradox stressed many years ago by Elie Halèvy, namely, that in English society in the nineteenth century two forces apparently so hostile should for a time combine in

> a moderate individualism, a mixture whose constituents are often mingled beyond the possibility of analysis, a compound of Evangelicalism and Utilitarianism.[47]

At the very end of the eighteenth century the complacent natural theology of William Paley was challenged by the *Essay on Population*. Malthus argued that population must necessarily be proportioned to the available subsistence; that population unchecked expands in a geometrical ratio, whereas food can be increased only in an arithmetical ratio; hence there must be checks on population growth in all societies. The checks are twofold: *positive* (misery, including infant mortality, starvation and disease; and vice) and *preventive*: 'the restraint from marriage which is not followed by irregular gratifications'.[48] In 1815 the argument was considerably sharpened by the claim, advanced by Malthus, Ricardo and West, that there is a diminishing rate of return from the land. To many it seemed that an Anglican clergyman had published a libel on God's providence, while the use of his theory to condemn the operation of the Poor Laws was regarded as an attack on the Gospels designed to bring Christian charity into disrepute. It was left to J. B. Sumner to reconcile the population thesis with 'the wisdom and goodness of the Deity'.[49]

Sumner accepted the latest results of the science of political economy, and assimilated them to Evangelical theology. God's creatures are depraved, weighed down by original sin. Life is an arena of moral trial by which we are sorted out into saints (deserving the literal felicity of Heaven) and sinners (deserving the literal eternal torments of Hell) at the Day of Judgment. Each soul is naked before God: intermediaries are of little avail. Redemption depends on conscience. The means are provided by Christ's Atonement on the Cross, which purchased ransom for our sins. Justification comes through faith in the Atonement. Good works and a good life are important but do not precede faith. The sermons of Joseph Butler were a major resource for Sumner. These emphasised the supremacy of conscience as an innate moral sense, contrary to the consequentialist outlook of theological or secular utilitarianism. For Paley, suffering is a byproduct of an essentially harmonious universe, whereas for Butler it reflects the fact that our earthly state is one of probation. Hilton notes that Butler deeply impressed figures otherwise widely divergent in their views: the Tractarians, notably Newman; Gladstone; and evangelicals like Wilberforce, Chalmers and Loyd as well as Sumner.[50] Wilberforce is representative when he complained that in Paley there is

> nothing of those tendencies of virtue to produce happiness, and of vice to produce misery, which are so judiciously collected and so unanswerably enforced by Bishop Butler . . . as proofs that the world is not now in the state in which it originally proceeded from the hands of the Creator, but that it is evidently in a state of degradation and ruin – that the Creator is a moral governor.[51]

For Sumner, population increase accords with God's design. Procreation is the direct or indirect cause of all labour. Overpopulation provides the spur to industry. It was the result of human corruption that pain and misery had been the human lot. A balance between population and subsistence would occur when men understood the individual obligation to labour as well as the biblical injunction to be fruitful and multiply. Smith had himself provided a corrective to Malthus in his demonstration of the productive power of the division of labour. The fact of a diminishing return from the land should spur us even more to exercise prudential restraint through abstention from marriage until its results could be afforded. Private property and social inequality are the results of the desire to better our condition. The social ladder forces us to exert all our capacities to emulate those above us in the order. Poverty (but not indigence) is necessary that we may labour. After 1816, church prelates learnt their Malthus from Sumner. Copleston took up Sumner's theme:

> It is the high distinction of the *Essay on Population* to have demonstrated . . . that all endeavours to embody benevolence into law, and thus impiously . . . to effect by human laws what the author of the system of nature has not affected by his laws must be abortive.[52]

The poor must learn prudence, frugality, self-respect and a dread of dependence.

Boyd Hilton has convincingly argued that evangelical models of individualism made a far greater contribution than either classical economics or utilitarianism to the public morality which provided context and sanction for economic policy before 1850.[53] However, he pushes the analysis further than Waterman or Stanley had done by drawing a distinction between moderate and extreme evangelicalism. The major relevant difference concerned the way in which providence worked: while the extremists thought of God as working by special intervention, the moderates envisaged God as working in a regular and predictable manner through the natural laws of causation.[54] Hilton suggests that in general the extremists were open to state intervention in the economy, whereas the moderates matched 'their *laissez-faire* or neutral conception of providence with a similar approach to the "Condition of England"'.[55] T. B. Macaulay thus berates Southey:

> We do not see either the piety or the rationality of . . . confidently expecting that the Supreme Being will interfere to disturb the common succession of cause and effect. We, too, rely on his goodness . . . as manifested, not in extraordinary interpositions but in those general laws which it has pleased him to establish in the physical and in the moral world.[56]

Hilton distinguishes two free trade models: the Ricardian, which was industrial, progressive and expansionist; and the moderate evangelical, essentially agrarian, static or cyclical, and national, in which competition is a means to moral education rather than economic growth. The Ricardian view was optimistic, and a secularised evangelical like Macaulay spoke of the natural tendency of society to improvement. We are so used to viewing the period in terms of bourgeois triumphalism that it is difficult to realise that it was not yet clear whether the unprecedented changes were irreversible or part of a cycle which would lead to disaster. The latter view was reinforced by the static world-view of evangelicalism.

Thomas Chalmers' *On Political Economy* (1832) exemplified this perspective. He supported Catholic Emancipation, an income tax, the repeal of the Combination Acts and the Corn Laws. But he was obsessed to the point of hysteria with the evils of the Old Poor Law and the redundant population he supposed it to encourage. For Chalmers a stationary state of population and wealth was preferable to the progressive state. Except for agriculture all sectors of the economy were prone to oversupply. The problem of poverty would be solved by sound Christian education and the building of churches. His book was poorly received, though McCulloch's review was a pale reflection of his private condemnation: 'a tissue of abominable absurdities . . . a more thorough piece of quackery never came into my hands'.[57] Yet it was through Chalmers that political economy was mediated to the evangelical world.[58]

The moderate evangelicals were confident that *laissez-faire* policies, including free trade, would reveal a providential order that was also just. But believers in God's perpetual superintendence by means of special providences rejected these claims (for instance, Shaftesbury, Drummond and Sadler) and advocated interventionist measures such as Factory Acts. The difference is also reflected in their attitude to events. The extremists had seen the cholera epidemic of 1831 as punishment for the sin of Catholic Emancipation in 1829, and were later to see the Irish potato famine as God's punishment on the Irish for being Catholics. The moderates were more prepared to see the famine as the mechanical outcome of general causes. Commercial crises were at first interpreted as the punishment of immoral speculation, but as recurrent crises became a feature of the economy the very regularity of the occurrence (1825–6, 1837–9, 1847–8, 1857, 1866) suggested a normal rather than special providence. The central point to note is that the moderate perspective could lead the evangelical to the same policy conclusions as were reached by the secular political economist. Thus Poor Law reform saw a conjunction between evangelicals who wanted to make individuals directly responsible for their actions, and political economists who believed that there would be no genuine unemployment once a truly free market was in place.[59]

Hilton notes that the evangelical model lost ground rapidly in the 1850s to the optimistic Cobdenite vision. The enactment of general limited liability legislation (1855–62) symbolised a dramatic change in attitudes.[60] Evangelicals saw limited liability as a derogation from full individual responsibility and as a license for fraud. McCulloch agreed. A free market involves autonomous agents who bear the consequences of their actions to the full limit of their resources.

In the scheme laid down by Providence for the government of the world, there is no narrowing or shifting of responsibilities . . . But the advocates of limited liability proclaim in their superior wisdom that the scheme of Providence may be advantageously modified . . .[61]

But most leading economists supported the measure (J. S. Mill and Senior), and so did Christian Socialists like Maurice and Ludlow. Both groups saw limited liability as a necessary legal step for the development of working-class enterprises. It was also the goal of a rentier class determined to minimise their risks: 'the middle classes suddenly opted out of the capitalist system *at the point where it stood to damage themselves*'.[62]

But the 1850s were also a period in which theological emphases shifted. The idea that God had inflicted suffering on his Son as a vicarious sacrifice for the sins of mankind gave way to an interpretation of the Crucifixion as a noble but symbolic gesture. The Incarnation, in the life of Jesus, becomes central. The theology of F. D. Maurice is crucial here. The Christian Socialists urged that God became man that we might learn a new ethical code. Maurice also argued that biblical expressions indicating Hell as a place of literal eternal agony were but metaphors for a state of alienation from God. As Hilton puts it, Maurice had limited the liability of sin.[63]

CONCLUSION

It is time to draw together the threads of our discussion. Paul sticks to 'high theory', and classical economics is related to the values of either natural rights or utility. It is implied that not only does a claimed change in moral perspective lead to a changed view of state intervention, but also that *actual* state interventions are the result of a changed view of policy by the classical economists. The repercussion on actual legislation is assumed, not argued. We have given cause to doubt the Paul version, while Hilton would be sceptical about there being any direct relation of theory to policy. In his version, 'high theory' takes a back seat: even Malthus is mediated through interpreters like Sumner and Chalmers. Theological and economic views are related to a large gallery of political figures. The general claim is that if X is a moderate evangelical, then it is probable that he will accept policy A. 'Probably' because clearly there are those who do not fit. Vansittart was an evangelical and a High Tory who opposed economic liberalism. Drummond and Irving were extreme evangelicals, but pleaded 'the mystery of providence' about slavery, and opposed emancipatory intervention. Hence Hilton does not commit himself to stating a causal direction, but confines himself to the fact that pessimistic moderate evangelicalism and utilitarian optimism lead to the same policy conclusions. Too many 'oscillated ambiguously between the two modes' for us to be more definite.[64] Macaulay and Fitzjames Stephen are perhaps representative of an intermediate category: figures who rejected the religious evangelicalism of their childhood, but retained a moral evangelicalism and accepted at least the legal theory of Benthamism.

Does this link between moderate evangelicalism, *laissez-faire* and political economy have any contemporary resonance? Hilton points to certain parallels, but finds them ultimately superficial. A commitment to the Victorian values of personal independence, individual responsibility, thrift and hard work have been much in evidence in the speeches and writings of those who have so zealously forwarded the free market philosophy in the last ten years. Politicians like Margaret Thatcher and John Selwyn Gummer emphasise the link between their religious and moral convictions and their political and economic prescriptions, a connection made even more bluntly by that licensed court jester of *The Sunday Telegraph*, Peregrine Worsthorne:

> 'Repent so ye be saved' . . . from the Christian viewpoint, the most pressing need in the inner cities . . . is for ordinary people to be shocked into . . . the paths of righteousness for fear of eternal damnation . . . Thatcherites [see poverty] to be God's will – divine retribution for past sins . . .[65]

But there is no providentialism, and the hedonism of the 'enterprise culture' has no counterpart in the pessimism of the early nineteenth century. There is no acceptance of Thatcherism by the Church of England: no bench of bishops to spread the economic gospel from the pulpit. The Thatcherite theology is *ersatz*, its intellectual level low, its grasp on reality tenuous. But this should not mislead us into thinking that the political and social attitudes expressed in that theology are not important and influential in their appeal to Mrs Thatcher's national constituency, which is after all the main thing for any politician.

NOTES

1. J. S. Mill, *Principles of Political Economy with Some of their Applications to Social Philosophy*, ed. J. M. Robson (Toronto: University of Toronto Press, 1965) V.xi.1 (p. 936) V = book; xi = chapter, 1 = paragraph number. Hereafter *Principles*.

2. T. Carlyle, 'Chartism' (1839), in *English and Other Critical Essays* (London: Dent, n.d.), p. 207.

3. J. B. Brebner, '*Laissez-faire* and State Intervention in Nineteenth-Century Britain', *Journal of Economic History* 8 (1948) supplement, 60.

4. D. Roberts, *Victorian Origins of the British Welfare State* (New Haven: Yale University Press, 1960), p. 100.

5. G. Watson, *The English Ideology: Studies in the Language of Victorian Politics* (London: Allen Lane, 1973, p. 73).

6. T. B. Macaulay, 'Southey's Colloquies on Society' (January 1830) in *Critical and Historical Essays Contributed to the Edinburgh Review by Lord Macaulay*, 3 vols (London: Longmans, Green and Co., 1906) vol. I p. 269.

7. S. Gordon, 'The Ideology of Laissez-faire' in A. W. Coats (ed.), *The Classical Economists and Economic Policy* (London: Methuen 1971) pp. 196, 201.

8. H. Spencer, *An Autobiography*, 2 vols (London: Williams and Norgate 1904) vol. I pp. 340–66.

9. *Contra* Watson, *The English Ideology*, pp. 73–4.

10. H. Spencer, *Social Statics* (London: John Chapman, 1851) pp. 195, 275, 295.

11. H. Spencer, *Social Statics*, chs 21–9.

12. H. Spencer, *Social Statics*, p. 406.

13. A. Smith, *An Inquiry into the Nature and Causes of the Wealth of Nations* (1776), ed. R. H. Campbell, A. S. Skinner and W. B. Todd, 2 vols (Oxford: Clarendon Press, 1976). References in text are to book, chapter and paragraph, thus: W.N. I.ii.1.

14. A persuasive account of this is given in V. Brown, 'The System of Natural Liberty and the Wealth of Nations', paper presented at the History of Economic Thought Conference, Groningen, September 1989.

15. A. Smith, *The Theory of Moral Sentiments* (1759), ed. D. D. Raphael and A. L. McFie (Oxford: Clarendon Press, 1976) III, 5.10. Hereafter TMS.

16. Halèvy's distinction between the *artificial* identity of interests in the political and legal sphere, and a *natural* identity of interests in the economic sphere, merely confuses the issue. See E. Halèvy, *The Growth of Philosophic Radicalism* (with a preface by J. Plamenatz) (London: Faber and Faber, 1972) pp. 127, 498–9. cf. L. Robbins, *The Theory of Economic Policy in English Classical Political Economy* (London: Macmillan 2nd ed. 1978) pp. 190–4.

17. B. Corry, 'The Theory of the Economic Effects of Government Expenditure in English Classical Political Economy', *Economica* 25 (1958), 34–48. On the 'Treasury View', see P. Clarke, *The Keynesian Revolution in the Making 1924–1936* (Oxford: Clarendon Press, 1988) ch. 3 and *passim*.

18. J. S. Mill, *Principles*, V.xi.7 (p. 945).
19. J. S. Mill, *Principles*, V.xi.8–11 (pp. 947–71).
20. R. L. Crouch, *Laissez-faire* in Nineteenth Century Britain: Myth or Reality?', *The Manchester School*, 35 (1967), pp. 199–215, suggests that we need to distinguish crude (Bastiat) and sophisticated (Smith) *laissez-faire*.
21. N. W. Senior, 'J. S. Mill on Political Economy', *The Edinburgh Review*, No. 178, (October 1848) pp. 331–2.
22. See Spencer, *Social Statics*, pp. 336f. for his answer to Mill on education.
23. Robbins, *Theory of Economic Policy*, pp. 24, 177. He takes his cue from D. Buchanan, *Observations on the Subjects Treated of in Dr. Smith's Inquiry into the Nature and Causes of the Wealth of Nations*, (2nd ed., Edinburgh: Oliphant, Waugh and Innes, 1817), who suggested of the French School of economists 'that however consistently they maintain the doctrine of freedom of trade, they seem to deduce it from the principles rather of abstract right, than of general expedience . . .' D. H. McGregor, *Economic Thought and Policy* (London: Hutchinson, 1949) p. 79, makes the same point.
24. E. F. Paul, *Moral Revolution and Economic Science: The Demise of Laissez-Faire in Nineteenth Century British Political Economy* (Westport, Conn: Greenwood Press, 1979).
25. Paul, *Moral Revolution and Economic Science*, p. 34.
26. See especially, WN.I.xi. p. 8–10 (pp. 265–6).
27. WN.IV.ix.28 (p. 674); IV.ii.43 (p. 471).
28. WN.I.x.c.12 (p. 138); IV.v.b.16 (pp. 530–1); IV.v.b.39 (p. 539); IV.vii.b.44 (p. 582).
29. WN.II.ii.91–4 (pp. 323–4). Here Smith justifies the need to prohibit the issue of small banknotes which, on the face of it, might not seem to 'endanger the security of the whole society'.
30. TMS.III.5.10. (p. 168). See T. D Campbell, 'Adam Smith and Natural Liberty', *Political Studies* 25 (1977), 523–34; and T. D Campbell and I. S. Ross, 'The utilitarianism of Adam Smith's Policy Advice', *Journal of the History of Ideas*, 42 (1981), 73–92.
31. For an interesting recent effort to explicate this, see J. Evensky, 'The Two Voices of Adam Smith: Moral Philosopher and Social Critic', *History of Political Economy*, 19 (1987), 447–68.
32. TMS IV.1.10 (p. 185).
33. TMS III.5.7. (p. 166).
34. TMS VI.ii.3.i. (p. 235). Part VI was written for the sixth edition and sent to press in December 1790. We cannot take Viner's line and argue that TMS and WN represent respectively the work of the immature and the mature Smith'.
35. TMS Introduction, pp. 5–10, 19–20; II.ii.3.12. (pp. 91–2).
36. TMS VII.vi.36 (p. 341); VI.ii.2. 9–10 (pp. 230–1).
37. WN IV.iii.c.8–9 (p. 493).
38. J. S. Mill, *Essays on Some Unsettled Questions of Political Economy* (London: John W. Parker, 1844) p. 124; N. W. Senior, *An Outline of the Science of Political Economy* (London: W. Clowes and Son, 1836) p. 3.
39. Paul, *Moral Revolution and Economic Science*, pp. 122, 91, 102, 161.

40. Paul, *Moral Revolution and Economic Science*, p. 219.
41. W. S. Jevons, *The Theory of Political Economy* (1871), ed. R. D. Collison Black (Harmondsworth: Penguin Books, 1970) p. 111.
42. B. Hilton, *The Age of Atonement: The Influence of Evangelicalism on Social and Economic Thought 1795–1865* (Oxford: Clarendon Press, 1988) p. 6.
43. TMS VI.ii.3.5. (p. 236). See the illuminating discussion in O. H. Taylor, *Economics and Liberalism*, (Harvard: Harvard University Press, 1955), chs 1 and 2.
44. WN.I.vii.
45. E. Burke, 'Thoughts and Details on Scarcity' (1795) in *The Works of the Right Honourable Edmund Burke*, 16 vols. (London: C. and J. Rivington 1826) VII, 404.
46. A. M. C. Waterman, 'The Ideological Alliance of Political Economy and Christian Theology 1789–1833', *Journal of Ecclesiastical History*, 34 (1983), 231–43.
47. E. Halèvy, *A History of the English People in the Nineteenth Century. I. England in 1815*, 2nd (revised) ed. (London: Ernest Benn, 1949) p. 537.
48. T. R. Malthus, *An Essay on the Principle of Population* (1798), ed. A. Flew (Harmondsworth: Penguin Books, 1970) p. 77.
49. J. B. Sumner, *A Treatise on the Records of the Creation*, 2 vols (London, 1816). Sumner (1780–1862) was Bishop of Chester 1828–48 and Archbishop of Canterbury 1848–62. He served with Blomfield (Bishop of London) on the Poor Law Commission in 1834.
50. Hilton, *The Age of Atonement*, pp. 170–8.
51. Quoted Hilton, *The Age of Atonement*, p. 178.
52. Quoted R. A. Soloway, *Prelates and People: Ecclesiastical Social Thought in England 1783–1852* (London: Routledge and Kegan Paul, 1969) p. 137.
53. In his previous book Hilton had argued that in 1815–30 government policies constituted pragmatic responses to economic problems rather than the clear application of economic theory, and suggested that a significant difference between the Liberal Tories and their paternalist colleagues lay in the evangelicalism of the former. B. Hilton, *Corn, Cash, and Commerce: The Economic Policies of the Tory Governments 1815–1830* (Oxford: Clarendon Press, 1977).
54. B. Stanley writes as if *all* evangelicals subscribed to the latter claim: '"Commerce and Christianity": Providence Theory, the Missionary Movement, and the Imperialism of Free Trade, 1842–1860', *Historical Journal* 26 (1983), p. 72.
55. Hilton, *The Age of Atonement*, pp. 13–16.
56. Macaulay, 'Southey's Colloquies on Society', p. 265.
57. McCulloch-Napier, 3 August 1832, quoted Hilton, *The Age of Atonement*, p. 64.
58. Stanley, '"Commerce and Christianity"', p. 74.
59. This is true in other areas. Thus the evangelical and the Benthamite coincided in their attitude to the corrupting influence of imaginative literature. K. J. M. Smith, *James Fitzjames Stephen: Portrait of a Victo-*

rian Rationalist (Cambridge: Cambridge University Press, 1988) p. 15; Hilton, *The Age of Atonement*, p. 245.

60. Hilton, *The Age of Atonement*, p. 255.
61. J. R. McCulloch, *Considerations on Partnerships with Limited Liability* (London, 1856) p. 10–11.
62. Hilton, *The Age of Atonement*, p. 267.
63. Hilton, *The Age of Atonement*, p. 277.
64. Hilton, *The Age of Atonement*, p. 245.
65. see *Sunday Telegraph* editorials, 7 October 1984, 8 December 1985, 7 September 1986. For Thatcher's speeches, see 'I believe . . . A speech on Christianity and Politics' (30 March 1978); and more recently, speech to the assembly of the Church of Scotland, 21 May 1988.

2 Markets and Communities – a Romantic Critique

Ursula Vogel

> Lands should be as much in commerce as any other goods
>
> (Adam Smith)[1]

> Men talk of 'selling' land. . . . but the notion of 'selling', for certain bits of metal, the Iliad of Homer, how much more the Land of the World Creator, is a ridiculous impossibility!   (Carlyle)[2]

ROMANTIC PERSPECTIVES ON COMMERCIAL SOCIETY

Arguments about the relationship between market and state are today usually referred to the competence of specialised knowledge within the political and economic sciences. Historical expeditions, on the other hand, which seek to excavate earlier forms of such arguments from the past will often have to move into foreign territory. Evans's contribution to this volume (p. 13–18) has shown how much nineteenth-century doctrines of laisser-faire owed to the influence of theology. This chapter will look at the polemical opposition of 'markets' and 'communities' that developed from an essentially aesthetic viewpoint in the tradition of German and English romanticism.[3] Most readers will associate the characteristic features of romantic art or, more generally, of a romantic temperament with a disposition of intense introspection and exuberance of feeling. Overshadowed by such preconceptions, the ideal of community can easily be misrepresented as but the projection of 'romantic' nostalgia – of the poet's flight from the prosaic realities of the modern world: 'Rosebushes and poor rates, rather than steam engines and independence'.[4]

However, when reconstituted in the original historical framework of an avantgardist theory of art and culture, the romantic 'community' can become the strategic reference-point for a comprehensive critique of commerical civilisation. As such, it offers a unique perspective upon the wider political and cultural meanings bound up in the process of economic modernisation. This perspective relates the crises and dislocations of a transitional period directly to the erroneous assumptions of the new science of political economy which, as the critics see it, has broken the unity of civil society into the separate spheres of market and state, private and public life, economic and political knowledge. The romantic critique seeks to reverse the process of division and fragmentation by claiming for the 'state' a field of meaning far more extensive than the institutional domain of law and government. It draws all the manifestations of a nation's particular identity – its language, religious beliefs and moral customs, its economic practices and characteristic art forms – into a common focus. In thus stressing the integrative, rather than the specialised, nature of political knowledge, romanticism points to a problem that readers will encounter in other chapters of this book. Cross-national comparisons of the market-state relationship will habitually invoke the imponderable effects of 'political culture' in order to accommodate the residues of inexplicable differences in an otherwise homogeneous pattern of regularities. Although notoriously elusive, the concept has a definite function. It suggests the need for a vantage point of historical understanding, outside the boundaries of a given field of analysis, which could transmit the interdependence and interconnectedness of all of society's institutions and collective practices. This extra-territorial domain of *Kulturkritik* is the homeground of romantic theorising. (From here, to quote Schumpeter, the romantic literati 'roamed all over those parts of philosophy and social science that happened to attract them'.[5]).

The next section will outline the main ideas that define the historical origins of romanticism as an all-encompassing theory and critique of modern culture. I shall concentrate, in the first instance, on the initial romantic programme expounded in the closing decade of the eighteenth century by a group of German poets and philosophers – the brothers August Wilhelm Schlegel (1767–1845) and Friedrich Schlegel (1772–1823), Novalis (1772–1801), and Schleiermacher (1786–1834). Later sections will be concerned with the process in which those aesthetic ideals and modes of theorising came to bear upon the tension between market and community. The writers most relevant here are, on the one hand, Adam Müller (1773–1825) and, on the other, those English romantics who, like Coleridge

(1774–1834) and Carlyle (1795–1881), were directly influenced by the German school.

The main part of the chapter will relate the romantic critique of the market to a paradigmatic case – the commercialisation of land. We must remember that in the still largely agrarian societies of early nineteenth century Europe the dynamic of economic modernisation was experienced, above all, in the rapidly changing conditions of rural life. The whole institutional order of the *ancien régime* rested on the privileged status of landownership which formed the as yet undivided centre of economic and political organisation. In France, these remnants of 'feudalism' were destroyed in the course of the Revolution; elsewhere – as in Prussia, during the Napoleonic Wars – they were undermined by liberal land reforms; in England, romantic writers could illustrate the social and moral costs involved in the commercialisation of agriculture by pointing to the consequences of the Highland clearances (in the decades after 1765.) In this particular historical context, the central tenet of a developing market economy – that 'lands should be as much in commerce as any other goods' – required, above all, the full privatisation of property rights. And we need to recall the far-reaching social and political implications of this process if we want to understand why land could become the catalyst in the romantic reflection on the divisions and antagonisms of modern society. To free landed property for the market meant to dissolve a complex web of entrenched collective rights, such as the traditional forms of tied ownership (the family trust entail and the *fideicommissum*) which secured large family estates against alienation, division and mortgage debts. Market forces spearheaded by individual property rights had, further, to break up the whole network of customary social obligations inherent in the manorial nexus between lord and tenants. Finally, landownership had to be de-politicised – by stripping the aristocratic estate of its quasi-public functions as an autonomous unit of jurisdiction and military recruitment, of church and welfare organisation.

In response to these developments – and paradoxically, at first sight – romantic writers, the pioneers of cultural modernism, rallied to the defence of economic backwardness. However, the case that they brought against the commercialisation of land differs significantly from, and extends beyond, the familiar conservative entrenchment of the status quo. The romantic critique is not predicated upon the quest for social stability as such, nor on the mere sanctity of institutional traditions. Rather, it postulates the incommensurable value of land – its unique, non-commercial qualities as the repository of 'living nature', on the one hand, and the intrinsically political purposes of landownership, on the other. In short, because of its special importance for the whole community land must be insulated against market forces and, similarly, against the hegemonic demands of political economy. Bound up in this claim are certain negative principles which encapsulate the romantic nightmare vision of a fully commercialised society: assimilation of all forms of social organisation to the uniform structure of market exchanges; hegemony of instrumental reason which treats all goods as commodities and all human relationships in the image of the cash nexus; erosion of communal loyalties consequent upon the ascendancy of private property; and, most important for our purposes, dislocation of the political sphere in the *laissez-faire* conception of the modern state.

> Adam Smith has delivered the whole state to the discretion of industry; he has turned all human pursuits into marketable trades, all services into wage labour; he knows but one form of community – the market.[6]

The images conjured up in this negative vision bear little resemblance to the historical features of market society at the turn of the nineteenth century. Nor can they be considered a reliable guide to the intentions and achievements of the *Wealth of Nations*. In this latter respect romanticism is deeply implicated in the 'sorry story of distortion and over-simplification' that marked the reception of Adam Smith's work in the nineteenth century, especially in Germany.[7] Political economists, whether hostile or sympathetic to the romantic temperament, have been agreed on one point – that romantic writers committed 'extraordinary blunders' when they moved into a domain for which most of them could claim no technical competence.[8] It would thus be futile to search in the romantic critique for evidence of an alternative system of political economy. What it does offer, however, is an imaginative projection of certain historical tendencies. In drawing out the most extreme implications of market principles, the romantic critique exposes the tenuous nature of the harmony-assumption that underpins the common understanding of *laissez-faire*. It challenges the belief that markets can be trusted to act as self-contained, self-regulating systems of competitive exchanges.

The emphasis on community in the romantic re-formulation of the market-state relationship will draw attention to a more general question which has been the subject of much recent debate: given that, historically, markets have depended upon a supportive framework of older moral traditions, what will guarantee the cohesion and stability of the system once those legacies of the past have been depleted by the very dynamic of market expansion?[9] From the perspective of the romantic critique, such guarantees cannot be expected from the modern state. Indeed, the latter is itself intimately bound up in the crisis of commercial society. Whether reduced to the minimal scope of law-and-order functions, or expanded in the military and welfare bureaucracies of enlightened absolutism, in neither form can the merely regulatory state sustain the collective fund of social trust that market society has inherited in the communal structure of non-market institutions.

THE ROMANTIC PROGRAMME: UNITY IN DIVERSITY

What preconceptions and values did romanticism bring to contemporary arguments about commercial society? A distinctly 'romantic' viewpoint emerged initially as the new perception of an old problem much debated in eighteenth century literary circles: how to revitalise the ideal of beauty and harmony once attained in the exemplary works of classical antiquity but then irretrievably lost in the inferior and corrupt art forms of the modern age.[10] Into this old debate entered a novel element, as German romantic thinking – most decisively under the influence of Schiller's philosophical writings – began to free itself from the 'tyranny of Greece' as the exclusive norm of beauty and perfection. It moved towards a sharper conceptualisation and, eventually, a sympathetic appreciation of those diffuse and disharmonious tendencies that had once been associated with 'modern' as degenerate art. The centre of poetic and, subsequently, of political inspiration shifted towards medieval literature ('romance') and towards the spirit of Christianity that it embodied.

In this process of fundamental reorientation, romanticism gradually disconnected the principles of aesthetic judgment from any authoritative model of excellence. It came to stress originality, spontaneity and the power of the artist's imagination as the only authentic qualities of the creative process. It similarly established individuality, diversity and organic (complex) unity as the normative categories that were to guide the understanding of art and, beyond it, of life in all its manifestations. The perception of the present epoch as an age of profound crisis changed accordingly. No longer measured solely by its distance from the simple unity lost in the past, it contained in its very dissonances and fragmentations the dormant forces of future regeneration. The envisaged integration of all modern experiences into a new universe of creative art found expression in the ideal of *progressive Universalpoesie*:

> Romantic poetry is progressive poetry oriented towards universality. Its purpose is not only to re-unite all the divided and separate genres of literature and to relate poetry to philosophy. It further intends. . . . to make poetry alive and sociable, and to render life and society poetic. . . . It alone can become the mirror of the whole surrounding world, a picture of the age.[11]

The aspiration of the poetic ideal towards all-inclusiveness and the simultaneous commitment to the values of diversity and unity can explain why the protest against uniformity (*Gleichförmigkeit*) remained the dominant and most passionately argued concern of romantic *Zeitkritik*. The craving for uniformity was blamed for many baneful developments in modern society, from the lifeless regularity of neo-classical art to the formalism of laws and administrative practices in the bureaucratic state (in both its monarchical and republican forms). Uniformity, as the romantics saw it, had triumphed in the analytical and quantitative procedures of the natural sciences. It was, equally, evident in the reductionist methods of the new doctrines of political economy which, for the sake 'of deceptive conciseness and unity'[12] pressed the many-faceted character of human experience into the single category of efficiency calculations.

Two implications of romanticism's original aesthetic programme need to be stressed here. First, in the romantic theory of modernity the present faces both the past and the future. Indeed, in the position commonly characterised as 'romantic medievalism' the two poles of orientation will often converge. The past, that is, may be part of the future – a site for the imaginative location of contrasting images and values.[13] It is important not to eliminate this tension between the backward-looking elements in the romantic critique and its utopian dynamic. Residues of the latter survived in the aesthetic reconstruction of feudal agriculture and landownership. And it was the continued impact of the original dual perspective, as well as a language resonant with modern sensibilities, that enabled a seemingly anachronistic model to reflect the moral and political deficits of a modern market economy.

Second, the contrast between uniformity and diversity contains within it a normative distinction between different modes of knowledge – between the 'calculating faculty' of analytical reason, on the one hand, and the 'synthetic power' of the imagination, on the other.[14] While the former will obliterate difference in order to obtain a homogeneous measure of calculability, the latter establishes affinities and reconciliation between the most discordant qualities. The imagination involves 'a going out of our own nature, and an identification of ourselves with the beautiful which exists in thought, action, or person not our own'.[15] The postulate of imaginative understanding portrays the relation of the knowing subject to the world as an encounter of personal intimacy and reciprocity. We shall see that the opposition between communicative structures and the advance of instrumental, or dominative, orientations recurs on all levels of the romantic argument against the market. The paradigm of the dialogue – which has absorbed the emotive intensity of the romantic cult of friendship and sociability – is used against the externality of nature presupposed in the commercial exploitation of land. The paradigm returns in the critique of private ownership and of the strictly contractual, rather than personal, quality of property relations in the market. The contrast between communicative and instrumental institutions, finally, casts the *laissez-faire* state as but the market's coercive agent. It is a state to which individuals are bound by the fragile links of self-interest and thus, in the last instance, by nothing more than force.

THE NON-COMMERCIAL NATURE OF LAND

> The Hill I first saw the sun rise over, when the Sun and I and all things were yet in their auroral hour, who can divorce me from it? Mystic, deep, as the world's centre are the roots I have struck into my Native Soil . . .
> (Carlyle)[16]

Romantic arguments about the intrinsically non-commercial character of land draw on pantheistic and mystical traditions of thought which perceive 'man and Nature as essentially adapted to each other'.[17] Land is part of 'living Nature' and related to human beings by reciprocal bonds of affinity. Such family resemblances, however, are accessible only to intuition and empathy – that is, only if we treat Nature in a 'personal', not instrumental way.

One would think that this sense of fellowship with Nature – the characteristic inspiration of romantic poetry – need in no way exclude the different treatment of the natural world for the purpose of economic analysis. Moreover, the romantic emphasis on the unique qualities of land seems but to reiterate assumptions that were widely held among political economists of the time. That in agriculture nature itself is a productive agent ('Nature labours along with men'[18]) yielding to the owner of land a pure gift in the form of a net surplus – this belief underlies the explanation of rent in the theories of the Physiocrats as well as in Adam Smith's *Wealth of Nations*. Neither school, however, sees in the intrinsic productivity of the soil a barrier to the modernisation of agriculture. The philosophical premise of commercial land use – that nature is external and subordinate to the designs of men (and that land can be owned and controlled just like any other ensemble of material objects) – is taken for granted.

The romantic critic, by contrast, will claim the communicative structure of interpersonal bonds also for the 'dialogue' between human beings and the land:

Since it [agriculture] communicates with living products of nature, such as plants and animals and with the living atmosphere and the chemical forces of the earth operating in their natural state it is much less disposed to a crude manipulation by machines than any other trade of the world. In agriculture, living nature will always be better worked upon by the hand of man as himself a living sensitive being.[19]

What are the political implications of romantic Nature mysticism? As in the passage above from Adam Müller, it might lend spurious scientific legitimacy to an outright attack against technological innovation and, more pointedly, to the interests of landowners who stood to lose from the advance of commercial agriculture. But the poet's Nature could also sustain political demands of an altogether different kind. Offer's study of the political debates about landownership in late nineteenth-century England has shown how much the intense emotional commitment to the cause of land reform owed to the residues of the romantic mood.[20] A whole generation of middle-class radicals learnt their politics from the 'ethics of Wordsworth'. To

bring the beauty of the unspoilt countryside and Nature's power of
spiritual and moral regeneration within reach of the urban masses
was the dominant inspiration behind the struggle for the preservation
of the commons, for public access to forests and mountains, and the
establishment of the National Trust. Romantic orientations – with
their peculiar fusion of Nature-worship, backward-looking nostalgia
and radical politics – lived on in the England and German garden city
movements and in numerous utopian projects that sought release
from the ills of modern civilisation in the exodus from the city, in land
settlements and alternative life-styles.[21]

Some of these experiments, in which the crusade against fertilisers
might 'go hand in hand with the search for the new god',[22] would
seem to afford easy proof that romantic ideas naturally aligned
themselves with profoundly anti-modernist attitudes. In its original
historical setting, however, the orientation of romanticism is much
more ambivalent. It is true that the romantic critique of modern
political economy is part of a concerted attack upon the legacies of
Enlightenment rationalism which implicates Newtonian physics and
associationist psychology as well as utilitarian ethics. The intention,
however, is not to return to a pre-scientific state of innocence but,
rather, to mobilise those forces which can counteract and contain the
inexorable advance of a scientific culture. The romantics comprehend
their own time as an age of crisis because 'our calculations have
outrun conception.'[23] The accumulation of scientific and technical
knowledge is driven by a dynamic of its own, while our capacity to
assimilate these new powers to the inner law of our nature has not
kept pace. Science has, indeed, expanded man's empire over the
external world but 'man, having enslaved the elements, remains
himself a slave'.[24] That the division of labour and the mechanisation
of the work process have only exacerbated the burden of the labouring classes, or that an abundant harvest will, in market terms, count
as a calamity – such developments are, in the eyes of the romantic
critics, the symptoms of a fundamental corruption of the relation
between means and ends. And it is against the growing disparity
between scientific progress, on the one hand, and the impoverish-
ment of our moral and political imagination, on the other, that they
assert the regenerative power of the poetic faculty.

We want the creative faculty to imagine that which we know; we
want the the generous impact to act that which we imagine, we
want the poetry of life . . .[25]

LANDOWNERSHIP AS TRUST FOR THE COMMUNITY

Agriculture is a trade which . . . . aims at producing a net gain or at making money. The rational doctrine of agriculture must demonstrate how, under given circumstances, maximum gain can be obtained from an estate.

(Albrecht Thaer, a German political economist)[26]

That Agriculture requires principles essentially different from those of Trade – that a gentleman ought not to regard his estate as a merchant his cargo, or a shopkeeper his stock – admits of an easy proof from the different tenure of Landed Property, and from the purposes of Agriculture itself, which ultimately are the same as those of the State of which it is the offspring.   (Coleridge)[27]

The key principle of romantic aesthetics – unity in diversity – recurs in the distinction between agriculture and trade as the two opposed yet complementary spheres of civil society. It is not a distinction that merely names two different sectors of production within a commercial economy. Rather, it refers to substantive, qualitative differences which place agriculture, as a 'public office', outside the market and in direct relationship to the state. The line of differentiation identifies two contrasting purposes of economic activity to which correspond different modes of ownership and different kinds of social relations. The dominant thrust of the romantic argument is thus directed not against the market as such but against the 'overbalance of the commercial spirit' as the main source of 'existing distress'.[28] So far from taking refuge in an ideal of primitive social homogeneity the romantic critique seems to claim the very opposite: a fully commercialised society would cast the whole of social life into one single mould and deprive the state of those resources of strength that flow from conflict and interplay between different social forces.[29]

In order to insulate land against the intrusion of commercial interests without, however, insulating society as a whole against the advance of market forces, the romantic argument required a definite institutional focus that could mediate between traditional agriculture and the needs of modern society. The reformulation of biblical and medieval ideas of landed property as an 'office of trust'[30] may be considered as one of the most fruitful and constructive ideas in the romantic critique of liberal political economy. In the peculiar form of rights and obligations that define the nexus between trustee and

beneficiary – as 'a relation between two persons, based on confidence, by which property is held by one on behalf or for the benefit
of another'[31] – entitlement to the land could be made conditional
upon political purposes. It was, according to John Stuart Mill', 'the
greatest service that Coleridge has rendered to politics . . . . reviving
the idea of trust inherent in landed property'.[32]

> . . . an absolute property in land, unknown to the constitution of
> the realm and in defeasance of that immutable reason which in the
> name of the nation and the national majesty proclaims 'The land is
> not yours; it was vested in your lineage in trust for the nation'.
> (Coleridge)[33]

> The soil must be cultivated in accordance with its peculiar nature as
> the permanent, eternal inheritance of the immortal family of the
> state, and it must be treated accordingly in all economic and legal
> relations. . . .   (Adam Müller)[34]

The romantic understanding of trust ownership recalls the original
entitlement of the whole community to the land. It does not, however, join this premise to any conception of distributive justice. The
issue is not – as in the case of radical land reformers like Thomas
Paine and Thomas Spence[35] – how modern society could restore such
collective rights. The romantic critique appeals to the moral conscience of the individual members of the landowning class, reminding
them of the duties that they owe to the community in return for the
'possession' of land. However, as Mill's own political commitment to
the land-question shows, the romantic trust could inspire the conceptualisation of institutions capable of reconciling individual property
rights with a special obligation to serve the public interest.[36]

In the concept of trust ownership, as the next section will show, we
can connect the romantic idea of community with distinct notions of
political space. The argument will focus on the intergenerational
community; on the feudal community as the paradigm of personal
and affective relations between economic agents; and finally, on the
state or nation as the guardian of society's collective identity. The
homogeneity of communal obligations along a continuum of familial
and friendship bonds defies any clear distinction between private and
public spheres, and thus challenges a core element in the liberal
construction of the market – state divide.

THE DIALOGUE ACROSS GENERATIONS

When romantic writers claim that, by contrast with movable goods, the value of a landed estate cannot be established within the confines of market categories, they refer to the incommensurable worth of relational qualities – to bonds of attachment that evolve in the continuous interaction between particular individuals and their property. Land, on this premise, is not merely an instrument of production nor a commodity to be measured by the impersonal, uniform indicators of the price mechanism. Its value derives from within, and is inseparable from, a particular nexus of ownership. The political dimension in such incommensurable qualities is owed to the time-resisting structure of land tenure. The romantic critique aims 'to construe time into the science of political economy'[37] by opening the concepts of value, wealth, property and contract to the representation of past and future generations. Land, as the romantics see it, is not only permanent itself, it lends permanence also to the individuals who own and work it. It counteracts and remedies the transience of human beings by connecting the members of successive generations into a chain – a community with a distinct identity.[38] Moreover, through the integrative capacities of landownership society as a whole accumulates that fund of collective 'credit' which alone can guarantee its existence over time:

> The mysterious and divine qualities of the land come to fruition only through continuous interaction between the same owner, the same family, the same sovereign and the same soil. From this relationship confirmed by whole centuries derive love, fidelity, trust in the community, and such a strong bond of credit that against it all associations among the contemporary members of society are but casual and loose.[39]

Considered by its immediate political intentions the argument is clearly designed to legitimate the privileged status of the aristocratic family estate (i.e. its traditional protection against alienation and division). But here, as elsewhere, the strategy of 'romanticising' anachronistic institutions can illuminate questions of wider import. Today, notions of trusteeship are frequently invoked in order to indicate society's collective responsibilities for the preservation of the natural environment. It is generally recognised that if left to market forces alone, the interests of future generations would count for little. One of the problems, as Steiner's argument demonstrates (p. 43ff), is how to construct a cogent link of obligations that could legitimately constrain the property rights of present individuals for the benefit of future members of the human species.[40] The romantic idea of an intergenerational community does not solve conceptual problems of this nature. It circumvents the notion of formal rights and strictly contractual obligations. It appeals, instead, to the lived experience of collective identity that individuals derive from the past; and it similarly calls upon the imagination to extend those links into the future. This conception of communal obligation, we might say, relies on human dispositions and motivations that are generally omitted from the rational-choice paradigms of economic and political theory. And yet such motivations may well have a role to play if we want political commitments to reach beyond the time-boundaries of individual right.[41]

THE FEUDAL COMMUNITY AND THE CASH NEXUS

> Ironcutter, at the end of the campaign, did not turn off his thousand fighters, but said to them: 'Noble fighters, this is the land we have gained; be I Lord in it . . . and be ye Loyal Men around me in it; and we will stand by one another . . . for again we shall have need of one another. Plugson, bucanier-like says to them: Noble Spinners, this is the Hundred Thousand we have gained, wherein I mean to dwell and plant vineyards; the hundred thousand is mine, the three and sixpence daily was yours: adieu, noble spinners . . .[42]

For Adam Smith and his followers the dissolution of the feudal nexus – the substitution of monetary exchanges for personal services in the evolution of commercial society – represents, above all, the advance of individual independence.[43] His critics judge the same process by the growth of social distance. The 'cash nexus' disguises a type of property relation which obliterates the distinction between persons and things as each individual is compelled to treat others, friends and strangers alike,[44] in an instrumental fashion. Contemporary developments, such as the catastrophic effects of land modernisation programmes on a great number of smallholders and tenants (and, related to this, the crisis of the system of poor relief in England) afforded romantic writers with powerful images of a world in which nobody is 'united manlike to you'.[45] Exposed to the impersonal operation of market forces individuals will, in times of adversity, have no claims on others except those specified in the formal commitments of the business or wage contract. Failure in the market – that is the main thrust of the romantic argument – results not only in material destitution. Worse than that, such individuals are cast from society like 'dead limbs' from a body: they have forfeited their place in the community.[46]

From the vestiges of feudalism the romantics construe a model of community in which economic exchanges are embedded in, and subservient to, a wider nexus of personal obligations. Tenants are bound to their lord by life-enduring commitments of service and loyalty. In return, he owes them protection, material assistance and moral guidance. On both sides the individual 'pays with his person'.[47] It is a salient feature in the romantic representation of the feudal community that it does not concern itself with the condition of ascribed inequality upon which that system was based. It beautifies an institution which, on the testimony of many contemporaries, had long degenerated into oppressive and inefficient practices. Restated in aesthetic categories and suffused with the colours of both medieval romance and modern sentiments of personal intimacy, relations of personal power and dependence take on the quality of 'beautiful reciprocity'.[48]

Nonetheless, two genuine dimensions of community can be excavated from the layers of ideological distortion. They recall communal dispositions of human nature which, the romantic critic claims, markets will never satisfy. First, in entering into economic exchanges with others, individuals strive for more than momentary satisfaction of their interests. They desire, above all, a secure place among their fellows – in our case, a guaranteed claim on the land – in order to ensure the conditions of future well-being. When Coleridge speaks of a landowner's obligation to safeguard 'the living and moral growth' on the land, he derives this obligation from a right of every member of society to the 'hope to improve his own condition or that of his children'.[49] Second, where rights of ownership are exercised under the constraints of trust and enveloped in reciprocal personal commitments, 'property guarantees itself'.[50] That is to say, the limited, contractual obligations in the market and the demarcation lines between the separate spheres of exclusive private property are secure only to the extent that they are enforced from outside (by the state). The community constituted by trust ownership, on the other hand, gains its order and stability from within.

THE MARKET AND THE STATE

> . . . as if a private life surrounded by armies could ever be called a
> state[51]

The contrast between social unity 'grown from within' and order
imposed from without shapes the romantic understanding of the
relationship between market and state in commercial society. Economic liberalism postulates the minimal state whose but residual law-
and-order functions will leave the private sphere of spontaneous
interaction free from coercive regulation. Romantic arguments turn
the common understanding of *laissez-faire* on its head in the paradoxical claim that a fully commercialised society requires a coercive
state. Where the state is understood as but a regulatory, external
power, and where its purpose is minimised to provide security for
private property, its rule will of necessity be one of force since it
cannot rely on any bonds of spontaneous trust and loyalty among its
citizens.

> If there is only one form of property, absolute private property . . .
> the government – however liberal and benevolent it may be – will
> be able to achieve its task of protecting property and its owners
> only through force, through an iron chain cast around the bundle
> of isolated owners who are not grown together through any per-
> sonal mutual obligations. All doctrines of state prevalent in our
> time . . . confirm the truth of my conclusions in so far as they do
> not acknowledge any other instrument of government than force.[52]

The romantic state is not the policeman for the market but the
guardian of society's collective identity. It represents what all its
individual members have in common in the shared property of their
cultural traditions – in their language, religious customs, legal and
political institutions, undisrupted patterns of landownership. True, if
we look for concrete institutional forms that could express and foster
that common identity in a modern pluralist society, the romantic
critique of the market has little to offer. The suggestion that the
process of commercialisation could be held in balance by keeping
land and agriculture out of the market betrays a curious lack of
realism in the face of accelerating historical changes. And that is even
more true when we consider that the demands of the community on

the landowner amount to little more than a moral obligation to sit still on his land and to refrain from commercial ventures. Moreover, since romanticism rejected the principles of equal right and democratic citizenship as but manifestations of the same spirit of uniformity that it combated in all other spheres of social life, it was left with a model of community that owed its appeal to the analogy with family and friendship bonds. Such a model, however, could not be transferred to the plane of the modern nation state. Neither the romanticisation of monarchy as the personal embodiment of the national community, nor the attempt to bind the commercial interest into a hierarchical order of different estates borrowed from the Middle Ages could close the gap between 'community' and state.[53]

But while the romantic community lacks a vision capable of practical realisation, it does have the qualities of a critical construct. It can focus attention on certain unstated or misconstrued assumptions in the common liberal understanding of the market-state relationship. In this capacity, it reminds us of the communal structures which actually sustain a system of market exchanges and without which it would not even be intelligible. It would, Müller argues, be impossible to explain the universal acceptability of money among 'strangers' (each of whom has but imperfect knowledge of distant times and places), unless we can assume some intangible bonds of trust.[54] Just as individuals are able to communicate with each other only because their language affords them a shared property of common meanings,[55] so market competition, contracts and security of private property must rest on something more than individual self-interest or state coercion. They must rely on trust; and it is in this emphasis on the place of trust that we will find romanticism's distinctive contribution to the debate about the market and the state.

NOTES

1. Adam Smith, *Lectures on Jurisprudence*, ed. R. L Meek, D. D. Raphael and P. G. Stein, *The Glasgow Edition of the Works and Correspondence of Adam Smith*, vol. V (Oxford: Oxford University Press, 1978) p. 70.
2. Thomas Carlyle, *Past and Present* (London: Oxford University Press, 1965) p. 180.
3. For the influence of German romanticism on English thinkers, cf. R. Wellek, *Confrontations. Studies in the Intellectual and Literary Relations Between Germany, England and the United States during the Nineteenth Century* (Princeton: Princeton University Press, 1965), chs 1 and 2.

4. Thomas Babington Macaulay, 'Southey's Colloquies on Society', in Macaulay, *Critical and Historical Essays Contributed to the Edinburgh Review*, 3 vols (London: Longman, Green and Longman, 1906) vol. I, p. 233.

5. J. A. Schumpeter, *History of Economic Analysis* (New York: Oxford University Press, 1954) p. 422.

6. Adam Müller, 'Agronomische Briefe', in J. Baxa (ed.), Adam Müller's *Ausgewählte Abhandlungen*, 2nd ed. (Jena: Gustav Fischer, 1931) p. 141.

7. K. Tribe, *Governing Economy. The Reformation of German Economic Discourse 1750–1840* (Cambridge: Cambridge University Press, 1988) p. 143.

8. C.f. Macaulay, 'Southey's Colloquies', p. 233; J. S. Mill 'Coleridge', in J. M. Robson (ed.), *The Collected Works of J. S. Mill*, vol. X (Toronto: University of Toronto Press, 1969) p. 155; Schumpeter, *Economic Analysis*, p. 421.

9. C.f. R. Plant, 'Hirsch, Hayek, and Habermas : dilemmas of distribution', in A. Ellis and K. Kumar (eds), *Dilemmas of Liberal Democracy* (London and New York: Tavistock Publications, 1983) p. 49 f.

10. Cf. A. Lovejoy, 'The Meaning of "Romantic" in Early German Romanticism', in A. Lovejoy, *Essays in the History of Ideas* (Baltimore and London: John Hopkins University Press, 1948) pp. 183–206.

11. Friedrich Schlegel, 'Athenäums Fragmente', in E. Behler (ed.), *Kritische Friedrich Schlegel Ausgabe* (München: Ferdinand Schöning, 1967) p. 182.

12. Cf. Müller, *Ausgewählte Abhandlungen*, pp. 32–40, 76–85.

13. Cf. E. P. Thompson, *William Morris. Romantic to Revolutionary* (London: Merlin Press, 1977) pp. 27–32.

14. Cf. P. B. Shelley, 'A Defence of Poetry', in. H. Bloom and L. Trilling (eds), *Romantic Poetry and Prose* (New York: Oxford University Press, 1973) p. 756; S. T. Coleridge, 'Biographia Literaria', ibid., S. 649.

15. Shelley, 'Defence', p. 750.

16. Carlyle, *Past and Present*, p. 180.

17. William Wordsworth, 'Preface to Lyrical Ballads', in Bloom and Trilling, *Romantic Poetry*, p. 604.

18. Adam Smith, *An Inquiry into the Nature and Causes of the Wealth of Nations*, ed. R. H. Campbell, A. S. Skinner and W. B. Todd, The Glasgow Edition, vols 2–3 (Oxford: Oxford University Press, 1975), vol. I, p. 363.

19. Adam Müller, *Die Elemente der Staatskunst*, ed. J. Baxa (Jena: Gustav Fischer, 1922) vol. II, p. 18.

20. A. Offer, *Property and Politics 1870–1914* (Cambridge: Cambridge University Press, 1981) pp. 328–49; quote, p. 333.

21. Cf. U. Linse, *Zurück, o Mensch, zur Mutter Erde. Landkommunen in Deutschland 1890–1933* (München: Deutscher Taschenbuch Verlag, 1983) pp. 7–36.

22. Ibid. p. 35.

23. Shelley, 'Defence', p. 757.

24. Ibid.
25. Ibid.
26. Albrecht Thaer, *Grundsätze der rationellen Landwirtschaft*, in W. Conze (ed.), *Quellen zur Geschichte der deutschen Bauernbefreiung* (Göttingen:Musterschmidt, 1957) p. 78.
27. Coleridge, *Lay Sermons*, in K. Coburn (ed.), *The Collected Works of Samuel Taylor Coleridge*, vol. VI (London: Routledge, 1972) pp. 214–16.
28. Ibid. p. 169.
29. Cf. Coleridge, *On the Constitution of the Church and the State*, *Collected Works*, vol. X (London: Routledge, 1976) p. 24.
30. Coleridge, *Lay Sermons*, p. 216.
31. *Osborn's Concise Law Dictionary*, 6th ed. (London: Sweet and Maxwell, 1976) p. 332.
32. J. S. Mill, 'Coleridge', p. 157. On the legal institution of the trust, cf. F. W. Maitland, 'Trust and Corporation', in Maitland, *Selected Essays* (Cambridge: Cambridge University Press, 1936) pp. 141–227.
33. Coleridge, *Church and State*, p. 51.
34. Adam Müller, *Elemente der Staatskunst*, vol. II, p. 26.
35. Cf. Thomas Paine, 'Agrarian Justice', in M. Beer (ed.), *The Pioneers of Land Reform* (London: G. Bell and Sons, 1920) pp. 179–206; Thomas Spence, 'The Real Rights of Men', ibid. pp. 5–16.
36. Cf. U. Vogel, 'The Land Question: A Liberal Theory of Communal Property', *History Workshop, XXVII* (1989), pp. 115–20.
37. Adam Müller, *Elemente der Staatskunst*, vol. I, p. 365.
38. Cf. Coleridge, *Church and State*, p. 24 f.
39. Adam Müller, *Über König Friedrich II und die Natur, Würde und Bestimmung des Menschen*, in R. Kohler (ed.). *Adam Müller, Schriften zur Staatsphilosophie* (München: Theatiner Verlag, 1923) p. 131.
40. For a comprehensive account of the problems under discussion here, cf. E. Partridge (ed.), *Responsibilities to Future Generations. Environmental Ethics* (Buffalo, N.Y.: Prometheus Books, 1980), passim.
41. Cf. N. Rosenblum, *Another Liberalism: Romanticism and the Reconstruction of Liberal Thought* (Cambridge, Mass.: Harvard University Press, 1987).
42. Carlyle, *Past and Present*, p. 199.
43. Cf. Adam Smith, *Wealth of Nations*, vol. I., p. 420f.
44. Cf. Coleridge, *Lay Sermons*, p. 169.
45. Carlyle, *Past and Present*, p. 281.
46. Cf. Adam Müller, *Ausgewählte Abhandlungen*, p. 129.
47. Ibid. p. 157.
48. Ibid. p. 164.
49. Coleridge, *Lay Sermons*, p. 216.
50. Adam Müller, *Ausgewählte Abhandlungen*, pp. 181 ff.
51. Adam Müller, *Über Konig Friedrich*, p. 91.
52. Adam Müller, *Versuche einer neuen Theorie des Geldes mit besonderer Rücksicht auf Großbritannien* (Leipzig und Altenburg: F. A. Brockhaus, 1816), pp. 24ff.

53. Cf. Coleridge, *Church and State*, chs 7–8; Adam Müller, *Elemente der Staatskunst*.
54. Cf. Adam Müller, *Theorie des Geldes*, p. 28f.
55. Cf. Adam Müller, *Ausgewählte Abhandlungen*, p. 39; *Elemente der Staatskunst*, vol. II, p. 29f.

3 Markets and Law: The Case of Environmental Conservation

Hillel Steiner

Markets have, of course, always had their critics. And though the past two decades have witnessed an unprecedented global resurgence of market advocacy and the rapid dismantling (through privatisation and deregulation) of commerce-restricting legal provisions in countless countries, there is one policy area that has emerged as a formidable redoubt from which those critics have proved particularly difficult to dislodge. Notwithstanding the singularly abysmal environmental record of the Eastern European command economies, it seems to be widely accepted – even by Mrs Thatcher – that environmental values must be statutorily insulated from determination and allocation by competitive market forces. The world must be forced to be 'greener' than sovereign consumers apparently would allow it to be. Why?

ARGUMENTS FOR CONSERVATION

There can be no doubt that fears of eventual environmental exhaustion are considerably substantiated by the available empirical evidence. We clearly do confront the prospect of not only the depletion of natural energy resources but also the complete despoliation of the Earth's habitable environment through the elimination of plant life, pollution of the air and water by radioactive and other industrial wastes, erosion of the ozone layer and so forth. Nor does a Pollyanna-like faith in providential technological innovations seem a credible response. So it is not surprising that governments find themselves subjected to ever-mounting pressure to extend their regulation of activities affecting the environment, in the interests of conservation. A vast array of enforced measures is proposed and adopted to curb ecological prodigality. These measures create complex packages of legal rights, duties, powers and liabilities. And in so doing, they lend themselves to moral evaluation.

But surely, one might protest, the moral case for such measures is unimpeachable and hardly warrants any scrutiny. One does not need to be an expert in statistical extrapolation to perceive the broad outlines of the impending catastrophe. Green concerns are now so widely shared by politicians across the ideological spectrum and the public at large that doubts about any aspect of the case for state action can quickly be dismissed as misanthropic and perverse. Yet, as I shall attempt to show, a closer look at one prominent part of this case reveals it to be somewhat more elusive than is generally supposed.

On the face of it, one might think that a service so highly desired as environmental conservation would be readily supplied by the private sector (markets and/or voluntary non-commercial activity). After all, most highly desired goods and services are. Indeed, many individuals and organisations tirelessly and voluntarily devote themselves to the cause of conservation without recourse to supportive intervention by the state. And growing numbers of manufacturers – no doubt under pressure from those individuals and organisations – are constantly endeavouring to make their products and processes environmentally friendly. So what is the case for introducing the heavy hand of legal compulsion?

Clearly it can only be that the kinds and amounts of conservation secured by private sector activity are insufficient. There is, let us say, an *optimal level of conservation* (hereafter OLC) which this activity fails to secure and which therefore can only be brought about by enforceable measures. Such measures basically consist of state regulation of environment-affecting practices and the levying of taxes to fund the cost of conservation services supplied either by the state itself or by state subsidised agencies in the private sector.

Why does realisation of OLC require such measures? Why can it not be left to the private sector? Presumably the answer here is the same as for any other advocated state programme of provision: namely, because although highly desired, OLC is insufficiently desired by any coalition of persons able and willing to incur the restrictions and sacrifices needed to secure it. But this type of explanation borders on the trivial. What we want to know is why there is this shortfall of resources and/or motivation, since state action is presumed able to overcome it. There are, I think, three standard ways of accounting for such puzzles.

One is what I will call the 'aesthetic' argument. On this view, OLC is simply ranked too low on society's preference schedule to induce its members voluntarily to bear its costs. Supporters of this view maintain that OLC has greater value, irrespective of other people's valuations of it. Much the same sort of argument has sometimes been advanced on behalf of the state subsidising (and regulating?) cultural and research activities. For the moment I am going to put this argument to one side, not because it is absurd – on the contrary, it makes perfect sense and has much to commend it – but because we shall have reason to return to it later in the light of our consideration of the third argument.

The second argument is an economic one, based essentially on the claim that OLC is a 'public good'. That is, OLC is a good which *does* occupy a high ranking on society's preference schedule but which nonetheless cannot be profitably supplied by the market because its consumption cannot be confined to only those who would voluntarily pay for it. And the latter cannot afford to bear the costs of OLC incurred by those who would free-ride on it, i.e. consume it without paying. There is much that is sound in this argument, though it should be noted that a demonstration that the market cannot deliver does not amount to a demonstration that the state can. The afore-mentioned Eastern European experience stands as a salutary warning in this regard. There are indeed serious questions, both empirically and theoretically motivated, about the capacity of public officials' incentive structures to induce the appropriate supply of public goods.[1] And there are persuasive theoretical and empirical grounds to suppose that much environmental degradation would be curtailed by privatisation of the resources involved: that its occurrence is in part attributable precisely to the absence of private resource ownership which would empower persons with a financial stake in restricting the otherwise free access currently enjoyed by many degraders. That said, it seems clear that some scope for state conservation measures is successfully underwritten by the second argument.

Finally, there is the argument that OLC needs state action because society's preference schedule does not assign it sufficient priority: not, as in the first argument, because OLC has insufficiently appreciated value, but rather because society's preference schedule is not properly constituted. Whereas the aesthetic argument laments the *content* of society's preference schedule, this third argument takes issue with its *construction*. On the third argument, what is wrong with this schedule is that it fails to include the preferences of *future generations* of human beings.[2] It fails to take account of the interests and entitlements of those future persons whose existence is sufficiently remote in time from that of currently living persons as to preclude the former's having any prospect of confronting the latter to demand compensation for the deprivations they will have imposed upon them. We, through our ecological prodigality, are depriving our great-great-grandchildren and their descendants of OLC. And state intervention is required to stop us from doing so.

Each of these three arguments can readily be found in standard statements of the green case for state action. And each, it should be noted, presupposes a slightly different interpretation of what OLC is. The kinds and amounts of environmental conservation dictated by the aesthetic argument and the future persons argument are undoubtedly more extensive than those suggested by the public goods argument, the latter presumably being a subset of the former.[3] Of these three arguments, it is the third – the concern for future persons – that figures most prominently in green rhetoric since the suffering of whose who, unlike ourselves, can have neither voice nor recourse must clearly exert a greater pull on our consciences than our own want of aesthetic sensitivity and economic efficiency.

What I propose to show is that this third argument does not make sense. Close scrutiny will reveal its concerns to be essentially aesthetic, and not the entitlements and preferences of future persons. Indeed, future persons figure only in an exotically attenuated sense in the future it mandates the state to secure.

MORAL PRINCIPLES AND STATE POLICY

Governments implement policies by attaching legal duties to persons and enforcing their compliance with them.[4] Broadly speaking, there are two sorts of moral principle which can be used to assess these legal duties. Utilitarian principles determine the content and incidence of duties by reference to instrumental considerations. They prescribe that distribution of those duties that would be maximally or at least more productive of some specified desirable end. In contrast, justice principles treat the content and incidence of duties as intrinsically justifiable – as constitutive of desirable ends rather than as means causally contributive to a desirable end.[5]

It is this difference that accounts for both the appeal and the intractability of justice principles. On the one hand, the duties they impose are – unlike utilitarian ones – not subject to the test of instrumental efficacy, and whatever personal rights they prescribe are therefore immune to revocation under changing empirical conditions for maximising the production of what is desirable. On the other, the difficulty of determining the content and location of duties which are constitutive of desirable ends is evidently much greater than is the case for duties which serve a purely instrumental role with respect to an already specified desirable end. For it is much easier to defend the ascription of a duty (let alone its enforcement) by empirically demonstrating that compliance with it is likely to bring about more good, than by claiming that compliance with it is good *per se*. Though it is also true that the desirable end to be produced by compliance with instrumental duties gives rise to similar justificatory problems – 'Granted that compliance with duty D will produce more of end E, what's so good about E?' – and in any case, that the specification of utilitarian good is itself beset by conceptual puzzles.[6] One of these will indeed be found to lie at the heart of the third argument for state conservation action.

Why then be just? Or rather, what is the proper way of justifying the duties imposed by justice principles? The answer to this is suggested in the previous paragraph. A person affirms a justice principle if he/she believes that persons ought to enjoy some element of inviolability: that is, that there are certain things which ought not to be done to any individual regardless of how much good may have to be forgone by not doing those things.[7] It is not that complying with the duties of justice *brings about* such personal inviolability. Rather, such compliance is simply identical to not violating persons in the specified respect. Not taking other persons' lives or possessions amounts to treating them as inviolable in certain respects, whereas the utilitarian justification for such forbearances would be that their occurrence tends to bring about more good than evil *under certain circumstances*. In the absence of those circumstances, such forbearances would lack a utilitarian justification and might even be prohibited by utilitarian principles.

In imposing these duties of personal inviolability, justice principles locate correlative rights to that inviolability in all persons. What, we may well ask, is the location of the rights correlative to the duties imposed by utilitarian principles? Utilitarianism implies that whether some particular forbearance should or should not occur entirely depends upon which one, of those two alternatives, will bring about more good. Accordingly, whether you should knock down my garden wall or take my life or do neither of these things or do both of them or pay compensation for doing them or be punished for doing them depends, for utilitarianism, not upon my wishes in these matters but rather upon what would be better for the set of persons with reference to whom good is to be maximised. It is in this set of persons – or in the subset of them that is best able to ascertain and bring about the conditions of maximisation (typically, the state) – that utilitarianism locates rights. Under justice principles each individual necessarily has rights. Under utilitarianism, no individual necessarily has rights, while the rights that they may have are entirely contingent upon their efficacy in bringing about a greater amount of good. In this sense, utilitarian rights are hypothetical ones, while those dictated by justice are categorical.

Now questions about the nature of persons' moral rights are normally thought to be ones about their categorical entitlements and not about what kinds of entitlement it might currently be useful for society or its agents to assign to them. It is true that achieving a utilitarian maximand is morally good and, thus, that whatever is necessary for that achievement (including some particular allocation of rights and duties) must be derivatively morally worthy. So the suggestion here is simply the uncontroversial one that the notion of 'moral rights' is usually reserved for those rights whose moral worthiness is non-derivative in the sense of not being based on instrumental contingencies. Moral rights categorically belong to their owners, and the duty to respect them is something which each of us owes directly and non-derivatively to each other rather than to society or the state, though the state may be authorised to enforce compliance with that duty.

Legal systems create legal rights. How do we assess whether a legal system is just, whether the rights it creates are moral ones? Trivially, by ascertaining whether those rights have the same content and personal location as moral rights. But what is the content of moral rights? In the last twenty years we have witnessed something like a population explosion in theories of justice and moral rights that shows little sign of abating. Nominations for the position of being a moral right now greatly exceed the number of places available.[8] In an effort to redress this particular ecological imbalance, I shall offer reasons why the rights of future persons – those rights which unfettered markets are said to violate and which enforced conservation is supposed to protect – are not moral rights. If this is correct, then the future persons argument cannot employ justice principles to justify state action on behalf of conservation. Nor, moreover, can the future persons argument for enforced conservation find any purchase in utilitarian principles. Enforced conservation *can* be justified on maximising grounds, but these grounds have nothing to do with the wellbeing of future persons, i.e. the maximand involved is quite unrelated to the wellbeing of persons as such.

Enforced conservation policies transfer environmental resources from present persons to future ones. Such transfers are enforced on the presumption that they would not occur if left to the free choice of individuals in their market transactions and their private conservation activities. Enforced transfers are usually justified either as protections of persons' rights or as requirements of increased wellbeing. My argument is thus that the enforced transfers involved in legislated conservation policies satisfy neither of these descriptions.

JUSTICE AND ENFORCED CONSERVATION

There are evidently a number of tests which can be applied to any proposed right, to discover whether compliance with its correlative duty is a demand of justice: that is, whether it is a moral right. Each of the many competing theories of justice can generally be found to offer a variety of such tests. Perhaps the most fundamental and least contestable test consists in ascertaining whether a proposed right possesses the analytic or formal characteristics of rights in general. Exactly what these characteristics are is itself a matter of some dispute. But it seems reasonably safe to say that, whatever they are, they cannot be such as to imply that the notion of 'a right' is entirely redundant in our moral and legal vocabulary. That is, they cannot allow the complete reduction without remainder of rights-statements to duty-statements. It was, for example, Bentham's belief in this very reducibility that logically underpinned his dismissal of the notion of foundational moral rights as 'nonsense' and thence his denial that the demands of justice could ever conflict with those of maximising social utility.[9] Since we know that these two kinds of demand sometimes *do* conflict – that what is best overall may require some individual's moral rights to be sacrificed – rights must have characteristics that preclude their subsumption by the calculus that determines the content of the general duty to do what is best. We shall look at these characteristics in a moment. The point of this is that, in order to discover whether future persons have a moral right to conservation by present persons, we have to see whether such a right possesses the formal characteristics of rights in general. I suggest that it does not.

The most significant formal features of a right are all implied in the fact that we speak of rights as being *exercised*. A right entails the presence of a duty in someone other than the right-holder. And the exercise of that right consists in the right-holder's either invoking that duty – in her choosing that the dutiful performance or forbearance shall occur – or in her waiving that duty. If she invokes it, non-occurrence of the performance or forbearance is impermissible. If she waives it, non-occurrence is permissible. Rights can thereby be conceived as spheres of protected personal discretion.[10] Because this discretion is protected, rights are considered to entail a further entitlement – called a *power* – to enforce compliance with the duties correlative to them. Acts which are non-compliant with unwaived duties, being impermissible, are *liable* to enforcement measures in the form either of prevented performance or penalisation.

These quite general facts about rights give us an important lead in our quest. Since a right entails a power to enforce its correlative duty, rights must be such that it is not logically impossible for their holders to exercise these powers or, at least, to authorise others (such as the state) to do so. Having a power to enforce compliance with a duty correlative to a right does not, of course, imply that the possessor of that power is actually able to exercise it by personally wielding the requisite force. But it does at least presuppose that there is nothing logically absurd or inconceivable about her doing so, or about her conferring that power on someone else better qualified to do so. And in this regard, it is perhaps worth emphasising that such a power can be conferred – its exercise by another can be authorised – only by the right-holder herself. For White's enforcing of Red's duty to do A to count as an exercise of the power entailed by Blue's right that Red do A, it must be the case that Blue conferred that power upon, i.e. authorised, White. If White's possession of that power did *not* presuppose Blue's authorisation, it would be an open question as to why anybody might not equally claim to be possessed of that power and hence to decide whether to enforce or waive Red's compliance with his duty to do A. To be possessed of the power to uphold a right is either to be or to be authorised by that right's holder.

It follows fairly readily from these considerations that whatever duties present persons may have to future persons, those duties are not correlative to any rights on the part of future persons. There can be no such rights. Future persons are unable to enforce present persons' compliance with the latters' duties. And this inability is not merely a physical incapacity, an empirical impossibility. It is a logical impossibility. A future person is necessarily incapable either of preventing a present persons's non-compliance with his duty or of penalising him for it, because two such persons lack any element of contemporaneity. Nor is this lack of contemporaneity a merely empirical or contingent fact, one which could conceivably be otherwise. For a necessary constituent of each person's identity – of what makes a person that particular person – is her temporal location or, at least, the temporal location of her origin. A standard element in all accounts of personal identity is that I am who I am partly by virtue of my being the offspring of certain persons. To suggest that this is a merely contingent aspect of my identity, to say that I would still be identifiable as the same person even had I been born two hundred years earlier, is to imply that I could have been my parents' ancestor. And this does not make sense.

Future persons' lack of contemporaneity with present persons implies the logical impossibility of the former enforcing the latter's compliance with their duties. By the same token, it also implies the logical impossibility of future persons authorising some present persons (such as the state) to enforce other present persons' compliance. Hence such enforcement cannot be regarded as an exercise of powers implied by rights held by future persons. In short, future persons have no rights against present persons. And they can therefore have no rights that present persons conserve anything for them.

Nor, at a less formal level of argument, is this entirely surprising. It is certainly conceivable and morally acceptable that present persons might prefer that their own living standards be lower and those of future persons higher than they otherwise may be. Conservation is very far from being either irrational or immoral. But correspondingly, it is neither inconceivable nor morally unacceptable that future persons might entertain (however impotently) symmetrical preferences with respect to their own and present persons' living standards. Just such a wish may well be entertained, for example, by many Russians today as they contemplate the horrific rigours to which their ancestors were subjected during the Stalinist industrialisation programmes of the nineteen-thirties. Rawls has noted the inequities that appear to be involved here:

Herzen remarks that human development is a kind of chronological unfairness, since those who live later profit from the labor of their present predecessors without paying the same price. And Kant thought it disconcerting that earlier generations should carry their burdens only for the sake of later ones and that only the last should have the good fortune to dwell in the completed building.[11]

Hence, even if future persons could be said to have rights against present persons, there could be no *a priori* presumption that they would demand compliance with, rather than waive, the duties correlative to those rights. And if they were to waive those duties, there could be no rights- or justice-based justification for any present person nevertheless enforcing other present persons' compliance with those duties. Indeed if, as seems plausible, such a waiver were part of a transfer by future persons to present ones of the rights involved, another present person's forceable intervention would actually constitute a violation of those future persons' rights.

It is precisely because rights are domains of choice that we cannot prejudge – independent of any indication of right-holders' wishes – which actions of others are violations of rights. And it is precisely because future persons are necessarily incapable of choice, that they cannot be said to have rights against present persons. It is simply self-contradictory to identify one person's duty as correlative to another person's rights, and then to remove it from that right-holder's control by denying her the choice as to whether or not it should be complied with.

UTILITARIANISM AND ENFORCED CONSERVATION

Government policies enforcing conservation cannot be justified on grounds of justice since that enjoins the protection of rights and future persons have no rights. What justification can there be, then, for enforcing conservation? What objective is served by enforced duties of this kind?

Enforced duties which are not owed to other persons are ones which, if owed at all, are owed to society or the state. It may be that such duties are moral ones but, if so, they derive from utilitarian principles rather than the demands of justice and moral rights. Now if enforced conservation duties are justifiable on utilitarian grounds, it must be because compliance with them is believed to bring about more social wellbeing than would otherwise be the case. What is the wellbeing to be gained from this compliance?

A general truth about the enforced duties prescribed by utilitarian principles is that the gain (in social wellbeing) from compliance is greater than its cost to compliers or, conversely, that the social cost of non-compliance is greater than the gain it confers (with all of these costs and gains being presumed to be greater than zero). That is why these duties are enforced, i.e. it is presumed that the compliers would not, given the option, choose to comply with them.

But although we may speak of gains and costs as 'social ones', it is normally presumed that they must ultimately accrue to individual persons. Thus the gains from enforced conservation accrue to future persons while its costs accrue to present persons who are denied consumption of the things they must conserve. For enforced conservation to be justifiable on utilitarian grounds, it must be the case that these gains outweigh these costs: that such a policy yields a *net* gain. What grounds can there be to suppose that it does?

Evidently, what enforced conservation does is to secure both *intra*- and *inter*-generational distributions of property rights that are different from those which would prevail in its absence. It brings about a different intra-generational distribution by more heavily encumbering those persons whose production and consumption activities, and whose assets, more directly impinge on the conservable environment. But apart from the fact that intra-generational distributions of property may be thought to be more appropriately governed by the demands of justice than by those of maximising social wellbeing, it seems reasonably clear that there can be no presumption of a net gain in wellbeing to be invariably secured from the intra-generationally redistributive effects of enforced conservation. Whether there are such gains to be had is an entirely empirical question. Net gains in wellbeing *may* be attainable through intra-generational redistributions. But there is no reason to suppose that enforced conservation must be one of these gain-yielding redistributions. It could equally be a loss-yielding one. Indeed, if any presumptions are to be made here, they favour this latter prospect. For if there is a wellbeing-enhancing distribution to be secured through conservation, it will be profitable for those who would gain from this distribution to offer sufficient compensation to those who would lose from it to induce the latter *voluntarily* to conserve. The fact that this distribution is one which can be brought about only by enforcement is *prima facie* evidence for believing that it promises no net gain.[12]

What net gain, then, is to be had from enforced *inter*-generational redistribution? We cannot casually assume, for instance, that it is an increase in inter-generationally averaged per capita living standards. Sacrifices of earlier persons' consumption do not necessarily produce disproportionately greater benefits for their successors. This cannot be an invariable effect of such redistributions since, as the Stalinist industrialisation case suggests, there is no reason to suppose that the resultant increase in later persons' wellbeing may not be offset or even exceeded by the associated decrease in earlier persons' wellbeing. And again, as I shall presently argue, any presumptions in this matter must lie on the side of such redistributions producing no net gain in social wellbeing.

THE ACTUAL DESTINATION OF ENFORCED CONSERVATION

What is left? What is the nature of the good actually secured by enforced conservation? What is augmented or enhanced by such policies? Apparently, only the number of future persons itself: that is, the number of them who are environmentally sustainable. But even this is not accurate. For the size of each future generation is determined by members of the generation preceding it. Much green rhetoric, and indeed much of our own unreflective thinking about the future, are permeated by the largely subconscious and utterly false assumption that the number of future persons is already determined: that there is, as it were, some gigantic fleet of space-ships 'already out there' and heavily populated by future persons who are even now anxiously awaiting either victimisation by our self-indulgent prodigality or salvation through our present self-denial.

But the fact is that whether there will be *any* persons to gain from others' conservation – and if so, how many – is determined by those others in their procreative decisions. And it would thus be odd to suppose that those others, having decided to bring members of a further generation into being, would not *voluntarily* choose to conserve sustenance for them.[13] At best, the possibility of such an irrational ordering of choices on any significant scale constitutes a rather implausible premise upon which to rest a justification of enforced general duties to conserve. It also holds out a less than promising prospect of those duties actually being enforced.

To this line of argument it might be objected that non-sustainable offspring could be the result of parental ignorance (i.e. parental overestimation of future available sustenance) rather than parental irrationality. But although this might be true, it fails on two grounds to count as a reason supporting enforced conservation. In the first place, it is by no means obvious that governments themselves cannot fall prey to the same ignorance and overestimation – particularly democratic governments elected by these same ignorant parents, as well as by non-parents. And secondly, even if it could be supposed that governments are better informed in these matters, the most that such a supposition licenses is a policy of public information and education, and not one of enforced conservation.

What an enforced duty to conserve accomplishes is not, therefore, the provision of sustenance for the children of any current generation, since current persons decide the number of children they will have and may be presumed willing voluntarily to conserve what would be necessary to sustain them. Rather, the effect of such a duty is more plausibly understood as providing sustenance for current persons' *grand*children and their successive descendants, whose numbers are *not* decided by those current persons. In other words, part of the case for this duty's being an enforced one is the presumption that, given the choice, parents would conserve less than would be required to sustain the number of children their own children (and/or their grandchildren and/or their great-grandchildren, and so forth) would choose to have.

But since the number of children each generation decides to have would (in the absence of *enforced* conservation) rationally be a function of the presumed lower proportion of resources they prefer to conserve rather than consume, the effect of enforcing greater conservation on successive generations is simply to increase the *number of sustainable human generations* beyond what it would be in the absence of such enforcement. What is augmented or enhanced by an enforced duty to conserve is thus to be understood as nothing other than the durability of the human species as such. *Enforcing conservation increases species-longevity.*

It is of the utmost importance to appreciate, however, that an increase in the number of sustainable generations cannot be identified with an increase in the number of sustainable future persons. Procreative decisions are (rationally) positively influenced by children's sustainability prospects. It follows that the impact of enforced (and hence, greater) conservation on current persons is to increase those prospects and thereby to provide current persons with a reason to adjust *upwards* the number of sustainable children they can have. But the enforcement of conservation on those children in turn, entails that they cannot consume all that was conserved by their parents. Hence the number of them that could be sustained is less than if no conservation were to be enforced on them. Since current persons know this, they correspondingly adjust *downwards* the number of sustainable children they can have. Enforcing conservation on rational choosers increases, not the number of their sustainable descendants, but rather the number of generations – the number of successively docking space-ships – containing their descendants.

CONCLUSION

Everyone likes a parade. And it is clearly beyond the scope of this chapter to assess the value of the pageantry in an extended procession of human generations, much less, to estimate whether that value exceeds the costs thereby entailed in enforceably restricting the choices and living standards of actual persons. The longevity of the human species and the longevities of actual persons are, no doubt, two quite incommensurable goods. So the purpose of the foregoing argument is simply to show not only that enforced conservation is neither a just nor a utilitarian demand, but also that its benefits accrue literally and irreducibly to the species rather than to individual persons. They do not accrue to individual persons because, in the absence of the prospect of sufficient sustenance for those persons, they would not have been brought into existence.

Acknowledging the incommensurabilities here, I suppose we can still ask what kind of good human species-longevity is. What sort of value does it represent? Presumably the motivations for its pursuit are not too dissimilar from those which prompt persons to take up the cause of preserving other animal and plant species. These naturalist inclinations cannot be regarded as other than *aesthetic:* species-preservation is good in itself and independently of any benign effects it may have for us. As was observed earlier, this kind of claim is perfectly intelligible and most of us, I would guess, say similar things about one sort of object or another: we choose certain things because they are beautiful – they are not beautiful because we choose them.

Yet the idea that the good of species-preservation might be independent of its benefits to us seems somehow a little harder to grasp when the species in question is our own. Perhaps not. Perhaps this reaction merely bespeaks the sort of impaired detachment which so bedevils much of our ethical and political deliberation. Still, in view of the non-negligible costs imposed on actual persons' living standards by enforced conservation, one might be forgiven for wondering whether states might not pursue this goal of extending human species-longevity more economically. After all and strictly speaking, the life of the human species (like that of any other species) is guaranteed immortality as long as there are always just enough appropriate specimens alive to ensure reproduction. We might say that, as far as species-longevity is concerned, a zoo will do.

Those who argue for market regulation in the interests of conservation have offered clear and cogent reasons for believing that, in its absence, there exists a real threat to continued human life on this planet. What they have been somewhat less clear and cogent about is the question of *who* is thereby threatened.

NOTES

1. Cf. Hillel Steiner, 'Prisoner's Dilemma as an Insoluble Problem', *Mind*, 91 (1982) 285–6.
2. We might, I suppose, alternatively describe this complaint as being (like the first) about the content of the preference schedule. That is, it can be read as an objection to the low-ranking assigned to the wellbeing or entitlements of future generations. This way of interpreting the third argument still leaves it distinct from the first, whose proponents attribute intrinsic high value to OLC independent of the preferences of both present and future generations.
3. Thus the first two arguments might suggest state curbs on both energy resource depletion and atmospheric pollution, whereas the public goods argument would apply to only the latter.
4. Enforcement takes the form either of *ex ante* forceable prevention of non-compliance or of *ex post* forceable penalisation for non-compliance.
5. Of course, adherents of justice principles can and usually do acknowledge that there are also moral duties of an instrumental kind. It is in this sense that moral codes containing justice principles are 'pluralistic' whereas utilitarian codes are not. Cf. Hillel Steiner, 'Reason and Intuition in Ethics', *Ratio*, 25 (1983), 59–68 and *An Essay on Rights*, (Oxford: Blackwell, forthcoming) chs IV and VI.
6. Cf. Derek Parfit, *Reasons and Persons*, (Oxford: Oxford University Press, 1984), Part Four.
7. What those forbidden things are varies from one proposed justice principle to another.
8. For an account of the formal conditions restricting the number of such places see Hillel Steiner, 'The Structure of a Set of Compossible Rights', *Journal of Philosophy*, 74 (1977) 767–75 and *An Essay on Rights*, ch. III.

9. Cf. Jeremy Waldron (ed.), *Nonsense upon Stilts*, (London: Methuen, 1987) ch. 3.

10. Cf. W. N. Hohfeld, *Fundamental Legal Conceptions*, ed., Walter Wheeler Cook, (New Haven, Conn.: Yale University Press, 1919); H. L. A. Hart, *Essays on Bentham: Studies in Jurisprudence and Political Theory*, (Oxford: Oxford University Press, 1982) chs VII and VIII; Carl Wellman, *A Theory of Rights: Persons under Laws, Institutions and Morals*, (Totowa, N.J.: Rowman and Allanheld, 1985); L. W. Sumner, *The Moral Foundation of Rights*, (Oxford: Oxford University Press, 1987); Steiner, *An Essay on Rights*, ch. III.

11. John Rawls, *A Theory of Justice*, (Cambridge, Mass.: Harvard University Press, 1971) pp. 290–1; though Rawls then proceeds to dismiss this appearance of inequity and to propose a principle of (enforceable) 'just savings'. My explanation of why his theory of justice thereby ascribes rights to future persons is that it fails to take adequate account of the formal features of rights.

12. The case of 'public goods', previously discussed, is the main exception.

13. Adam Smith long ago observed the dependency of procreative decisions on prospective living standards (wage levels) when he remarked that 'the demand for men, like that for any other commodity, necessarily regulates the production of men'; *An Inquiry into the Nature and Causes of the Wealth of Nations*, vol. I, (eds R. H. Campbell, A. S. Skinner, W. B. Todd) (Oxford: Oxford University Press, 1976) p. 98. See also Gary Becker, *The Economic Approach to Human Behaviour*, (Chicago: University of Chicago Press, 1976) ch. 9.

4 'The Fruits of Labour' – Private Property and Moral Equality

Norman Geras

A justificatory belief system is a complex of interdependent themes and arguments. The whole, typically, has an intricate life: evolving, subject to piecemeal addition or subtraction, to internal shifts rearranging its constituent elements, to critical stricture, defensive reinforcement, creative modification, and so on. It is not always easy in the circumstances to estimate the exact importance of a given element of the whole, to know how much depends on its particular strength. Yet some elements are obviously more central strategically than others, and if it can be shown of any such central element that it is in fact intellectually flimsy, then, other things equal, this weakens the chain of justification in which it is a link.

I shall focus here on what I believe to be a link of this normatively strategic sort, an argument commonly associated with the name of John Locke and used in attempts to legitimate (great) social inequality. The argument derives original moral entitlements to private property from the labour expended by free individuals on virgin natural resources – or, as Locke himself expressed this, the labour 'mixed' with them – and it functions, for many who use it, as a polemical weapon against government interference with private property and the transactions between private proprietors; hence as a weapon against state encroachment upon the 'free' market. Since property titles of such origin, as well as any derived in turn from them by voluntary transfer, are held to be a matter of fundamental *right*, the state may not impinge on them or on the legitimate dealings of their holders other than in the way of vouchsafing protection.

The argument to be examined I shall call the labour-mixing argument. To suggest that its difficulties had gone unnoticed hitherto would not be right. They have been commented on many times. Given how serious and important they are, though, there is something odd about the way they are generally dealt with. Writers note them briefly – whether because they do not think them overwhelming, or because they think them too obviously so to be worth troubling over – and then pass on to what is of more immediate concern. With one exception to my knowledge, there has been no concentrated effort either of decisive rebuttal or of careful vindication (if the latter is indeed possible). The exception is an article by Jeremy Waldron, the substance of which is now also incorporated in his formidably impressive *The Right to Private Property*.[1] What follows takes the same direction as Waldron on this point: it impugns the labour-mixing argument. But there is more, in my own view, to be said about that argument than Waldron says, if we are to understand both its apparent strength, its widespread appeal, and the full extent of its actual weakness.

This is how I proceed. First, I exhibit the chain of moral reasoning in which I am interested, with one of its key consequences. I then comment briefly on features of it which I either do not challenge in this context or else do not wish to consider, and I say why I do not. That leaves, by elimination, the argumentative link which matters here, and I indicate why I think it really does matter. I go on to examine it: criticising the labour-mixing argument and related justifications of very unequal private property.

SELF-OWNERSHIP IN AN UNOWNED WORLD

(1)　Individual persons are the full and rightful owners (henceforth, for short, just 'owners') of themselves.

(2)　It follows that they are the owners of their capacities and talents and of their labour.

(3)　Expending their labour upon previously unowned things, or mixing it with them, yields a moral entitlement to, equivalent to ownership of, those things.

(4)　In a world of initially unowned resources, inequality of property holdings will emerge as a consequence of applying these norms; and given the differential ability, luck, efforts and so forth, of different individuals, not to speak of their different positions in the sequence of generations, such inequality is likely to be extreme.

(5)　It is mitigated, sometimes, in stories of this kind by a proviso on original acquisition: to the effect that the result of anyone's appropriation either must leave a sufficiency available to be acquired by others or must not make anyone worse off than they would have been had that appropriation not occurred – or something similar.

That some of this comes down from Locke may be seen from the following well-known lines of *The Second Treatise of Government*:

> Though the earth and all inferior creatures be common to all men, yet every man has a property in his own person; this nobody has any right to but himself. The labour of his body and the work of his hands, we may say, are properly his. Whatsoever then he removes out of the state that nature hath provided and left it in, he hath mixed his labour with, and joined to it something that is his own, and thereby makes it his property.[2]

The inegalitarian tendency of such premises has been emphasised by G. A. Cohen: 'The claim people can make to the fruits of their own labour is the strongest basis for inequality of distribution, and the claim is difficult to reject as long as self-ownership is not denied.'[3]

I for my part will not challenge the self-ownership thesis. This is primarily for tactical reasons. Even allowing full self-ownership, I think this whole line of justification is inadequate. Conceding as much as reasonably can be conceded to it for the sake of discursive compression, I try to show that it fails anyway on account of one ineradicable deficiency. If there are then other weaknesses as well, so much the worse for the justification.

I do not, in any case, believe the principle of self-ownership to be logically problematic. J. P. Day has urged otherwise, on the grounds that ownership is an irreflexive relation, but this seems an arbitrary stipulation philosophically. The notion of rights of exclusive use, control, power of transfer and so on, involved in full ownership of external things, seems to be extendable without undue semantic or logical strain to people's disposition over themselves.[4]

As to how ethically compelling the principle is, this is more debatable. Proponents of it see it as a principle of liberty. It erects a moral barrier against the holding of property rights, whether partial or total, in the persons of others without their consent; a barrier, therefore, against slavery in the limit case, and, short of that, against relations sharing something of the essence of slavery. Critics of the principle, on the other hand, say that it is precisely self-ownership that would morally permit slavery, via the voluntary alienation by individuals of what they own and so have a right to alienate, in this case themselves.[5] Formally there is no contradiction, of course, since what the principle excludes is only enslavement without consent, slavery involuntarily instituted.

It is at least arguable that we can do without slavery, period. It is a moral abomination, however instituted, and the freedom sacrificed by forbidding consent to it outweighed by the freedoms so secured. Locke himself, it may be noted, in effect restricts individual self-ownership by ruling out enslavement by consent. As God's creatures we are entitled neither to destroy ourselves nor to court our own destruction by putting ourselves under 'the absolute, arbitrary power of another'. Our ownership of ourselves is limited by God's owner-ship of us, as being his workmanship.[6] I set aside, however, all such qualms about unqualified self-ownership, religiously or otherwise inspired, and rest content here with the not altogether reassuring hypothesis that few if any self-owners will ever consent to be en-slaved.

The suggestion is often met with also that it is the principle of self-ownership which protects people against the awful contingency of having their organs (an eye, a kidney, etc.) compulsorily con-fiscated – for the benefit, say, of others less well off than themselves in the way of organs.[7] Were it to be pointed out that exacting a pint of blood each from (healthy) people, in circumstances where it might be critically important to do that, also compromises their self-ownership without being on the face of it quite so horrible, the 'slippery slope' would doubtless be invoked: once you can contemplate anything of this kind, who knows where you will stop? A clear boundary is needed. Let us discount the possibility that other principles might supply one.

I go along, then, with (1), the self-ownership thesis. And I abstract in doing so from the problems that will be generated by asking whether it is, exactly, one's person (as according to some commen-tators it was for Locke)[8] or one's body or indeed one's 'self' that one owns. I take it simply that each individual is the owner of everything encompassed by his or her physical frame.

I shall accept also the derivation from this – (2) – that individuals own their capacities, their talents and their labour. In relation to the latter, I disregard again Day's objection: that it is logically improper to speak of owning an activity such as labour. Though the semantic strain is perhaps greater here than in the case of ownership of oneself

('She owns this kick' being odder than 'He owns this leg'), the sense of an exclusive right of control or decision over something can as well be applied to the activity as to the bodily means of it.[9]

Bypassing for the time being (3), the labour-mixing argument, I now want to explain how I shall handle the premiss contained in (4), of an initial non-ownership of natural resources. I explain via a brief comment on Locke.

In the passage quoted above and at several other places in the *Second Treatise*, Locke speaks variously of the world, the earth and the things of nature as having been given by God to humankind in common. He does not, however, intend by this a condition of genuine joint ownership. He intends, in effect, one of non-ownership. For it is central to Locke's purpose to insist that nobody requires the consent of others – as they would so require it with real joint ownership – to appropriate from this common gift for their own private use.[10] At the same time, the condition is not one of, so to say, 'pure' non-ownership. A shadow of the principle of joint rights hovers over it in the shape of Locke's stipulation that anything appropriated must be for use, must not be allowed to waste or spoil.[11] The reason behind this is that his justification of private property is guided by a teleology of, broadly, welfare. Private appropriation for Locke is the means, and it serves the ends, of survival and flourishing. The preservation of humanity is a 'fundamental law of nature' and each person's right to preservation a right to the means of subsistence – including, in circumstances of extreme want, to the surplus or plenty of others.[12] That this amounts to a residual common property right is highlighted by Locke's saying that to take more than one can use is to take what 'belongs' to others and that to waste anything is to 'rob' them.[13]

I shall not challenge, nor shall I, as Locke does, qualify, the premiss of original non-ownership of natural resources. I shall accept it. But I accept it *only as an initial premiss*: as a point of departure in discussion. Some kind of joint ownership or, for that matter, private ownership otherwise founded than on labour-mixing, might well be a *conclusion* of such discussion. But it is unfruitful to treat these simply as alternative premisses to that of non-ownership. For, if private property through labour-mixing requires justification, an effort of moral foundation by means of normatively relevant argument, so too does any kind of joint ownership or differently conceived route to private property. The assumption of original non-ownership of the earth's resources clears the ground for an examination of the moral claims of one putative route away from that condition as compared with others.

I illustrate by addressing myself to an issue raised by Robert Nozick. Amongst a number of other questions about the labour-mixing argument, Nozick asks why mixing what one owns with what one does not should be a way of gaining the latter rather than of losing the former.[14] Suppose, then, that I am the undisputed owner of a small sea. I spill a cupful of my sea into an unattended can of tomato juice and claim the mixture. If my moral title to the sea is indeed sound, why *should* I lose my cupful of it rather than gain the tomato juice? Perhaps someone else already owns this. But what if nobody does?

Imagine, instead, that one member, L, of a low-tech community of committed self-owners gets his leg caught in a high-tech trap from which it cannot be removed. The trap is unowned, remnant of a dead civilisation. It is, for L's community, a virgin 'natural' object. L owns his leg, now fastened in the trap. No one else makes, or has, any moral claim on the trap: no one needs or even wants it, has ever made any effort to get it, nor deserves it for any other kind of reason; everyone else, as it happens, already has an identical trap, found earlier; etc. If L's right to his leg is incontestable – as for this community, and us here, it is – and no one has any moral right to the trap, then L is surely entitled to the composite 'leg-trap', formed by his leg and the trap. This is one way of answering Nozick's question. L has a rightful claim on one component of something to whose other components nobody has any moral claim.[15]

Suppose, however, that other such claims, amounting to competing claims of (either full or partial) ownership, *are* now made to the hitherto unowned trap. Then, an argument will be required to establish whether L's claim to the trap – in virtue of its being irremovably attached to something he owns[16] – is more morally compelling than these other claims.

Our acceptance of the initial non-ownership of natural resources is not an acceptance that no other basis for ownership can be established than by labour-mixing. It is merely the concession that we do not begin by assuming the validity of another such basis. We leave the field clear both for labour-mixing and alternative types of claim. We allow that the principle underlying labour-mixing can be argued for, but also that it can be argued against. It is a fact, so far as we know, that there were once no people, so that everything was in the relevant meaning unowned. Taking this (pre)historic condition as also a normative starting point, we ask how labour-mixing fares against other putative foundational arguments for property.

This brings me to (5), the 'sufficiency' or 'not-worsening' proviso, sometimes held to limit original acquisition through labour. Where I have until now accepted without challenge the assumptions that frame the labour-mixing argument in the chain of reasoning under examination, this proviso I simply set aside as a detachable link of it.

Jeremy Waldron, it is relevant to note, has argued persuasively that there is no such proviso in the *Second Treatise*. That 'enough and as good', in Locke's phrase, is left for others, is merely an effect and not a condition of private acquisition in the early stages of this process in the state of nature.[17] Still, the exegetical point is not decisive. Our interest is in a family of Locke-*like* arguments, including but not only Locke's own; and other writers have taken such a proviso seriously. Our acceptance, however, of the premiss of original non-ownership of natural resources dictates that the proviso be set aside in the first instance, along with other qualifications of that premiss. For it does qualify it. If I cannot through my labour appropriate a given area of untouched land, because to do so would either leave insufficient for others or make them, in some specified sense, worse off, then these others have rights on that land and it is not altogether unowned.[18] I set aside the proviso *as an initial assumption*, whatever its precise content; and let the moral concerns which inspire it compete on an equal footing with the labour-mixing argument, from an original position of non-ownership of the world.

There are, it seems to me in any case, good reasons of expository 'purity' for so removing the proviso from the labour-mixing argument to which it is adjunct. This forces the argument to walk unaided, as it were, thus allowing us to estimate its independent strength. If it has little or none and the proviso is a crutch, we will be better able to see this. We prevent, by change of metaphor, a bad argument from hiding behind a good, or a less bad, one. But – it could be suggested – what if the argument is, not bad, but just partially adequate; in need, like many another argument, of supplementary support? Even were this so, viewing the argument on its own would enable us more clearly to perceive that, its strengths alongside its weaknesses, unobscured by other matter.

(Putting aside the proviso in order to focus on the argument it supplements, obliges me to meet a contention of G. A. Cohen's that the reverse is, in fact, better procedure. According to Cohen,

Nozick, who does take a version of the proviso seriously, is right to concentrate attention on it, rather than on the labour-mixing notion with which he is much briefer. For it is the impact of any acquisition, Cohen argues, more than how it was brought about, that matters. An acquisition will be 'difficult to criticise', and the basis of it by implication unimportant, if no one is harmed by it; if, in terms of Nozick's version of the proviso, nobody's situation is worsened. But Cohen himself goes on from here to show, with great clarity, that there is virtually no acquisition which will not make other people worse off relative to some morally non-arbitrary alternative dispensation.[19] His own demonstration reflects back on the observation made in introducing it. If, now, we cannot ever establish that an acquisition is harmless, then the moral basis of it may indeed be of concern.)

MIXING AND TRANSFORMING

My opening commentary on the rest of the sequence completed, I turn finally to (3), labour-mixing itself, as a basis for claims of private ownership. I shall examine it after one last preliminary, a brief answer to the question why I see it as meriting attention. Its importance may well be doubted. After all, this ideal story of acquisition through labour, from an original position of non-ownership of external things, bears a rather distant relation to the real history of the world; of private property in particular.[20] Why bother with the discussion of such a mythical route to economic-distributional patterns whose real genesis has plainly been different?

My answer is that, first, the issue of what is a normatively adequate genesis of property titles is a crucial one, irrespective of the actual history of actual property. For, as Hillel Steiner has put this point, 'it is a necessary truth that no object can be made from nothing, and hence that all titles to manufactured or freely transferred objects must derive from titles to natural and previously unowned objects.' Consequently, for anything at all ever to be owned, it, or the constituents of it, must have a first owner; and we may reasonably enquire just what it is that gives this person, or group, rights over the thing. If nothing does, all claims subsequently derived from the initial (*de facto*) title are put in question.[21] 'Original position' or 'state of nature' constructions of the process of appropriation are a methodological device for fastening upon such normative origins; a convenient way of focusing on the foundational conceptual moment by artificially treating it as a chronological one. They are a selective abstraction.

Second, the selection of precisely labour-mixing for scrutiny in this context, notwithstanding the fact that it is scarcely possible any longer with unowned resources, is motivated by my belief that the principle encapsulates, nevertheless, a normative idea of continuing currency and some apparent force. We have seen this idea formulated once already. It was expressed also by John Stuart Mill: 'Private property, in every defence made of it, is supposed to mean, the guarantee to individuals of the fruits of their own labour . . .'.[22] My interest here happens to be in anti-egalitarian usages of the idea. But it will not have failed to occur to readers that entitlement to the fruits of one's labour also has a socialist pedigree, and that the (or at least one) Marxist concept of exploitation depends on it: the concept, namely, that workers are exploited when, and in that, a portion of the value they create is appropriated by their capitalist employers. I examine the labour-mixing argument with a view also to assessing some cognate ideas.

In the *Second Treatise*, then, John Locke offers several labour-based justifications for acquisition. It is a moot point whether those other than labour-mixing as such were intended or understood by him as wholly distinct from it. That labour costs effort, for example, or that it makes things more valuable to people – were these meant as separate, additional justifications, or does the labour-mixing argument itself ride on them? Later, I consider the possibility that it does. But if it does, it is important to recognise this, for it has significant consequences. We need, first, to know how the argument fares on its own.

Locke in any case, in making that argument, repeatedly uses a style of formulation whose force is different from asserting that labour is effortful, or value-creating; or of any other particular quality. As the passage earlier cited says, what a man removes from its natural state he has mixed his labour with, 'and joined to it something that is his own, and *thereby* makes it his property' (my emphasis). Locke expresses this thought twice more in the same paragraph: '[the object] hath by this labour something annexed to it that excludes the common right of other men'; and 'this labour being the unquestionable property of the labourer, no man but he can have a right to what that is once joined to . . .'. Shortly afterwards, he speaks also of man 'lay[ing] out something upon it [the earth] that was his own, his labour'; 'annex[ing] to it something that was his property, which another had no title to, nor could without injury take from him'.[23]

That labouring on something entitles you to own it turns, in all these formulations, on what you have mixed into the virgin matter being, not your *labour*, but simply *yours*. It is that it is yours and mixed, not that it was hard or value-enhancing, that counts here. The inference from mixture to entitlement would work for any of your property you mixed – except, only, for one circumstance. For, though Locke does not make this explicit, it is critical to the inference that the mixing is irrevocable. What is joined cannot be disjoined. Otherwise, someone could just extricate the mixed-in stuff from what it was mixed into, and make off with the latter themselves, having returned to you what was yours; 'without injury'. The burden of the argument is that they cannot deprive you of the hitherto unowned matter without depriving you simultaneously of what you own.[24]

Now, in the article earlier mentioned, Waldron makes two powerful logical objections to this argument. The first is that it exploits what is merely a metaphor as though it were literally true. Labour is an activity, not a substance. It cannot actually be mixed with anything. When you genuinely mix two things, there are the two things and the activity of mixing them. Here, with the labour and the object laboured on, there is just one thing, the object, and an activity, labouring. Or else, if you do treat this as a second substance, then you still want an activity, the mixing; and so have to count the labour again, as activity as well as substance. The analogy will not work. Second, and overlooking this first objection, the derivation of entitlement from the metaphor presupposes a right to something – what you already own and mix in – that in the case of labour is no longer, after the mixing, even there: 'the labour, *qua* labour, no longer exists.' There can be no further right to what no longer exists, nor any entitlement consequently derivable from such right.[25]

Strong as they are, these logical objections deflect attention from something as important; more important, indeed, to the moral dimension of the question. It is easier to grasp if we pretend that Waldron's objections do not hold; that labour actually is a substance and still extant after being mixed. What better pretence than to replace it by a substance? This will help us also to forget labour's specific qualities as labour and to concentrate on (what is supposed to matter here) its being, merely, property.

I own a quantity of powder which I allow to be scattered over a lovely, unowned beach. This is powder-, not labour-mixing. 'Allow to be scattered' means just that : accidentally I let the wind do it, as I amble about and the powder trickles from a hole in my bag. It gets mixed with the beach, as good as inextricably. For though by luck I may locate some grains of it, I cannot possibly find them all. I claim the beach. Others are beginning to voice competing claims.

I shall not ask how potent, morally, my claim to the beach would be. I shall suggest, instead, you try to think of a *weaker* one. The suggestion is not just rhetorical. Really, what claim to the beach could be weaker? It may be urged that the example does not genuinely meet Waldron's second objection. Mixed the powder may be, but in effect it no longer exists. But this depends on what you think it was. If it was face powder, it no longer usefully exists as that. But if it was the remains of my recently-cremated donkey, it still exists as remains, and in a medium suitable to them. Or suppose that someone makes a large, nutritious cake, then abandons it to all comers. A group of such, which includes myself, is discussing putative shares, when I say, because it is true, that one of my eggs has been mixed into the cake – and this is, therefore, mine. My egg no longer exists as an egg, but its nourishing substances, my property under a description I favour, do still exist; only mixed. Again, what claim to the cake could be weaker than mine to all of it?

It follows from what was said about L's trapped leg that I would be entitled to the beach, or the cake, if there were *no* other moral claims on it. However: several people need this beach, for recuperative or self-developmental purposes; one person has travelled weeks to reach it; another would put it to great social benefit; others just think they have a right, with me, to some (use) of it. Or: we come upon the cake hungry; a child amongst us has her birthday today; everyone feels entitled to equal consideration in dividing the cake; and so on. Not only are claims like these clearly stronger, morally, than mine; even that someone just wanted some beach, or cake – not usually considered an especially powerful type of claim – would be, I contend, morally stronger. For, think what my claim amounts to: a right to all of something on account of a *bare physical conjunction*. To find a weaker claim you need other such morally arbitrary connections: 'I had a dream about a beach like this'; 'It is visible from my hill'; 'I said "cake" first'; 'My mother used to bake such cakes'. Of course, one *could* choose to commend or adopt one of these as a principle of acquisition. But to suggest they carry 'natural' moral weight is absurd. So it is, if subtracting from the labour-mixing argument the specificities of labour, as some of Locke's own formulations seem to do, you rest things purely on the fact of mixture.

I do not need to be told, incidentally, that these are particularly helpful examples for me. I chose them for that reason. Were it all mine, you see, the use I would actually make of the beach, *qua* resting place for my donkey, would be to stand there awhile, fondly remembering him; and of the cake, *qua* bearer of my egg's nutrients, would be nutritional; and otherwise, in both cases, none. So, I can be offered precisely this use of the beach and this, the egg's, nutritional equivalent in cake – plus whatever I might also be due on the sort of grounds informing other people's claims. One could certainly have different examples: in which what gets mixed in is of greater value to its owner, and invites a (pretty comprehensive) title for this individual to the whole 'mixture'. We already do have, of this ilk, L's trapped leg. But, then, it is L's *need* of his leg, or its irreplaceable value; generally, it is the specific quality of what is the person's in the mixture, that carries moral weight, when (as here) it does. It is not its mere physical conjunction with other things.

Exactly the same difficulty vitiates the suggestion by Hillel Steiner that Locke's metaphor can in fact be given effective, non-metaphorical sense, by taking it to be energy that gets mixed with things in labouring. A process genuinely akin to mixture does occur; and ownership of a quantity of expended energy forms the basis of the labourer's title to what is laboured on.[26]

I pass over briefly the point – developed, again, from Waldron – that this is not really an interpretation *of* labour-mixing, but an alternative proposal. Not all, sometimes perhaps none, of the energy expended in labour goes into the object laboured on. If you pursue a hare,[27] the energy you expend is not, or is hardly at all, *in* the hare. Moreover, quite apart from labour, energy is transferred by people to matter around them willy-nilly, as they come into contact with it, as their bodies give off heat, etc. Energy-mixing, could you monitor it, would yield another set of entitlements, overlapping only partially with any held to derive from labour.

Once more, though, ignore such logical objections and consider what strength of claim energy-mixing, just as such, could plausibly generate. We abstract, remember, from any moral purchase to be had from possible associations here with effort and its virtues. Your claim to own a tree because you had sat against it, warming it, or had so placed your radiator to do this, would not be at all compelling. Compare it with 'I spat [sic] somewhere on this beach – (or) I cut my hair here, letting it fall in the sand – so making the beach mine'. Try to think of weaker, more arbitrary claims.

Labour is not a substance and cannot be mixed. Even if it were and could be, the bare mixing of what one owns with unowned matter yields, at best, an extremely feeble moral claim to such matter, weaker than virtually any standard alternative. Reasons of interpretative charity suggest we should pick up another strand in Locke's argument.

An obvious strand to pick up is this. Labour-mixing is in reality labouring, and labouring changes its object. The point was made long ago by David Hume: 'We cannot be said to join our labour to anything but in a figurative sense. Properly speaking, we only make an alteration on it by our labour.' Perhaps, then, it is the transformation which labour effects in objects that establishes a title to them.[28] Some passages in the *Second Treatise* do appear to highlight this side of things. Thus, Locke writes that whoever has employed his labour 'about any of the spontaneous products of nature as any way to alter them from the state which nature put them in, by placing any of his labour on them, did thereby acquire a propriety in them'; and again, 'all that his industry could extend to, to alter from the state nature had put it in, was his'. Another Lockean locution has things 're-moved', through labour, from their original condition, where some-times the force of 'removed' seems to be, simultaneously, a taking away, a privatising of what was formerly 'common', and an alteration of things from their initial state.[29]

Now, from this angle one can, I think, give rough sense to the idea of 'mixing'. But the sense one can give it is not the sense Locke and its other sponsors need, to get the normative link they cherish between person and object.[30] Here, at any event, is the rough sense. If I change something by working on it, then it will have features it did not have before, and I can say these have been 'added' by me; though, of course, features have also been 'subtracted'. (Locke himself expresses labour-mixing in terms of addition: 'That labour put a distinction between them and common; that added something to them more than nature . . . had done.'[31]) The features added, if one thinks of it in this way, are not themselves labour; they are the effects of labour. But the elision of cause and effect is, so to say, short, and even encouraged by some ways of speaking. The 'work of his hands' is what his hands do, an activity, and it is also what they fashion, the effects or the product of that activity.[32] One can think of the effect as the cause, frozen.

Yet, for all that, the effect is not the cause, and ownership of the cause, labour, not equivalent to ownership of its effect, the alterations wrought by it, let alone of the whole object altered. We want pertinent ethical considerations leading from one to the other. It is easy to let oneself think this connection, cause to effect, is just obvious, undeniable. Imagine a sculptor. She takes a shapeless mass (as we say) of unowned matter, and struggles to give her vision form; bending her back, worrying, devoting her time, her effort, her best creative inspiration. Whose should the sculpture be?[33] But is it because her labour was the cause, and the sculpture the effect? If I remove a loose bit of bark from the abundant fruit tree you lately sat against; or pick a raisin from that cake; or take a pebble from the beach; are tree, cake or beach all mine, because altered by me – and against the moral claims (of need, desert, equal right, etc.) of others? Say 'yes', for argument's sake. In the state of nature, then, I accidentally surprise a herd of unowned animals. Do I now own the herd, being the cause of an alteration in its condition? Try to suggest a recognisable moral ground for saying people acquire exclusive rights over everything they cause to change.

Readers who have not already done so may begin to lose patience. The subject, they may say, was alterations wrought by labour – scarcely what these examples embody. The examples are merely of effects, not of labouring-effects. But the hypothesis we set out to explore was that labouring on things gives a title to them, *because* it transforms them. If you now object, in substance: transforming things gives a title to them (only) *when and because* it is labouring, well and good. We lack, consequently, having failed again to find here, a moral reason why labouring does this.

This second (altering) strand shares with the first (mixing) one a further difficulty, which should not be passed over. For, although well-known, it has never been satisfactorily met. It is the issue of boundaries. It is most crucial in relation to land. By turning a shovelful of earth, I alter or (assuming this did make sense) mix my labour with the earth turned by my shovel. But so – incontrovertibly – do I alter, mixing my labour with, the mound on which I dig; and the area visible from it; and the entire land mass on which it stands. To add to its other problems, this principle of appropriation is radically indeterminate. It could yield large first claims.

Locke, for his part, at least offered something on the issue. Our property, according to him, is bounded by our uses. Through labour, one may obtain ownership of as much as one can use 'to any advantage of life'.[34] Simply to enclose an area is insufficient: lying waste, it remains available for appropriation by others. 'As much land as a man tills, plants, improves, cultivates, and can use the product of, so much is his property. He *by his labour* does, as it were, enclose it from the common' (my emphasis).[35] But there is here a discrepancy between the formal criterion offered – use to any advantage of life – and the substantive specification of it, which is exclusively agricultural. Land can obviously be used otherwise.[36] The criterion will fail to place meaningful limits on appropriation. Just by setting foot on this big uninhabited island I alter it, and digging I mix my labour with it, thus beginning (immediately) to prepare it for use as a recreational facility, by me, my family and friends – and anyone else willing to pay me for the enjoyment of what I own. As this example also shows, to appeal to purposes here ('The extent . . . [is] naturally defined by the purposes for which one labours')[37] will help not at all.

The point is that there is no *natural* boundary, and so a conventional one has to be given.[38] But this is ruinous for the principle. The convention can be made to leave space for ownership rights founded on other moral bases than labour-mixing/transforming, if not to render the principle itself altogether nugatory. 'A beautiful sculpture. But you altered only the outside. As we are equally entitled to the inside, we'll retain occasional borrowing rights.' 'Sorry, but we need the inside.' '*Some* of the top-soil is yours.' It is understandable if those who still have time for the labour-mixing idea evade this difficulty. Nozick raises it; and passes on. Steiner concedes that it is 'well worth dodging'. Another writer wonders why 'vagueness' here should even matter.[39] Vagueness? This is not a case, as is indeed common, of some approximate way of drawing a line, with the unavoidable rough edges. It is a case of there being no line – except by appeal to considerations that are extraneous to the principle supposed to determine it.

(I include Nozick amongst those attached to the labour-mixing principle. It is Waldron's contention that he 'rejects it completely', but I think this is wrong. Nozick, it is true, is coy about actually accepting the principle, but some of his argument depends on it.)[40]

IDENTIFICATION AND DESERT

Logically void, uncompelling morally, and of indeterminate application to boot, the notion under scrutiny can evoke blank scepticism. Some express themselves quite unmoved by it.[41] And yet, others continue not merely to affirm it, but to affirm it as embodying an intuition whose power is, to them, manifest. One is bound to surmise that the affirmation draws strength from elsewhere. Earlier, I suggested with regard to Locke that the labour-mixing principle might ride on other things, related to but distinct from it. I now argue that that is so. Two other ideas are in play: one, (loosely) personal extension; the other, desert.

As to the first, I am not myself persuaded it is of much significance *in Locke*. But one commentator proposes so. Discounting that Locke's metaphor could be intended literally, he proffers instead a psychological meaning. The idea is of 'an extension of the personality to physical objects', so that they become 'part of our very selves'. We have a 'feeling of unification' with them. Through labour, 'something of the spiritual ego [is] infused into the object'; and for others than the labourer then to have a right to the object would imply 'a right over another free individual, which is out of the question.'[42] However it may be with Locke, this idea of something *of the person* (here their 'spiritual ego') *in* the thing, so the latter becomes part or extension of the former, certainly figures in other advocacy from labour-mixing to exclusive property rights. We are told by Murray Rothbard, for example, that Crusoe, in mixing his labour with the soil, is 'stamping the imprint of his personality and his energy on the land'; and that a man has 'the right to own the product that he has made, by his energy and effort, into a veritable extension of his own personality'; and (quoting earlier advocacy) that the product is 'an emanation from his being' – he 'has left a fragment of his own person in the thing'.[43]

I consider three possibilities suggested by these locutions. First, what there is of the person in the thing is an ineffable substance, not open to observation or discovery. The argument then rests on an arcane metaphysic and need not detain us. Second, what there is of the person in the thing is just the person's labour. Labour, however, is not a substance in the thing; it is an activity. Third, the meaning is entirely psychological. There is nothing of the person actually in the thing, but the person feels a powerful identification with it and would experience its loss as a wound; perhaps more grievously still. There is no question that working long or hard on something can produce this type of identification. Our earlier example of the sculptor partly traded on its likelihood; and in general those who have done practically any sort of work will be familiar with it.

But the feeling is also produced in other ways. Mere long possession can do it. (He writes each day at this bureau; periodically rearranges its contents. She has *lived* here so long.) Even wanting something badly enough can do it. Used in support of exclusively labour-based appropriative rights, this type of identification is illicitly exploited, for it is not special to labour. Further, if it carries moral weight, it must do so as a species of need, and has to be assessed, then, relative to other needs. Again, should one respond that need due to an identification formed through labour counts in a way that other kinds of identification or of need do not, the result will be that 'extension of the personality' is not, after all, the reason for labour-based property entitlements – labour is.

I turn to desert. Some writers conflate here two different notions: that of fair reward for effort; and that of an entitlement to what one produces or 'creates', be it the value or the thing itself.[44] I keep the two notions distinct. Each figures significantly in Locke's discussion of property in the *Second Treatise*. Much is made there of the taking of 'pains', of 'toil', 'sweat' and 'honest industry'; as also of the 'improvement' labour effects in things, its enormous value-enhancing powers.[45] In Nozick, by comparison, desert is but a shadow. This is not surprising, for desert can become the basis of a liberty-threatening distributional 'pattern', such as he disparages. That desert might weigh at the point of original acquisition would raise the (for him) uncomfortable question of why it should not also weigh at other points: such as at the inheritance of vast fortunes; or at the receipt of a wretched wage for long, painstaking work.[46] Yet, 'desert' does cast a shadow in Nozick, in a prized foursome with 'earning, producing, entitlement'.[47]

On the suspicion that this is what the argument from labour to exclusive property covertly depends on, I now explore the moral force desert carries in its different versions. I start with value, and a short story. The latter is about a performance rather than a physical product, but nothing turns on that. The story is entitled 'Wilt who?'

It concerns a once famous basketball player fallen on hard times. He conceives the plan of making a come-back and collecting, as he used to, a modest sum from each spectator – over and above the regular ticket price and just for himself. With difficulty, he finds a team to host the enterprise, and a game is arranged. Nobody shows. Basketball is thought of little in this place and Wilt (as is his name) not at all. His friends get to work, publicising his plight and his skills. For the next games, all well-attended, Wilt, chastened, seeks no bonus. But after turning in some brilliant performances, he tries again. A sum is added to the price of each ticket. The spectators, now flocking in, and apprised of the scheme, are happy to pay the extra if Wilt plays. And being of generous disposition, they are happy, too, for some of it to go towards helping him through his difficulties. But for the rest, they think his regular share of the gate a decent return for his game. The balance of Wilt's putative bonus they insist – and claim the right to insist – should be spent on improving the spectating facilities.

Wilt's idea is that he is entitled to the fruits of his labour. The value of his performance, which draws the fans, depends on him. But these same fans, somewhat taken with this value-creation theory of desert, say the value of his performance depends on them. It was worth nothing before they became interested in it. Value, they say, is not an objective property of his performance. It has value because *they* value it.[48] They will use the extra gate money towards better facilities. Wilt fumes. 'You just sit and watch. I exert myself every game to show you something worth watching. Every day I work out. I practise.' 'Hmmm . . . but that,' someone reflects, 'is a different argument; (most of) the other players also do their best.' Eventually, Wilt and his fans agree that the value-creation notion of desert is no good. It is a variant of the view that people have exclusive rights to whatever they have had a part in causing to be as it is.

Now, it may be suggested that it is not the value of Wilt's performance that is the point, it is the performance itself – or, *mutatis mutandis*, the physical product he makes. *This* is the fruit of his labour: it is, indisputably, its result, and he should get the benefit. But without further argument here, we still lack a reason why something's being the result of a person's labour matters morally. Is this the view, again, that one has exclusive rights over what one has caused to be as it is – altered? If so, it will be proper for me to own the beach, as I have removed a pebble from it. Why does it matter that something is the result of someone's actions? One could say, 'It just does', cleaving to the principle regardless. One could; but that is not cogent, and proponents of the principle clearly feel it is cogent. Or one could suggest that what matters is the *effort* labour involves: the product is due reward for effort. But this is, once more, 'a different argument'.

It lands us in quite another world of entitlements. The whole sculpture may be fair reward for the efforts of our sculptor; but the whole beach is not fair reward for mine. In general, the criterion will not yield the normatively solid link between person and object that the criterion's supporters aver. Further, it has large redistributive consequences where – as happens – some people expend their efforts transforming materials already claimed by other people, while these others, whatever else they earn and however else they do so, receive a return just from their (*de facto*) title to the said materials.

We are left, in the end, merely with the power of metaphor and association. It is testimony to their power just how often such devices crop up, to convey some veritable unity of substance between the person and the altered thing. Think of 'fruits'. They can be simply 'results', 'effects'. But fruits also grow upon the plant. From critics as from sponsors of the view which has been the subject of this essay, in exposition only or in commendation of it, those literary devices talk: of 'fruits of his body and capacities'; of 'noncontractual title to the fruits of others' labour, *hence* to the labour embodied in [the] objects, and *thus* by extension to the persons whose labour that is' (my emphases); of 'seizing the results of someone's labour' – as through taxation – being like 'seizing hours' from them, and like becoming a 'part-owner' of them; of 'steal[ing] the vegetables' some- one has raised being equivalent to treating this person 'like a slave'.[49] *But*: there is no bit of the person in the thing. If someone *is* wronged, as they may be, by not getting (part of) what results from their labour, this can only be shown by establishing why they are entitled to get it. Nothing is established by the use of metaphors and conti- guities which themselves just presuppose that entitlement, through virtual identification of person and thing.

People are wronged when their efforts are overlooked, discounted, ill-rewarded; as they are wronged when their vital needs are over- looked, discounted, not met. Why this is so, is another, bigger story. It has something to do with the principle of moral equality: of giving persons equal consideration as agents. Efforts and needs are a kind of burden and to let them go unrewarded or unmet fits ill with the commitment to giving equal consideration to their 'bearers'. So does it fit ill with that commitment, if the basic rights and freedoms of people are taken lightly. Proponents of labour-mixing and the like assert that such rights and freedoms *are* taken lightly in egalitarian viewpoints such as that just adumbrated. But the assertion depends on persuasively establishing the moral tie between self-owning per- sons and what they have transformed or 'mixed' their labour with – and this has never yet been done.

78 The Market and the State

NOTES

1. Jeremy Waldron, 'Two Worries About Mixing One's Labour', *Philosophical Quarterly*, 33 (1983) 37–44; and *The Right to Private Property* (Oxford: Oxford University Press, 1988), pp. 184–91. I refer, hereafter, to the second of these simply as Waldron.
2. John Locke, *Two Treatises of Government*, II, sec. 27.
3. G. A. Cohen, 'Self-Ownership, World Ownership and Equality', in Frank S. Lucash (ed.), *Justice and Equality Here and Now* (Ithaca and London: Cornell University Press, 1986), p. 117 – cited hereafter as Cohen I; and cf. his 'Marx and Locke on Land and Labour', *Proceedings of the British Academy*, 71 (1985) 362.
4. J. P. Day, 'Locke on Property', *Philosophical Quarterly*, 16 (1966) 216–18; and See Lawrence C. Becker, *Property Rights* (London: Routledge, 1977), p. 37, for the contrary view.
5. See A. M. Honoré, 'Ownership', in A. G. Guest (ed.), *Oxford Essays in Jurisprudence* (Oxford: Oxford University Press, 1961), pp. 129–30; and 'Property, Title and Redistribution', *Archiv für Rechts-und Sozialphilosophie*, 10 (1977) 107 n. 5; also James M. Smith, 'The Scope of Property Rights', in Samuel L. Blumenfeld (ed.), *Property in a Humane Economy* (La Salle Ill.: Open Court, 1974), p. 238.
6. *Two Treatises*, II, secs 6, 23.
7. See, e. g., Erick Mack, 'Distributive Justice and the Tensions of Lockeanism', *Social Philosophy & Policy*, 1 (1983) 149; Robert Nozick, *Anarchy, State, and Utopia* (Oxford: Blackwell, 1980), p. 206; and Fred D. Miller, 'The Natural Right to Private Property', in Tibor R. Machan (ed.), *The Libertarian Reader* (Totowa, N. J.: Rowman and Littlefield, 1982), p. 284.
8. James Tully, *A Discourse on Property* (Cambridge: Cambridge University Press, 1980), pp. 105–9; and Waldron, p. 178.
9. Day, 'Locke on Property', pp. 211–14; and see Andrew Reeve, *Property* (London: Macmillan, 1986), pp. 124–5, for the contrary view. Waldron seems inconsistent on this point: compare pp. 181–2, 184, 398, with p. 230 (and his 'The Turfs My Servant Has Cut', *The Locke Newsletter*, 13 (1982) 17).
10. *Two Treatises*, II, secs 25–8, 32, 34, 39, 44, 45, 51 (for the common gift); and secs. 28, 29, 32, 35 (for not requiring consent); and see Cohen I, pp. 129–30, on joint ownership and non-ownership.
11. See Alan Ryan, *Property and Political Theory* (Oxford: Blackwell, 1984), pp. 29–30, and Waldron, p. 155.
12. *Two Treatises*, I, sec. 42, and II, secs 25 and 134–5. On this, see Waldron, pp. 145–7; and his 'Enough and as Good Left for Others', *Philosophical Quarterly*, 29 (1979) 326–8; and cf. M. M. Goldsmith, 'The Entitlement Theory of Justice Considered', *Political Studies*, 27 (1979) 582, and Virginia Held, 'John Locke on Robert Nozick', *Social Research*, 43 (1976) 171–2.
13. *Two Treatises*, II, secs 31 and 46.
14. Nozick, pp. 174–5.
15. This line of thought was suggested to me by a marginal note in a book I

borrowed from Hillel Steiner. I take the opportunity of thanking him here also for helpful general discussion about these matters, which he has pondered as long as anybody.

16. For L also has a claim of need on the trap.
17. Waldron, 'Enough and as Good', pp. 319–26; cf. Waldron, pp. 209–18.
18. Some so-called libertarian writers therefore criticise Nozick for accepting such a proviso and allowing the shadow of common ownership to fall over full-blooded private property entitlements. See, e. g., Mack, pp. 134–5, and Fred Miller, pp. 283–4.
19. See Cohen I, pp. 122–3 and 133, and the matter in between.
20. Cf. Karl Marx, *Capital*, vol. I, ch. 26.
21. Hillel Steiner, 'Justice and Entitlement', *Ethics*, 87 (1977), p. 151. Cf. Cohen I, p. 119; and F. A. Harper, 'Property and its Primary Form', and George I. Mavrodes, 'Property', in Blumenfeld, pp. 11–12 and 185 respectively.
22. John Stuart Mill, *Principles of Political Economy*, book II, ch. I, sec. 3.
23. *Two Treatises*, II, secs 27 and 32.
24. See, for contemporary formulations of the point, Murray Rothbard, 'Justice and Property Rights', in Blumenfeld, p. 113; and Hillel Steiner, 'Slavery, Socialism, and Private Property', in J. R. Pennock and J. W. Chapman (eds.), *Nomos XXII: Property* (New York: New York University Press, 1980), pp. 262–3 n. 15; and cf. also his 'Capitalism, Justice and Equal Starts', *Social Philosophy & Policy*, 5 (1987), p. 54.
25. See note 1 above.
26. The suggestion was communicated to, and is discussed by, Waldron – at pp. 183, 187–8.
27. See Locke, *Two Treatises*, II, sec. 30.
28. David Hume, *A Treatise of Human Nature*, book III, part II, sec. 3. And cf. David Miller, 'Justice and Property', *Ratio*, 22 (1980) 5.
29. See *Two Treatises*, II, secs 37, 46 and – on the last point – 27 and 30 (first usage in each case). I am grateful to Geraint Parry for discussion of this point.
30. Cf. here Waldron, p. 186; and 'Two Worries', p. 41.
31. *Two Treatises*, II, sec. 28.
32. See text to n. 2 above; and Day, p. 209.
33. Cf. Rothbard, 'Justice and Property Rights', p. 109; or the same author's *The Ethics of Liberty* (Atlantic Highlands, N. J.: Humanities Press, 1982), pp. 47–8.
34. *Two Treatises*, II, secs 51 and 31.
35. Ibid., II, secs 38 and 32. Cf. Goldsmith p. 581 n. 13, Ryan, pp. 35, 37–8, and Waldron, p. 173.
36. David Lyons, 'The New Indian Claims and Original Rights to Land', in Jeffrey Paul (ed.), *Reading Nozick* (Oxford: Blackwell, 1982), p. 361.
37. Becker, p. 34.
38. Of interest here, albeit in connection with another notion of appropriation, is G. W. F. Hegel, *The Philosophy of Right* (Oxford: Oxford University Press, 1965), p. 238, addition to para. 55; and Marx's comment on it, *Capital*, vol. 3, ch. 37 n. 26. Rothbard (*The Ethics of Liberty*, pp. 33–4, 47) has no difficulty with the idea that the extent of one's 'true'

property is a 'natural fact' – defined for him, however, by one very specific kind of usage, what is 'brought into production'.

39. Nozick, p. 174; Steiner, 'Capitalism, Justice and Equal Starts', p. 61; Fred Miller, p. 285.

40. See Waldron, pp. 256–7; and, by contrast, Mack, p. 133, and Onora O'Neill, 'Nozick's Entitlements', in Paul, p. 312. Cf. Nozick pp. 150, 153, 174–5 and 178. And see the text to note 49 below.

41. See Thomas Nagel, 'Libertarianism Without Foundations', in Paul, p. 195; Honoré, 'Property, Title and Redistribution', pp. 107–8; and O'Neill, p. 314. Also relevant here are the telling remarks on formal principles of justice in acquisition (PJAs) by Waldron: pp. 265, 267–8, 270–1.

42. Karl Olivecrona, 'Locke's Theory of Appropriation', *Philosophical Quarterly*, 24 (1974) 224–6. Cf. Becker, pp. 48–9, for the suggestion of a psychological dimension to the labour theory of acquisition.

43. *The Ethics of Liberty*, pp. 33, 48, 67 n. 2; cf. his 'Justice and Property Rights', p. 109.

44. See Becker, pp. 34–6, 47, 50–3; David Miller, pp. 6–7; and Waldron, pp. 202–5.

45. *Two Treatises*, II, (respectively) secs 30, 34, 37, 42, 43; and 32–5, 40–43.

46. See David Miller, pp. 7, 9, 11.

47. Nozick, pp. 154–5. Puzzling also are the references to desert in Steiner, 'Justice and Entitlement', p. 152; and 'The Natural Right to the Means of Production', *Philosophical Quarterly*, 27 (1977) 44–5.

48. Cf. James Sadowsky, 'Private Property and Collective Ownership', in Blumenfeld, p. 89; and G. A. Cohen, 'The Labour Theory of Value and the Concept of Exploitation', in his *History, Labour, and Freedom* (Oxford: Oxford University Press, 1988), pp. 229–30, 237. For a view that one has the right to the value created or added by one's labour, see Baruch Brody, 'Redistribution Without Egalitarianism', *Social Philosophy & Policy*, 1 (1983), pp. 74–5, 78–9. And cf. Nozick, p. 161– I am aware that *his* story is not about value.

49. In turn: G. A. Cohen, 'Self-Ownership, Communism and Equality', *Proceedings of the Aristotelian Society*, supp. vol. 64 (1990) 25; Steiner, 'Slavery etc.', pp. 249–50; Nozick, p. 172; and John Exdell, 'Distributive Justice: Nozick on Property Rights', *Ethics*, 87 (1977) 144. Cf. G. A. Cohen, 'Self-Ownership, World Ownership and Equality: Part II', in Ellen Frankel Paul et al. (eds), *Marxism and Liberalism* (Oxford: Blackwell, 1986), pp. 90, 95–6.

5 Voices and Signals – Active Citizens and the Market-Place*

Geraint Parry and George Moyser

In democratic Athens it was the practice to use a vermilion-smeared rope to drive citizens from the market-place (the agora) to the assembly on the pnyx.[1] Thus it would seem that Athenians fell somewhat short of Rousseau's ideal that men would 'fly to the assembly' and that, even in this most politicised of communities, they were inclined to stay around in the market, trading for their own advantage. This reluctance to use one's political voice may, perhaps, be reflected in the ambivalent relationship between states and markets which has run through political thought. What is it that people can do or that they prefer to do through politics which they cannot do through the market?

One rather grand – and perhaps grandiose – view of politics divorces it entirely from the base affairs of the market. The major protagonist of this conception of the political in recent times has been Hannah Arendt. In classical Greek manner, she divorces the public arena from the private sphere in which the pursuit of economic interests takes place. One must emerge from the privacy of the 'household' which is the sphere of economic life. Politics is acting and speaking in which 'men show who they are, reveal actively their unique personal identities. . . .'[2] But the individual can only act fully and freely in association with others:

> This revelatory quality of speech and action comes to the fore where people are *with* others and neither for nor against them – that is, in sheer human togetherness.[3]

In the present, often justifiably sceptical, age, Arendt's vision of politics seems curiously remote. If politics is not about economic interests what, it might be asked, is it about? The answer seems to be that it consists in the heroic activities of the statesman who sets or changes the tone of public debate. There are also affinities with what has been called 'expressive participation' when people want to add their voice to a protest or announce their solidarity with others in a demonstration, or to be present on such politically resonant and history-making occasions as the destruction of the Berlin Wall. Speech is almost as important as any conclusion which might be reached.[4]

This rarified conception of politics has, needless to say, had but a limited impact on contemporary political science and thought, although it has its adherents amongst advocates of some versions of participatory democracy.[5] Much more common are approaches to the relation between markets and states in which politics is regarded as a secondary activity. In many cases primacy is given to the market as the major means of reconciling conflicting interests. Market transactions are presented as signals sent to the producers *via* the price mechanism from an unknown multitude of traders and purchasers as to the nature of demands. In politics, by contrast, voices are raised rather than signals flashed. One major reason why such voices are raised is, indeed, to call for repairs to the signalling equipment. As Jon Elster has put it in his discussion of the market and the forum:

> Politics . . . is concerned with the common good, and notably with the cases in which it cannot be realized as the aggregate outcome of individuals pursuing their private interests. In particular, uncoordinated private choices may lead to outcomes that are worse for all than some other outcome that could have been attained by coordination. Political institutions are set up to remedy such *market failures* . . .[6]

The state steps in when, in the phrase of K. B. Smellie, 'the invisible hand' has 'faltered in its cunning'.[7]

It follows, therefore, that one of the prime objectives of political participation is as a means whereby citizens can act individually and collectively to alter the positions that they find themselves in as a result of market forces. In one of the most notable contributions to the analysis of political participation, Pizzorno argued that

> the widening of participation seemed to be a contradictory phenomenon, because it contained a potentially egalitarian force, while at the same time it reaffirmed private privileges.[8]

The egalitarian aspect of participation is most clearly directed against market failure. When political participation was extended, especially through the winning of the franchise by the working class, it could be employed as a means of fighting against social and economic inequalities, as well as a mechanism for integration. The labour movement, in particular, sought political power in order to effect a more egalitarian distribution of income, wealth and welfare. The most significant means of participation in such a struggle was collective action. The lack of individual resources could be compensated for by solidaristic action through friendly societies and trades unions. Organisation would thus appear to be the weapon of the weak.

The contrary tendency of participation distinguished by Pizzorno was to reaffirm private privileges. Just as the working class could organise to ameliorate its position by political action, so the established classes and interests could organise to protect their own status. Citizens, as Pizzorno puts it, bring 'to the political process the weight of their property, prestige and capacity to mobilize resources'.[9] Those who have been successful in the market tend also to possess or to accumulate the resources which are useful in politics. Organisation generally requires finance and the skills which are acquired through more advanced education. In this way, to quote once more Pizzorno's account of the history of extensions of participation, there develops a process which 'puts back into the political system the inequalities rooted in "civil" society'.[10] Thus the egalitarian thrust is checked by the political organisation of private interests, which reproduces within 'political' society, 'civil' society's system of inequality.[11] The problem facing advocates of greater participation is, therefore, whether it will, as is often supposed, make for a more egalitarian political system.

One of the underlying concerns of much recent work on political participation – notably the classic studies by Verba and Nie and their partners[12] – has been to assess the extent of any 'bias' of participation. Thus Verba and Nie concluded that in the United States 'participation helps those who are already better off'.[13] Not only were upper-status persons disproportionately more active than other citizens, but participation appeared to be an effective means of getting their political messages across. Advocates of a more 'active citizenship' in Britain should ask, first, whether there are enough active citizens to go round in order to provide for a more politically involved society and, secondly, whether they will be the catalysts of a new society, or will be more likely to reinforce market advantages through political activity.

In the next section we shall use data from the British Political Participation Study to examine who it is that at present best employ their voices as citizens. Are they those who are already beneficiaries of the market, or can voice be some considerable compensation for individual economic disadvantage?

THE VOCAL AND THE NON-VOCAL

The nation-wide section of the British Political Participation Study was based on interviews with nearly 1,600 citizens in England, Wales and Scotland conducted in 1984–5 and covered activities over the previous five-year period.[14] Questions were asked about actions taken on the issue which was of most concern to the respondent, to his or her family, to the locality or the nation. The survey also asked whether, in addition, the individual had undertaken any of a number of activities including voting, contacting a representative or official, acting in an organised or an informal group, campaigning for a political party, and engaging in various forms of protest, from mild types such as petitioning to direct action such as stopping traffic.

The analysis concentrated on twenty-three such activities. Of these, four stood out as different from all the rest, if only in the fact that very large numbers had performed them. These were three voting activities (the General Election of 1983, the various local elections during the period and the European Election of 1984), and signing a petition. The vast majority of the sample (82.5 per cent) had voted in the General Election; 68.8 per cent said they had voted in most of the local elections; and 47.3 per cent claimed to have voted in the European Election. Signing a petition was the only other activity in which a majority (63.3 per cent) had been engaged.

These relatively common forms of participation present something of a problem in forming an assessment of what constitutes high citizen activism. It is in elections in particular that the *vox populi* is expressed. But elections are exceptional events. The voice of the people is activated by the voices of the political class. This is not to say that elections are insignificant examples of participation – from very many standpoints they are the most important in setting the political tone for a period of years. General elections also have the virtue that the high turnout means that they are the most egalitarian of forms of citizen participation. One person, one vote does not have its parallel in any other form of activity. On the other side, as Verba, Nie and Kim have pointed out, elections are not an effective means of transmitting the voice of the people on specific issues.

> Voting is a blunt act; the voter is limited to a small number of choices, none of which necessarily expresses his or her views on what is most salient.[15]

The relative ease and universality of voting mean that it is not a good test for distinguishing those with voice from the voiceless in Britain. The same applies to some degree to petitioning. For these reasons we have, for the present purposes, distinguished as the 'vocal' section of our sample those who took action on the issue of most importance to them (their 'prime issue'), and who also performed at least three of the remaining nineteen actions investigated after discounting the three voting items and signing a petition. Those who were 'voiceless' have been taken to be those who either did not even cite an issue or problem of importance, or who, if they mentioned a problem, did not act on it and who in addition took fewer than three of the nineteen types of action. The 'vocal' are, by this standard, very much a minority of the population – 16.5 per cent of the sample (or 260 individuals). The 'voiceless' are in total over half the sample (53.5 per cent). The remainder constitute a block of persons only moderately active.

As Table 5.1 shows, the mean number of activities out of the nineteen performed by the population was only one and a half (it should be noted however that some will have performed these types of activity more than once). The voiceless did less than half of one action (.41). By comparison, the vocal minority were quite distinct. They had done something about their prime issue and had on average undertaken just over five of the nineteen types of action (5.16).

Participation is, however, a term which covers a range of different types of activity. In Britain, as in other countries, it has several dimensions or modes.[16] It is far from being the case that people who are active in one dimension of participation, such as party campaigning, are necessarily also the most active in other dimensions, such as contacting an official or joining in direct action. Nevertheless, the vocal minority turn out to be above average in each of the dimensions of participation identified in the study.

It can be seen from Table 5.1 that there is no category of activity in

TABLE 5.1: *Voice and modes of participation*

	Vocal	Voiceless	Average	Maximum Possible
Collective action	1.90	.12	.52	5
Contacting	1.84	.19	.59	5
Party campaigning	.79	.04	.21	4
Direct action	.63	.06	.17	5
All four modes	5.16	.41	1.49	19

Figures represent mean number of actions performed.

which, on average, the whole population has performed more than one action. In the case of 'collective action', which comprised working in organised or with informal groups, attending a protest meeting and circulating, rather than merely signing, a petition, the average was half of one action (out of a notional maximum of five). The vocal minority had, however, performed almost four times the average number of collective actions (1.90). The voiceless had done a mere .12. A similar pattern is found with the other relatively more frequent form of participation – contacting national and local representatives and officials, and the media. The overall average score is slightly over half of one action (.59) out of a possible maximum of five. The activists were over three times as likely to contact the authorities (1.84); the almost voiceless scored on average only a fifth of one action (.19). In other words, the elites would scarcely have received any contact from over half of the population.

The two remaining categories of participation are often regarded as highly indicative of the quality of political life, yet are very rare in Britain. Campaigning actively for a party is something which only around 5 per cent of the population has done. There were four kinds of campaigning activity – raising funds, canvassing, clerical work and attending a rally. On average people had done a fifth of one such action (.21). Even the activists had done less than one (.79) and the voiceless were, it follows, scarcely evident (.04). Campaigners are a very rare breed.

Direct action was composed of political boycotts of goods and services, blocking traffic with a street protest, going on a march or demonstration, taking part in a strike which the respondent considered 'political' and employing physical force. With five types of action possible, the average British citizen had done .17 of them. The inactive scored .06. But even the super-activists had done on average only just over half of one action (.63). Thus the publicity engendered by direct action should not conceal its relative rarity in British political life.

WHO ARE THE ACTIVE CITIZENS?

Where, then, does voice come from? Who are those who most readily make themselves heard? Is it the case that those who participate are those who are seeking to compensate for market disadvantage or, alternatively, that advantage in civil society is translated into politics?

Market position may be, initially at least, defined by economic class. The class schema devised by Heath and Goldthorpe in particular defines class by reference to a person's place in the productive process.[17] The class bias of voice is clear even though there is not a linear pattern. As many as 42.2 per cent of the active minority are drawn from the salariat. Compared with their membership of the sample as a whole they are over-represented by almost 70 per cent.[18] Within this class the vocal higher professionals are twice as frequent as they are in the population. This skewed pattern is partially compensated by the fact that the second most prominent category is the working class, who comprise just over a quarter of the activists (27.2 per cent). Nevertheless, this means that the working class is under-represented by 27.6 per cent. The other classes – routine non-manual, petty bourgeoisie, manual technicians and foremen – are all very slightly under-represented. The voiceless show the converse pattern – the salariat are under-represented (by 33.7 per cent) but are by no means absent; the working class, who comprise 44.0 per cent of the total are somewhat over-represented (by 17.0 per cent).

The picture may be looked at from an alternative perspective. How prone are the various classes to raise their voices? The salaried class again appears the most active, with the other classes some way behind, all with very similar levels of involvement in public life. Thus 30.7 per cent of the salariat are in the voice category whilst only 13 per cent of the working class is active. This shows quite effectively that the activity of the salariat is only high relative to other classes – almost 70 per cent of the salariat are *not* amongst the most participatory. Indeed, a third are in the voiceless group. By comparison nearly 60 per cent of the working class is without voice, but this is not a significantly greater proportion than that of the petty bourgeoisie who are also generally uninvolved.

The pattern for class is, not surprisingly, repeated for wealth. The richest quarter of the population provide just over 40 per cent of the active minority but less than a fifth of the voiceless. The poorest quarter are 13 per cent of the vocal and just over 30 per cent of the voiceless – not a dramatic difference but confirming the general economic bias to participation. Looking from the other perspective at the propensity of the advantaged and the disadvantaged to participate, the contrast is quite marked. Over a quarter (28.3 per cent) of the wealthy are in the activist minority compared with just under a tenth of the poor. The vast majority of the poor (69.1 per cent) are in the least active sector of the population. At the same time, it is the case that a third of the rich are also politically uninvolved. Nevertheless the balance is quite pronounced. One is more likely to appear in the topmost ranks of participants the wealthier one is.

One way in which a person may promote his or her market position by political as well as economic action is through membership of a relevant union or staff association or of a professional society. Union members are more vocal (22 per cent) than non-members (12.6 per cent). As a proportion of the activists, union members and non-members are very similar, although this does imply an over-representation of members compared to the population. It does not, however, necessarily follow that unionisation is a means of collective action to compensate for market weakness. It is well-known that unions in Britain have changed and the balance shifted away from the former working-class dominance of the movement. This was true for the present sample – union members were rather above average in wealth and education. It was the unorganised who were less advantaged. Of course the working class does receive protection and gains collective expression through the unions, but other sectors of society including the salariat act in combination as well.

Voice is indeed generally associated with membership of a network of voluntary groups. Activists are also more likely to be office-holders in such associations. The result is that group membership (which is *not* for this reason taken to be a measure of participation) turns out to be one of the strongest predictors of participation in Britain. Affiliation to groups provides channels for action and permits mobilisation by the groups. Organisation and participation go closely together.

Perhaps not surprisingly, those who employ voice with what in British terms passes for regularity have a more positive orientation to politics. Only 10 per cent of the voiceless claim to be 'very interested' in politics and national affairs whereas over a quarter declare themselves to be 'not at all interested'. By contrast a third of those with voice are 'very interested' and less than 5 per cent admit to having no such interest. A similar pattern is found in the frequency with which people say they have discussed politics with family, friends and neighbours. The 'voiceless' confirm their description in that a fifth say that they 'never' discuss politics and only six per cent have done so 'very often'. Virtually all the vocal have indeed raised their voices in this way and a fifth 'very often'.

The activists also have, on the whole, a more supportive view of political institutions and practices than the inactive, and are less politically cynical.

The implication of the preceding analysis is therefore that those who are advantaged in the economic market-place are also well entrenched in the political arena. This is not to suggest that the less well-off are entirely 'locked out'.[19] However they do not appear to be able fully to compensate politically for their economic disadvantage to the same extent as the better-off are able to convert market strength into political pressure. The question is then how far this differential propensity for political action is likely to affect the agenda of issues in Britain.

ACTION AND AGENDAS

Although the British have been exhorted in recent years to look to market solutions for their problems, few respondents (8.7 per cent), said, when asked who ought to be responsible for tackling the problems they faced, that they ought to be tackled by such market organisations as business or the trades unions. There was a similar reluctance to name the individual as the responsible agent (8.2 per cent). Perhaps this is an indication that there still is some way to go before an individualist, market orientation can be built in this country.[20] It is best not to exaggerate this possibility since the focus of the investigation was on issues about which public action could be taken.[21] Nevertheless, it was the state, and especially the local state, which was seen as chiefly concerned with the issues facing people.

The vocal do not differ from the voiceless in their propensity to assign responsibility for solving problems to the market or the state. They do differ somewhat, however, in their perception of the success of the authorities in dealing with the issues which worry them. Whereas fewer than 10 per cent of the voiceless believed the relevant authorities to have been very successful, over double that proportion of the activists had formed this view. There are, admittedly, roughly equal numbers from each category with very negative views of the authorities, but there is here some indication that inactivity may reflect a pessimistic view of the potential for political action.

Generally the activists had a positive view of their own political involvement. Three-quarters believed that they had got their message across. Satisfaction with the results of their actions was less widespread – somewhat under half (44.5 per cent) were satisfied but, on the other hand, only 10 per cent were positively dissatisfied (the others had 'mixed feelings'). In nearly half the cases the respondents believed that the authorities had actually responded wholly as a result of that person's intervention. Thus one argument for participation is that, at some levels at least, it can pay off.[22] Given this success rate it is to be expected that the activists' sense of political efficacy (the sense that individuals or groups of like-minded people can exercise influence) was so much stronger than that of the inactive – past influence no doubt breeds political confidence.

In some respects the ultimate test of the importance of any bias to participation is the extent to which the issue agendas of the voiceless and the vocal differ. How far do the activists distort the picture that elites receive as to what most concerns the British public? Answering this crucial question is not straightforward. Taking the prime issue mentioned by our respondents,[23] some divergences between the priorities of activists and inactive surface. For the voiceless general economic issues (wages, inflation) were most frequently mentioned, followed by unemployment. Together, these categories of problem constituted over a third (37.8 per cent) of the issues mentioned by the inactive. By contrast, in the total agenda of the activists economic matters were only in fourth place and unemployment in sixth, with 14 per cent of the issues. In very clear first place were problems connected with environment and planning (a quarter of all their issues), whereas these were in third position, but some way behind, amongst the inactive. In second place for the activists was education (eighth for the voiceless), followed by transport and traffic (fifth).

Thus, whilst the inactive majority are primarily concerned about material issues of wages and unemployment, the active minority, which is relatively more affluent, is bringing to the attention of elites the 'quality of life' issues. Such a designation may, however, be partly misleading in that preservation of certain environments is often in the material interests of the affluent classes who live in them. But, even so, if the authorities had relied upon pressures from active citizens in order to form their own priorities they would have been misled as to public opinion.[24]

However, this divergence between activist and non-activist agendas is not entirely a matter of differences in priorities. It also reflects the political opportunity structure. Economic problems, such as inflation or unemployment, are not readily susceptible to effective citizen participation. Very few individuals take action over them. They are the issues of high politics. By contrast, planning problems, education and transport are, to a considerable extent, local responsibilities and there are several points of access for citizen complaints or pressures. The 'voiceless' are partly so because their demands are not ones which can be easily converted into citizen inputs. The use of voice, by comparison, reflects the instrumentally rational perception that some kinds of problems are less responsive to active citizens than others.

The issue agenda does, therefore, reflect a certain bias to participation. Voice is unrepresentative both in its accent and in the substance of what it speaks about. We would not, nevertheless, wish to exaggerate the bias. The social background of participants is not an entirely reliable predictor of political attitudes. It does not, moreover, follow from placing problems high on an agenda that those who do so agree upon their solution.[25] Furthermore, although one might be tempted to infer a conservative bias to political inputs from the social background of activists, the left are well-represented amongst British activists. Whilst Conservative identifiers formed the largest proportion of the activists (39 per cent), this merely matches their part of the overall sample. Labour supporters were a third and were very slightly over-represented, as were the supporters of what was then the Liberal-Social Democratic Alliance. A similar result is found when the activists are placed on a 'Left-Right' scale, according to their responses to a range of policy issues. Those on the hard Right are over-represented but so, to a lesser degree, are those on the hard Left. When, in other analyses of the data, the social and economic background of participants was controlled for, the leftward inclination of political action was further emphasised. Even in a period of Conservative electoral domination the voice of activists was often from left of stage. Thus, there are potentially countervailing forces amongst political activists.[26]

Limited though the participatory bias may be, a democracy should not be complacent about a situation where activism could actually increase inequality of political impact. It might be argued that the inequalities which exist will gradually diminish as the habit of participation spreads in a more educated society. There is some evidence that citizen activity has gradually increased over the last decade or so, although strictly comparable data are not readily available. But there are few signs of a radically more participatory society on the horizon. Measuring 'potential participation', or the readiness to consider participation in the future, is a hazardous matter.[27] There are too many gaps between intention and practice for predictions to be securely based. Even so, there remains a large number of British people who would not even consider *any* political participation (beyond voting and signing a petition) in the future. A substantial majority (60.8 per cent) of the voiceless would remain silent in that they could not say that they would 'probably' or 'certainly' consider any of the nineteen different types of action on offer.[28] By contrast, amongst the activists only 7.9 per cent had such doubts about any future activity. Indeed, over half of them (55.1 per cent) would 'probably' or 'certainly' consider doing five or more of the activities compared with a mere 10 per cent of the voiceless. The general pattern holds, moreover, across the various modes of participation, whether 'conventional' or 'unconventional'. There seems, on this evidence, little sign that people will break silence by erupting into protest. Thus, over three-quarters of the voiceless would 'never' consider going on a protest march. The inert seem likely, by and large, to remain so. Not a voice – scarcely even a whisper. The vocal seem likely to continue to speak up for themselves even if more citizens gradually join their numbers.

CONCLUSIONS

To the extent that there is a bias to participation, what are the possibilities of first, enhancing the sound of voice in modern politics and, second, of ensuring that the individual voices are heard equally? As has been implied, these objectives are by no means the same. Maximising voice may be at the expense of its equalisation.

One response to levels of participation might be that both goals would be better attained by extending the opportunities to vote. Even if one considers the lowest levels of turnout in Britain – in local elections and in the elections to the European Parliament – elections still involve more persons than any other political activity, with the exception of signing a petition. Thus one avenue of reform would be to extend the number of occasions on which people could vote. This might be for different offices or on a range of issues. It is sometimes alleged that there is an oddity about participation in the United States – high non-electoral participation yet exceptionally low electoral turnout. But this of course conceals the frequency of elections in the US and the range of offices (state governors, mayors, judges, city officials), for which one can vote.[29]

No other major country has followed the US example in providing so many opportunities for the vote. There are powerful reasons why actual turnout in these elections is, nevertheless, so low in the US. Some of these reasons (especially registration procedures) may help to explain why even electoral participation is biased towards those advantaged in the market, leaving an underclass which does not even vote.

This American phenomenon contradicts what should be one of the major advantages of the electoral mode of participation which is that its very ease renders it less subject to economic distortion. Admittedly such distortions may enter the electoral arena in other ways, through the greater capacity of certain parties and candidates to obtain finance from corporate organisations. This is a major argument for seeking to insulate the political realm more fully from the market by, for example, placing a ceiling on the contributions any individual or organisation may donate to a candidate. In Walzers' terms, there have to be 'blocked exchanges' to limit what money can buy politically, just as we limit open bribery.[30]

Allowing the economic distortion of the electoral process to be capable of limitation, the extension of voting opportunities might encompass the reintroduction or extension of very local, parish-level, elections (coupled with granting such bodies more powers), elected health councils and educational authorities (voting for school governors is perhaps a step in this direction). National and local referendums on issues would constitute a further such development. The most radical proposals of this nature have been for the installation of 'voting machines' within the home which, through the operation of modern communications technology, would enable the electorate to vote instantly not merely for representatives but also directly on particular issues. Some aspects at least of Athenian democracy can be re-created. There need be no vermilion-smeared rope to drive people to the place of voting. The 'polling booth' will be on the keyboard by the TV set. The public realm will have been transplanted inside the household.[31]

Perhaps more immediately promising ways of increasing partici-pation are through processes of decentralisation of both democratic inputs and outputs. In some respects the ultimate form of decentral-isation is the market. For marketeers, exit rather than voice is usually the more appropriate response to problems of service provision. Thus the instinct of the New Right is not to favour participation but the extension of consumer choice, through private health schemes, education vouchers, competing refuse collection services and the like. The citizen is perceived as a consumer of services and should be enabled to act like one wherever this is possible. Such consumers may enter or exit from competing services according to their perception of the nature and quality of provision. In some instances exit is com-plete, as with the privatisation of council houses. Here tenants, who previously complained to local government about slow repairs, be-come householders who go to the DIY store. The state, including the 'local state', retreats to a minimal role of regulating the operation of the new markets which are opened up.

From a market-oriented standpoint some of the schemes intro-duced by the British government in the 1980s must be seen as second-best solutions which favour voice over exit. These empower local groups who replace, or are agents for, the state. In some instances this implies an element of local participation, as in the case of the elected parent school governors in charge of opted-out schools. Community self-help groups are incorporated into service provision such as the management of housing estates which have not been privatised.

Whether this will constitute an upsurge of participation it is too early to tell. Will there be enough active citizens to go round? In some cases the local groups which are intended to run these ventures have had to be created from above rather than emerged from below. In their studies of local authority reforms, Hambleton and Hoggett have sought to distinguish forms of decentralisation which are con-sumerist in orientation, designed to improve relations with local authority customers (neighbourhood housing offices, for example), from what they term 'collectivist' solutions which seek to democratise local services.[32]

Who will the active citizens be, assuming sufficient numbers can be found? Hirschman's classic analysis of exit and voice suggested that exit drove out voice.[33] The option of private consumption offered by market solutions is generally most available to the better-off who are often also the better-educated and the most skilled in the use of voice to complain about quality. Remaining locked into the service would be the less well-off, the less-educated and the less-organised. On the other hand, where the advantaged do remain to employ voice it cannot always be assumed that they will do so in order to improve quality in some objective sense rather than to promote their own sectional interests. It seems likely that positions such as school governorships would require the time and the skills which are more readily possessed by the established salariat who could, conceivably, have different educational priorities from those shared by parents from the working class or from some ethnic minorities.

It is sometimes suggested that if active citizens are unrepresentative and threaten to distort the agenda, others will be stimulated to intervene in a countervailing manner.[34] This is, however, to assume that people equally readily cross the threshold of participation whereas, as has been seen, such persons are 'disproportionately found in a privileged part of the population'.[35] Decentralisation may make for greater participation – and in a sense greater democracy: but it may lead to localised domination by well-resourced interests at the expense of the disadvantaged.[36] Nevertheless, decentralisation would chime in with what might be regarded as the overwhelming tendency of citizen participation, in Britain at least, to take place at the local level. This is where more people can make their voices heard over issues about which they are informed and which they believe they can influence.[37] Localisation of arrangements does, however, raise other concerns. Many of the major issues of politics are over the general arrangements of society or over the authoritative allocation of values in an equitable manner. Decisions on such matters are national or, increasingly, transnational. These are the issues of high politics which involve minimal citizen participation other than through the ballot box. In this sense citizen participation has a hole in the centre. Localised participation by itself may increase voice but over less important matters, leaving the professional politicians deciding high politics, not in conditions of silence of course but in circumstances where citizen voice can be severely distorted and where they may be inclined to pay excessive attention to market signals. The market certainly has its place in the decision-making of

individual consumers. The problem facing democratic theory is that
of finding appropriate levels of decision-making institutions (from
neighbourhood councils, through referendums to transnational
forums) in which voice can be articulated to balance signals from the
market.[38] As Walzer has put it, 'The morality of the bazaar belongs in
the bazaar. The market is a zone of the city, not the whole of the
city'.[39]

NOTES

*We acknowledge with gratitude the support of the Economic and Social
Research Council under Grant No. E0022003.

  1. Aristophanes, *The Akharnians*, ed. A. H. Sommerstein, (Warminster:
     Aris and Phillips, 1980) lines 19–22. For interpretations of this device see
     R. K. Sinclair, *Democracy and Participation in Athens* (Cambridge:
     Cambridge University Press, 1988) pp. 116–17.
  2. H. Arendt, *The Human Condition* (Chicago: University of Chicago
     Press, 1958) p. 179.
  3. *The Human Condition*, p. 180.
  4. The importance of speech or dialogue and communication in Arendt and
     in the work of Habermas is interestingly discussed by R. Beiner, *Political
     Judgment* (London: Methuen: 1983) pp. 11–30; M. Canovan, 'A Case of
     Distorted Communication: A Note on Habermas and Arendt', *Political
     Theory*, 11 (1983), 105–16; D. Miller, *Market, State and Community:
     Theoretical Foundations of Market Socialism* (Oxford: Oxford University
     Press, 1989) pp. 261–7.
  5. This is despite inadequacies in Arendt's own understanding of ordinary
     democratic processes. See B. Parekh, *Contemporary Political Thinkers*
     (Oxford: Martin Robertson, 1982) pp. 18–20.
  6. J. Elster, 'The Market and the Forum', in J. Elster and A. Hylland (eds)
     Foundations of Social Choice Theory (Cambridge: Cambridge University
     Press, 1986) pp. 103–4 (emphasis in the original).
  7. K. B. Smellie, *A Hundred Years of English Government* (London:
     Duckworth, 1950) p. 10.
  8. A. Pizzorno, 'An Introduction to the theory of political participation',
     Social Science Information, 9 (1971), p. 36.
  9. Ibid.
 10. Ibid., p. 33.
 11. Ibid., p. 35.
 12. S. Verba and N. H. Nie, *Participation in America: Political Democracy
     and Social Equality* (New York: Harper and Row, 1972); S. Verba,
     N. H. Nie and J-O. Kim, *Participation and Political Equality: A Seven-
     Nation Comparison* (Cambridge: Cambridge University Press, 1978);
     N. H. Nie, S. Verba, H. Brady, K. Schlozman and J. Lunn, 'Partici-
     pation in America: Continuity and Change'. Paper presented at the

Annual Meeting of the Midwest Political Science Association, Chicago, Illinois, 1988.

13. *Participation in America*, p. 338.

14. In addition there were local studies of six specially selected communities covering a further 1,600 citizens and some 300 local leaders. Full details will appear in G. Parry, G. Moyser and N. Day, *Political Participation and Democracy in Britain* (Cambridge: Cambridge University Press, 1991. See also G. Parry and G. Moyser, 'A Map of Political Participation in Britain', *Government and Opposition*, 25 (1990), 147–69.

15. *Participation and Political Equality*, p. 306. See also Verba and Nie, *Participation in America*, pp. 326, 341–2.

16. See Parry and Moyser 'A Map of Political Participation', pp. 147–54 for the formation of the modes of participation.

17. See A. Heath, R. Jowell and J. Curtice, *How Britain Votes* (Oxford, Pergamon Press, 1985) pp. 13–16. We use here their five-fold scheme distinguishing salariat, routine non-manual, petty bourgeoisie and farmers, manual technicians and foreman, and working class.

18. Figures for over or under-representation here and elsewhere in the chapter are computed using the following formula:

$$R = \frac{(Yi - Xi)100}{Xi}$$

Where R = the extent of over (positive value) or under (negative value) representation;

Xi = % of the entire sample within the given social group;

Yi = % of the same social group within the given category of Voice.

19. See S. Verba, N. Nie and J-O Kim, *Participation and Political Equality*, pp. 80–93 for a discussion of processes of political exclusion.

20. Compare K. Schlozman and S. Verba, *Injury to Insult: Unemployment, Class and Political Response*, (Cambridge, Mass.: Harvard University Press, 1979); H. McClosky and J. Zaller, *The American Ethos: Public Attitudes toward Capitalism and Democracy*, (Cambridge, Mass.: Harvard University Press, 1984.)

21. Whilst the relevant question did not employ the term 'political', it did ask about 'issues, needs and problems that people might consider taking action on: actions such as contacting a local councillor or official, signing a petition, joining in a national protest march or working in a group'. It is the case that the vast majority of respondents did not think of the actions taken as 'political'. See G. Parry and G. Moyser, 'What is "Politics"?: A Comparative Study of Local Citizens and Leaders', in D. Sainsbury (ed.), *Democracy, State and Justice: Critical Perspectives and New Interpretations* (Stockholm: Almqvist and Wiksell International, 1988) pp. 33–54.

22. For a further discussion see G. Parry and G. Moyser, 'A Map of Political Participation in Britain', pp. 164–6.

23. This is the issue listed as most important by the 'voiceless' who did not act on the matter and the issue on which most action was taken in the case of the activists.

24. Compare Verba and Nie, *Participation in America*, pp. 268–9.

25. It should also be noted that when, in addition to the prime issue, all other issues listed by respondents are taken into account, the divergences between the active and inactive are further attenuated, although not eliminated. This is examined more fully in Parry, Moyser and Day, *Political Participation and Democracy in Britain*, forthcoming.

26. G. Parry and G. Moyser 'A Map of Political Participation in Britain', pp. 160–3. There are somewhat comparable findings for the Netherlands, West Germany and the United States in M. Kent Jennings and J. van Deth *et al.*, *Continuities in Political Action: A Longitudinal Study of Political Orientations in Three Western Democracies* (Berlin and New York: de Gruyter, 1990) pp. 364–71.

27. See S. Barnes, M. Kaase et al., *Political Action: Mass Participation in Five Western Democracies*, (Beverly Hills and London: Sage, 1979); See also C. Rootes, 'On the Future of Protest Politics in Western Democracies – A Critique of Barnes, Kaase et al, *Political Action*', *European Journal of Political Research*, 9 (1981), 421–32.

28. Compare the analyses in R. Jowell and C. Airey, *British Social Attitudes: the 1984 Report* (Aldershot: Gower, 1984) pp. 20–7; R. Jowell, S. Witherspoon and L. Brook, *British Social Attitudes: the 1987 Report*, (Aldershot: Gower, 1987) pp. 55–9.

29. See R. J. Dalton, *Citizen Politics in Western Democracies: Public Opinion and Political Parties in the United States, Great Britain, West Germany and France* (Chatham, N. J.: Chatham House, 1988) p. 40. See also I. Crewe 'Electoral Participation' in D. Butler, H. Penniman and A. Ranney, *Democracy at the Polls: A Comparative Study of Competitive National Elections* (Washington: American Enterprise Institute, 1981) pp. 216–63.

30. See M. Walzer, *Spheres of Justice: A Defence of Pluralism and Equality*, (Oxford: Martin Robertson, 1983) pp. 95–128; R. A. Dahl, *Dilemmas of Pluralist Democracy: Autonomy vs. Control* (New Haven: Yale University Press, 1982) pp. 170–2.

31. We necessarily concentrate here only on the egalitarian aspects of such democratic technology. There is a host of arguments for and against such devices – technical, moral and logical. For some discussions see for example F. C. Arterton, *Teledemocracy: Can Technology Protect Democracy?* (Newbury Park: Sage, 1987); I. McLean, *Democracy and New Technology* (Cambridge: Polity Press, 1989); B. Barber, *Strong Democracy: Participatory Politics for a New Age*, (Berkeley: University of California Press, 1984) pp. 273–90; G. Sartori, *The Theory of Democracy Revisited* (Chatham N. J.: Chatham House, 1987) pp. 111–20, 246–7.

32. See P. Hoggett and R. Hambleton (eds), *Decentralisation and Democracy: Localising Public Services* (University of Bristol, School for Advanced Urban Studies, 1987) pp. 9–28, 53–83; R. Hambleton, P. Hoggett and F. Tolan, 'The Decentralisation of Public Services: A Research

Agenda', *Local Government Studies*, (1989) 39–56. Also, R. I. Hadley and S. Hatch, *Social Welfare and the Failure of the State* (London: Allen and Unwin) 1981.

33. A. O. Hirschman, *Exit, Voice and Loyalty: Responses to Decline in Firms, Organizations and States* (Cambridge Mass.: Harvard University Press, 1970).

34. See comments reported in G. Parry, G. Moyser and M. Wagstaffe, 'The Crowd and the Community: Context, Content and Aftermath', in G. Gaskell and R. Benewick (eds), *The Crowd in Contemporary Britain* (London: Sage, 1987) pp. 248–50.

35. J. Elster, 'The Market and the Forum', p. 114.

36. For an examination of the drawbacks as well as the claims on behalf of decentralisation see B. C. Smith, *Decentralisation: The Territorial Dimension of the State* (London: Allen and Unwin, 1985).

37. See Parry and Moyser, 'A Map of Political Participation', (1990).

38. See R. Dahl and E. Tufte, *Size and Democracy* (Stanford: Stanford University Press, 1974) pp. 134–42.

39. M. Walzer, *Spheres of Justice*, p. 109.

6 From Party-state to Political Market-place in Eastern Europe: the Collapse of the Power Monopoly

Michael Waller

An entire postwar generation has grown up with a notion of a Europe divided into an East and a West, with the Berlin Wall serving since 1961 as a graphic symbol of the division. That notion of Eastern Europe, born in the crisis of the onset of the cold war in 1947–8, came to an end in 1989 with the fall of the regimes in the region that had been maintained for almost half a century by a guarantee of Soviet support. With them fell a particular configuration of state power, economic and political. That structure of power, together with the thinking that provided its ideological underpinnings, has frequently been called monopolistic. In this chapter the appropriateness of that metaphor will be demonstrated by a brief examination of the roots of the political system that the Eastern European states have shared for the past fifty years, and by a more detailed account of its demise or, in some cases, fundamental transformation.

The emphasis will be on political rather than economic change, and on Eastern Europe rather than the Soviet Union. The changes associated with *perestroika* in that country have, of course, been massive enough to alter the course of European history, and it was the withdrawal of Soviet support for the regimes of Eastern Europe that was the chief factor in bringing about their downfall. But the events of 1989 in Eastern Europe, where communism had, in most cases, sat awkwardly since its imposition after the Second World War, deserve separate study in their own right. What was wished on those societies at the point of their origin was a system of political and economic monopoly. That monopoly in the hands of the party-state has now been abandoned, and the market has begun to replace it –

literally, in the case of the economy, and figuratively in the case of the political system. The forum or marketplace has throughout the ages stood for the exchange of both goods and opinion. In what follows, the formation of a 'new forum' in Eastern Europe will be examined.

No sensitive account of recent change in the east of Europe can dispense with some statement about the central characteristics of the system that has been rejected. For its roots we have to search not in the dependent territories of post-war Eastern Europe, but in the Soviet Union itself and in its experiences since the revolution of 1917. Those experiences provided a model that was adopted by communist parties that came autonomously to power in other countries, and which was imposed on the societies of Eastern Europe after the Second World War.

THE POWER MONOPOLY

A remarkable feature of the Russian revolution, and a feature also of future communist revolutions, was the extent to which the revolutionaries, as a result of a number of factors, of which their Marxist thinking was but one, broke up existing islands both of economic and political autonomy, creating a single pool of power. Monopoly, both economic and political, was in that sense a product of the revolution. It gave rise, in Najdan Pasic's words, to 'the basic dilemma of public ownership, which is therefore the basic dilemma of socialism: who controls the great economic power materialized in public property and social capital'.[1] In some cases, amongst which Pasic's own Yugoslavia is prominent, the initial monopoly came to be heavily qualified relatively soon. But in the revolutionary party's arrogation to itself of control over that pool of economic and political power, and its patrimonial attitude to that collective pool, lies the clue to an understanding of all communist regimes. It also provides the essential key to understanding what has been happening in recent times in Eastern Europe, where revolution, and with it the power monopoly, was imposed from without, and where the factors that shaped the Soviet Union, China or indeed autonomous Yugoslavia were in many cases absent.

The communist power monopoly can usefully be seen as having four interconnecting components, three of which are now familiar, but another perhaps less so. First, it comprises an economic monopoly that has found its expression in the system of central command planning. A graphic illustration, drawn from Soviet experience, of the economic power monopoly was provided by the measures that Gorbachev was able to adopt in bringing the Lithuanian leadership to heel in 1990. Having control of Gossnab, the state procurement agency, the government could simply switch off the oil supply. It had no need to worry about other channels through which sanctions could be applied, or to which the Lithuanians could turn, for there were none.

A second, and equally familiar, component of the power monopoly is the political counterpart of the system of central command planning: the 'leading role of the party'. If the expression sounds somewhat general, the various crises to which communist regimes in Eastern Europe have been subject have shown it to involve two very particular mechanisms. The first of these is the party's control over elite recruitment, operated through the *nomenklatura*. The second is the monopoly exercised over the spoken and written word, which lies with the party's departments of propaganda. The way in which these mechanisms work has been amply illustrated in recent events in Eastern Europe. The party first and last never allowed Solidarity time on the Polish television to explain its position between August 1980 and the declaration of a state of war in December 1981. That and the party's interference in electoral candidacies and official appointments were two of the major issues of the Solidarity period, and it was seen as a sign of radical change when the party was brought to abandon its practice of presenting 'portfolio' candidates in the election of delegates to the Polish United Workers' Party's extraordinary ninth congress in June 1981. Again, on two prominent occasions – in Czechoslovakia in 1968 and in Yugoslavia in 1974 – a call for 'normalisation' was spelled out in terms of a reinstatement of the party's leading role, to be effected expressly by greater attention on the one hand to censorship, and on the other to the 'selection of cadres' – or 'trusted comrades' as *Kommunist* put it in the Czech case.[2]

These political mechanisms have been a prominent part of the furniture of communist political systems, and will be recognised as such by the reader. A third feature of the power monopoly is somewhat less familiar. It has an economic dimension – autarky – which in turn has generated a political dimension in the closed frontier and an obsession with borders in general. When applied in the context of the smaller nations of Eastern Europe, these ingredients of the power monopoly have created particular problems and generated particular resentments.

Autarky and a closed frontier are, as a little reflection will reveal, both corollaries of the system of central command planning and of the party's monopoly of power. They are the sluice that holds the monopoly in place as a system. Competition from abroad in terms of both goods and ideas must be kept out, or at least reduced to a minimum; whilst trained manpower, which is being paid at rates determined by the power monopoly and not by an international market, must be kept in. These aspects of the power monopoly have been particularly difficult to sustain, and have only existed in an extreme form in equally extreme cases: the Soviet Union during the Stalin years, Yugoslavia until 1948, Albania still today.

The destruction of the Berlin wall in 1989 was reasonably interpreted as symbolising the end of the party's leading role in Eastern Europe and with it a turn to a market economy. But in a very real sense the significance of the breaching of the wall was much closer to the physical fact. It spelled an end to autarky and isolation, and as the history of the past twenty years is put together it is becoming ever more clear that the driving force behind Gorbachev's reforms, and therefore behind the end of communist party rule in Eastern Europe, has been the Soviet Union's need to end its economic isolation. One of the first acts of the Gorbachev leadership was to move towards abolishing the system whereby all foreign trade had to pass through a single governmental department. It was an easier step to take than to reform the economic or political system, but it was also in a sense prior to those more momentous tasks. Like the perforation of the Berlin Wall, it represented the opening of a sluice.

The fourth and final feature of the power monopoly is the most important, in that it has provided the ideological bonding for the other three features. This is the collectivist psychology associated with the 'Leninist principle of democratic centralism'. Democratic centralism is often presented as a set of rules, or as a practical guide to action, but in fact it is more usefully seen as a particular way of thinking about social, political and economic relationships. It concerns the image of its role in society that the party has presented and the pattern of social relations that it has fostered through its control over the means of communication. It is an image that promotes and justifies the power monopoly; it justifies also the mechanisms that have held the monopoly in place. What results therefore is a closed system – which, of course, is what has given that system its monopolistic character.

Central to the orthodox theory of democratic centralism has been a notion of organic unity, that a house divided against itself will fall, that the ranks must be closed to prevent the enemy slipping through, that discussion breeds disunity and saps the efficacy of the political and social organism. It is all-embracing, and – so long as the ruling party can sustain it – all-powerful. It renders any distinction between the economic and the political monopoly irrelevant, simply by reducing the value of choice, autonomous competition and even initiative in whatever realm. There is presented a single, collective social interest, and one single collective voice should speak for it. Elections cannot involve choice, but must consecrate the unity of the people around the collective national spokesperson: 'I vote so that my country may prosper', as one poster of the Brezhnev period had it.

As important as this image of the party's role, is the machinery of propaganda that has been employed in generating and sustaining it because it has itself benefited from the monopoly of power that the party enjoys. That is, the party's propaganda is not randomly produced, but is itself the product of a monopoly of information.[3] Not surprisingly, the propaganda has extolled the value of political and economic behaviour that support's monopoly. Since it is a monopoly and neither subject to correction nor influenced by rival ideas, it has been possible for it to be internally quite consistent, whilst having at times little connection with reality.[4] This point is of the utmost importance when it comes to understanding the inflexibility inherent in the way in which the leading role of the party has functioned and the manner in which change is inhibited from taking place until either it is too late, or until some major upheaval, such as a change of leadership, jolts the ideologists and power-holders alike into an abrupt reaction. This explains why the process of de-Stalinisation has proceeded in a series of fits and lurches. In the words of Ogden Nash:

Shake and shake the ketchup bottle,
None'll come and then a lot'll.

THE POWER MONOPOLY UNDER PRESSURE

Such, in broad-brush profile, was the monopolistic structure of power that fell in Eastern Europe in 1989 after a little more than forty years of existence. Just as it had been transplanted into the region by Soviet power, it was the withdrawing of Soviet support from the communist regimes of Eastern Europe that brought about its downfall. The story, however, is a good deal more complicated than that. That the power monopoly also had inherent weaknesses that were gnawing at it from within is witnessed by the process of reform in the Soviet Union itself, where no outside agency was involved.

The power monopoly was, in any case, and in fact, at certain points quite leaky. This leakiness, however, did not detract from its essence as a monopoly, but rather confirmed it, as two simple examples will show. First of all, replacing the market by an administered system of allocating resources opened the way to bureaucratic impediments which would have brought the economy to a halt if the actors in economic life had not found ways of by-passing the monopoly, most simply through a black market. Secondly, the officials of various hierarchies in a given locality were able to make common cause against the centre, and thus frustrate the political power monopoly.

Other leakages in the power monopoly were not inherent in it but developed over time. The attempt to maintain a monopoly over communications, for instance, was doomed by technical developments, as ever more shortwave radios became available; by cultural development, as ever more people spoke foreign languages and as cultural exchanges became more frequent; and by economic developments, such as the growth of a tourist industry.

The political leadership did all it could to minimise the incidence and the effects of these examples of what might be termed the pathology of the power monopoly, but with diminishing success. Of far greater historical significance were the proposals that came to be made to reform the economic system, and with this we enter upon the story of the gradual dismantling of the power monopoly.

The story of the various proposals that have been made for economic reform in the Soviet Union and Eastern Europe must, for reasons of space, be left to be related elsewhere. But economic reform on its own was insufficient to bring about the demise of the power monopoly. It was the challenges to the political monopoly that provided the main interest in the events of 1989, and it is to the prelude to these challenges that we must now turn.

Here the key sequence of events runs from the Hungarian uprising of 1956, through the Prague Spring, through the Solidarity episode in Poland, to Gorbachev's scuttling of the monopoly in the country of its birth after 1986.

In the Hungarian events of 1956 the issue was not the nature of socialism, nor the extent to which the Soviet economic or political model was susceptible of adaptation; it was the existing boundary of Soviet power in the region that was being contested, and which was in the event confirmed.

The Prague Spring and the Solidarity episode of 1980–81 in Poland, whilst they each regenerated resentments about Soviet power in the region, did not contest it. But each of them, in very different ways, did contest the communist power monopoly in their own country. The Prague reformers were categorical in this: the success of economic reform depended upon political change. 'Socialism with a human face' was a socialism in which both the economic and the political monopoly had been abandoned . Solidarity, by contrast, was deliberately modest in its actual demands. In claiming, at the outset, to constitute a 'self-limiting revolution', it expressly renounced any intent to challenge the party's leading role.[5]

This stance, however, if not deliberately disingenuous, was unrealistic, and it is important to understand why. In setting out to achieve legal registration as an autonomous organisation, Solidarity was by that very intent proposing to breach the power monopoly, by forcing the acceptance of a measure which, however small in itself, would none the less represent the first element of a law on association, and therefore an effective end of the power monopoly. Solidarity was finally registered on 10 November 1980, and although the gains of those hectic sixteen months of the Solidarity episode were to be clawed back when Jaruzelski imposed martial law after 13 December 1981, it none the less remained a landmark.

Space allows only the briefest mention of a further element in the process whereby the political monopoly was dismantled. This developed during the period between the Prague Spring and the Solidarity crisis, and it concerned the evolution of the pattern of dissent during those years.

Was it the gradual easterly movement of the ideas of 1968? Or was it the awareness on the part of Eastern European – or more precisely Central European – dissidents that pressure from the West on Eastern governments was beginning to count in the political equation? Or was it simply one manifestation of the shrinking of the world that ever-improving communications was bringing about? For whatever reasons there took place in the 1970s a significant shift in the nature of dissent in Central Europe. It was not a shift that could of itself bring about the downfall of the power monopoly – in fact it developed against that power monopoly, aware of the latter's power to portray and condemn the dissenter as a traitor or a madman because of his resistance to a social interest and a scientific truth articulated by the party.

It was in good part this inability to make any impression on the power monopoly that drove dissent in those years to develop the notion of a cultural secession. The anti-politics of a Michnik or a Konrad, the counter-public sphere of an Agnes Heller, were based upon a strategy of secession, which consisted in abandoning to the party the high ground of politics, where it had shown itself to be invincible, and to develop a separate set of values. This strategy had an immense appeal above all to youth, and in Czechoslovakia in particular, but elsewhere also, jazz and rock became vehicles not so much of protest as of a rival world to that to which the party was so strenuously enjoining loyalty.[6]

At the same time movements such as Charter 77 in Czechoslovakia had found a new stick with which to beat their governments. The Soviet Union's expressed commitment to the Helsinki agreements of 1975 meant that not only the Soviet government, but the governments of Eastern Europe too, could be held to task within the international community if cases of infringement of human rights could be revealed – as they were thenceforth, assiduously, in the face of severe police harassment. The workings of the power monopoly could thus be made public, and the monopoly itself perhaps weakened. It is important to note what was not often pointed out at the time, that this strategy depended upon a gradual shift in the Soviet Union's own stance in Europe, from one of outright coercion to one of diplomacy. It was this shift in the Soviet Union's strategy, rather than any success of Charter 77, that ultimately brought down the power monopoly in the whole of Eastern Europe.

THE YEAR OF CHANGE

The date that deserves to go down in history as the symbol of the collapse of the power monopoly in Eastern Europe is Tuesday, 2 May 1989, when, with no great fuss, the barbed wire of the frontier between Hungary and Austria was snipped near Hegyshalom. But before that a sequence of events had taken place in Hungary and Poland that heralded the process and set it well on its way.

In Hungary, the fall of Kadar at the conference of the Hungarian

Socialist Workers' Party (HSWP) of May 1988, and the entry of the reformers Imre Pozsgay and Rezso Nyers into the Politburo set the ball rolling. The fateful year of 1989 opened with the passing of a law on the Right of Association, which set a constitutional seal on the demise of the power monopoly. This was followed on 26 January by the government's announcement that it had consented to the exhumation and re-interment of Imre Nagy and other leaders of the 1956 uprising, which, in Bill Lomax's term, 'set political life ablaze'.[7] In March the party's Central Committee adopted an 'action programme', and this was followed by 'triangular talks' between the representatives of the HSWP, of the official mass organisations and of the opposition movements. When the party dissolved itself at its extraordinary congress in October, to form the Hungarian Socialist Party, this was but the culmination of the process that saw the end of the power monopoly in Hungary.

In Poland, the crucial turning-point was the tenth plenum of the Central Committee of the Polish United Workers' Party at which, on 18 January 1989, Jaruzelski forced through, apparently by threatening to resign, a resolution of 'political pluralism and trade union pluralism'. On 6 February there began the 'round table' talks, involving representatives of the party, of the official unions, of the opposition (dominated by Solidarity) and two priests. The object of the discussions, in the words of General Kiszczak, the Minister of the Interior at the time, was 'not the principle of pluralism, but its form'. In an interview with *Le Monde*, the Polish prime minister announced that the party was 'renouncing its power monopoly'. The way was open for the re-registration of Solidarity, and for the national elections of 4 June, at which 35 per cent of seats in the lower house, and all those of a newly-created Senate, were opened to free election.[8]

In Bulgaria, the turning-point came on 10 November when, amid intense popular demonstrations, Petar Mladenov replaced Todor Zhivkov at the head of the Bulgarian Communist Party, to embark on a strategy of controlling and as far as possible guiding very vigorous public pressures for change. But the party had to pay for remaining at the head of events in the coin of its monopoly of power. On 17 November Article 273 of the criminal code, banning propaganda hostile to the party, was abolished. This symbolic but none the less juridical blow to the monopoly was followed at the end of November by the drafting of two laws guaranteeing freedom of association.

The crisis naturally came more abruptly in the three regimes that had chosen outright resistance to the pressures of the time: Czechoslovakia and the GDR, the two industrial leaders of the bloc, where the pressures generated by the Soviet reforms were particularly sharply felt and equally severely repressed; and Ceausescu's Romania. In the case of Czechoslovakia, a particularly savage show of police brutality at a demonstration on 17 November led to a massive upsurge of popular feeling, and the entire Politburo resigned en bloc on 24 November. Both the Central Committee and the Politburo of the GDR's Socialist Unity Party were to follow suit on 3 December, as the flow of GDR citizens through the now perforated iron curtain threatened the government and party with catastrophe.

The Romanian Communist Party dissolved when the dictator fell at Christmas time, and was at one point actually outlawed by the Council of the Front of National Salvation which had taken over the reins of power. It was reinstated very shortly afterwards, apparently through pressure from the party's regional apparatus, whose role could not be so swiftly ended as that of the Conducator himself and his immediate family. In the case of Romania, more than in that of any other country of the bloc, there lingered during the months following the fall of Ceausescu the possibility that the power monopoly of the communist party might come to be replaced by an authoritarianism scarcely less monopolistic, or indeed that the communist party might reconstitute itself in another guise. But elections were held, as promised by the Council of National Salvation, in May 1990, and at that point at least it could still be hoped that Romania was to share in the general wave of change that had swept the region.

In these crowded events of a single year the power monopoly of the communist party fell in Eastern Europe. But for a full understanding of this historic moment of change, the events themselves and their immediate sequel must be put in an analytical framework.

If the entire process is surveyed, from the mid-1980s on, it can be seen that the fall of the political monopoly in Eastern Europe flowed in a variety of channels. First, a process of aggregation of dissenting opinion had taken place in the period from 1977 which was to prepare the way for the political parties that were to spring into life, or to be resuscitated from some forty years of suspended animation, in 1989. Second, a process of party formation was already under way in all the countries of the region by the time the ruling communist party fell, and this was to gather momentum after the fall of the power monopoly. Third, the years up to 1989 saw the development of a great many new initiatives over individual issues or involving distinct sections of society – and in particular youth. Finally, any analysis of the crisis of the power monopoly must deal with developments within the ruling party itself, and the way in which it responded to the exceptional challenge posed.

If the history of the period from the mid-1970s to 1989 is examined it can be seen that a process of aggregation of dissident opinion predated the coming of Gorbachev by a decade. If a date is to be sought for its established emergence, it must be 1977 when Charter 77 was created in Czechoslovakia. One year later the Evangelical churches in the GDR emerged as a further aggregating centre around which alternative views and indeed political action could cluster.[9] By the end of 1989, the baton had been passed by these two earlier centres to the New Forum in the GDR and the Civic Forum in Czechoslovakia, although the influence of the Evangelical churches and of Charter 77 has been strong within these new organisations. By then, too, Bulgaria had acquired a Union of Democratic Forces which was playing a similar aggregating role, and a Group for Dialogue had come into being in Romania.

But the most prominent case of a broad movement that aggregated under a single organisational umbrella the demands arising from civil society was of course Solidarity in Poland. Indeed, the path travelled by Solidarity since its inception in 1980 is quite extraordinary. From being in August of that year a workers' movement with a relatively limited aim, it found itself within a year representing in a sense the entire nation against the party in power, until Jaruzelski rang down the curtain on this first stage of Solidarity's existence in December 1981. During the ensuing period of underground activity divisions developed, which became more marked with the roundtable talks of 1989. By the time of the elections to the Sejm of 1989 the movement was made up of a number of strands that were distinct in terms of organisation, leadership, constituency and perceived role. But it was the 'parliamentary' Solidarity, enjoying the patronage of Walesa himself, that went on to form the first non-communist government in Eastern Europe for forty years, in coalition with the Democratic and United Peasant parties.[10]

The Solidarity story contained an element that was reproduced in most countries of the region. Once the monopoly position of the communist party was seen to be vulnerable, there was a natural tendency for movements to arise that made a general appeal to society as a whole against the ruling party rather than to sectional interest or specific issues beyond that simply of achieving or restoring democracy and civil rights. That is, there was a certain ecumenism in the general movement to displace the power monopoly, which was often reflected by the use of the term 'forum' in a movement's name (the New Forum in the GDR, Democratic Forum in Hungary, and Civic Forum in Czechoslovakia).

This use of a marketplace metaphor is revealing, but should be properly understood. The forum in question developed within the movement that was opposed to the power monopoly. The development implied that a degree of organisation among the elements that compose civil society had taken place. But these forums could not – or not necessarily – be taken to represent the shape of things to come, a model of a new pluralist polity. At the moment of their appearance they were the creation of a particular conjuncture in Eastern European history. Their precise future will only become clear with the passing of time. Some of the more important factors that will influence that future are succinctly presented in Peter Mair's chapter.

In some cases these broad movements went on to fight elections as a political party, as with Solidarity. At other times they remained movements outside the electoral field, preferring to continue to be a more detached source of ideas. But in other cases they have been unable to decide on the matter. This has led at times to reversals of policy (on 5 December 1989 the Czechoslovak Civic Forum said that it would put up candidates in the scheduled election, only to decide in mid-January that it would not) or splits (the GDR's New Forum decided at its constituent congress on 27–8 January 1990 not to take part in the elections of March, but a dissident Deutsche Forumspartei in Karl Marx Stadt formed itself at that point to fight them). In the event New Forum went on to become one element in the Alliance that was victorious in the elections of March 1990.

When the books are written on what was then happening in Eastern Europe, the Polish experience will no doubt be seen to be the first illustration of a widely shared initial stage in a process of party formation in Eastern Europe out of the cocoon of the traditional power monopoly: a rallying of society, without at this stage too much concern for sectional interests, against the power monopoly. The new at this stage seems to reflect the old. The opposing movement confronts the communist party as bloc against bloc, the shape of the one determining to some extent the shape of the other. In the Czechoslovak case, Vaclav Havel described in a celebrated passage how party and dissidents, in the pre-perestroika phase, saw themselves as 'drawn into the same game', where 'we are a little bit "them", whilst "they" are at the same time a little bit us'.[11] It was from this initial simple confrontation between the party and the forces for change that the new political and party systems of Eastern Europe have emerged. The end of this social face-to-face confrontation that the events of 1989 brought no doubt explains to some extent the lack of enthusiasm for the newly established electoral process, as witnessed in the low turn-out in the Hungarian elections of March 1990 (64 per cent in the first round and 45 per cent in the second) and the Polish local elections of May of that year (42.1 per cent). The battle having been won, it was not clear what value voting would thereafter have.[12]

A second channel in which the fall of the power monopoly has flowed is the actual process of party formation itself, together with a parallel process of party revival.

Perhaps the least surprising feature of that process has been the revival of the parties that had enjoyed an autonomous existence before the onset of the cold war. Many of these had been either directly or indirectly suppressed at that point (for example, the Hungarian Smallholders Party, and the Romanian Liberal and National Peasant Parties, and the Bulgarian Agrarian Party). Others had played in the intervening period a subservient role within a bloc dominated by the communist party (examples here are the Democratic Party and the United Peasant Party in Poland, the Christian Democratic Party in the GDR, and the Socialist Party, the People's Party and the Slovak Freedom Party in Czechoslovakia). Whilst their association with the pre-communist past was at first a strong asset, guaranteeing them a role in the making of a new polity, these parties were in many cases soon revealed to be in a Rip van Winkle position, awakening after a long enforced slumber to find that the world had changed, and that other forces were moving more dynamically on the political chessboard. None the less, the Hungarian Smallholders Party was from an early stage a significant competitor in the elections of spring 1990 in Hungary, winning itself a role in the government that stemmed from those elections, whilst the Polish United Peasant Party played a prominent part in the Polish elections of 1989, albeit in the shadow of the mightier and newer Solidarity.

Among these resurrections from the past the social-democratic parties are in a very particular situation. Forced into mergers with the communist parties in the late 1940s, they find attempts at independent revival hampered by reformist communists who are themselves seeking salvation in a version of social-democracy. The fact that the

CPSU itself ever more clearly sees its future in some form of social-democracy (Sweden and Austria are the models most frequently mentioned) further complicates the situation.[13] But the social-democratic parties undoubtedly have a future as independent parties in their respective political party systems, and can benefit from having partners immediately available in Western Europe which can help to secure their contemporary identity and offer them the organisational benefits of an international network.

Side by side with these revivals of the past, a whole plethora of new political parties emerged and, in the new climate, duly had themselves registered. In Hungary by the beginning of March 1990 there were no fewer than fifty parties, and in Romania over seventy parties competed in the elections of May 1990.[14] The number was soon considerably whittled down, either through an electoral system framed deliberately to produce that result (as in Czechoslovakia) or simply through the succumbing of the least fit in the elections themselves as they one by one took place.

Worth noting is the creation of green parties in every country of the bloc. Given the very grave environmental problems that confront most Eastern European countries, the development of green parties is perhaps not surprising. Eco-glasnost in Bulgaria was at the forefront of the democracy movement, and was itself the product of widespread public concern over environmental problems. The Polish Ecological Party, formed in September 1988, sent a representative to the fifth congress of European Green Parties in Paris in April 1989.

On the whole, however, the green parties are not large, and with the possible exception of eco-glasnost are not likely to be a major political force in the near future. In Eastern Europe, as elsewhere, environmental issues are now on everyone's agenda, and no green party can hope to monopolise them. But the appearance of green parties in all the countries of the region is interesting for less obvious reasons. First, there seems to have been something of a demonstration effect at work, which is the fruit of the growing links between radical groups of Eastern and Western Europe. Secondly, they have a particular appeal to the younger generation, and the element of youth in the events of 1989 in Eastern Europe has been particularly prominent.

But this account of the emergence of broad aggregating movements and of the formation of political parties gives no real impression of the immense upsurge in political activity of one sort or another in the region in the era of perestroika. There was change, for instance, within organisations that in the past had functioned as an integral part of the power monopoly. This was particularly striking in the case of the party-sponsored youth movements, but it affected also the 'peace councils', erstwhile faithful ambassadors for Soviet defence policies. It was the Czechoslovak Socialist Youth League that in 1988 orchestrated a celebrated protest action against the building of a dam in the Berounka Valley at Krivoklat; whilst the Hungarian peace council under Barabas even applied to join the council of European Nuclear Disarmament (END).[15]

As the 1980s progressed these official bodies came to be flanked by a great number of new and totally independent movements and organisations concerned with particular issues (the Danube Circle in Hungary was and remains but one major example of a vast array of environmental groups and movements), or rallying particular sections of society, and in particular the young.[16] Hungary again provides a prominent example of the latter, in the Association of Young Democrats, known by its acronym FIDESZ.

But FIDESZ was far from the only case. Further illustrations were provided by the tribulations of the Jazz Section of the Prague Musicians' Union in the mid-1980s, the part played by the students in the revolution in Romania, and the fact that the Evangelical churches in the early 1980s in the GDR were undoubtedly doing the SED a great service in catering for the energies and aspirations of young people in a way that the SED's youth wing appeared unable to achieve. On the lighter side, a Czechoslovak Society for Merrier Times Today together with the Polish Orange Alternative staged an 'Unsuccessful Action by Merry Policemen' in Prague on 15 August 1989, and attacked a political demonstration with truncheons made of salami and cucumbers, water melon helmets and inflatable elephants. It has indeed been argued that the events of 1989 in Eastern Europe represented an Eastern version of the Western European 1968, and somewhere in the vast historiographical exercise that sorting out that view would involve there would undoubtedly be found more than a grain of truth. What the future of these often anomic initiatives will be in the emerging political systems remains to be seen, but it is worth noting that FIDESZ stood as a political party in the Hungarian elections of March 1990, and achieved a score of 9 per cent of the poll.

Finally there is the other side of the equation – the communist parties themselves which have been led by internal pressures, stemming in turn from the withdrawal of Soviet support, to cede all or a part of their monopoly of power. Where the communist party took the step of allowing rival parties to form and to contest elections, they themselves have had to adapt to this radically changed situation. Three strategies can be discerned, although they are far from distinct and elements of all three are present in certain cases.

The first strategy was that followed by the Polish United Workers' Party (PUWP) – which was the first voluntarily to invite rival political organisations into the political arena. This strategy consisted in giving up to the opposition a part of the arena, on condition that the party could retain the rest, and hoping either to withstand further demands, or with luck allow the coming hard economic times to create a need for the party's administrative skills. Thus, as we have seen, the Polish party ceded 35 per cent of the seats in the Sejm and all the seats in a new Senate for open election, and Eastern Europe acquired its first non-communist government in forty and more years.

The second strategy, which was pioneered by the Hungarian party, was to adopt a policy of purposeful reform within the party, and to mark the turn by renaming the party. The Hungarian Socialist Workers Party's change of name and transmogrification into the Hungarian Socialist Party at its fourteenth (extraordinary) congress was recorded above. The rump then went on to hold a 'true' fourteenth congress of the HSWP.

A third strategy is that followed by the Bulgarian party, although it had already been adopted forty years earlier by the Yugoslav League of Communists. This strategy has consisted in making – from above – wide-ranging adjustments to the way in which the political system works, without radically altering its character. That is, the monopoly was retained, but with a high level of tolerance. In the case of the Bulgarian party, the timely palace revolution of November 1989 enabled an alternative leadership, resting on the existing structures, to bend to the political wind, invite the opposition to roundtable talks, and pay out as little to its demands as possible.

There remain the cases where popular pressure and a failure to adapt in time to circumstances left the communist party with no alternative but simply to react to events, and to salvage what it could from a situation of which it was no longer master. In the extreme case – that of Romania – the party foundered entirely. But the Romanian case is indeed extreme, and in the two other cases – Czechoslovakia and the GDR – the chances of having a future role, whilst obviously restricted, none the less exist. The Communist Party of Czechoslovakia and the French Communist Party were the two largest and most influential of the Comintern parties in Europe in the interwar period, whilst the German KPD was the party of Rosa Luxemburg and Karl Liebknecht. It would be romantic to imagine that the past will redeem the recent memory of 'really existing socialism'; but it would be foolish to deny altogether the power of folk memories belonging to a not-so-very-distant past. It may not be long, as the excitement of 1989 recedes, before folk memories will begin to assert themselves against a new reality that will not be particularly enchanting.

It remains to focus on the key moments at which the power monopoly was either negotiated away or collapsed. In the foregoing, certain points at which freedom of association came to be given juridical form were mentioned. But, significant as those moments were in historical terms, it was not they that were seen as the prime symbols of the demise of the power monopoly. Of greater symbolic importance were: first, the constitutional rescission of the party's leading role; second, the decision to abolish the party's militia (often termed the 'workers' militia'); third, the abandoning of the communist party's practice of organising in the workplace as opposed to the place of residence; and fourth the acceptance that the intervention in Czechoslovakia had been a political error. These may seem minor events when compared with the formation of a non-communist government in Poland (12 September 1989), or the conversion of the Hungarian Socialist Workers Party into the Hungarian Socialist Party (7 October 1989), or the resignation or dismissal of individual leaders and political bureaus in Bulgaria, the GDR, Czechoslovakia and Romania. But they involved practices and institutions that were clearly seen by society as symbols of the power monopoly.

Thus, the clause in the constitution that enshrined the party's leading role was rescinded or amended by the Hungarian Assembly on 18 October, in Czechoslovakia on 29 November, in the GDR on 1 December, in Poland on 29 December, and in Bulagaria on 15 January 1990. In Romania the Communist Party was so totally discredited that it was not seen necessary to revoke its leading role.

The workers' militia (the 'workers' guard') was abolished in Hungary on 20 October and in Poland (the 'Civic Militia Voluntary Reserve' – ORMO) on 23 November. On 25 November the Bulgarian militia dissolved its sections concerned with 'struggle against ideological diversion'. On 17 December the GDR's hated Stasi was abolished. This was, in fact, a police force formally independent of the party, but the Kampfgruppen, which was the true party militia, was abolished at about the same time. The Romanian Securitate – which was originally a party militia, but was gradually converted into a national political police force – fell with the dictator in December. The Czechoslovak party militia was abolished on 21 December.

As for the condemnation of the intervention by the Warsaw Pact forces in Czechoslovakia in 1968, the Hungarians and the Poles were first in the field on 11 August (though the Hungarians had condemned the intervention of 1956 in their own country on 28 January). They were followed by the Bulgarians in November, with the GDR making its declaration on the last day of that month. The Czechoslovaks themselves, under a new government and a new party leadership, condemned the invasion on 1 December; whilst three days later the Warsaw Treaty Organisation as a body followed suit.

Having through these various steps either divested themselves or been divested of the baggage of the past, the communist parties of Eastern Europe entered on their long Calvary, their eyes fixed on a day when present animosities had died down, when economic hardship and the failure of successor governments to solve them had possibly rekindled some respect for their organisational abilities in the minds of the people and when, in an ever more united Europe, and in a very much humbler role, they might hope to forge a new relationship with the continent's social democratic – and possibly green – parties. But their monopoly of power had gone for ever.

NOTES

1. Quoted in Dennison Rusinow, *The Yugoslav Experiment, 1948–74* (London: Hurst, 1977), p. 139.
2. *Kommunist*, 12, 1968.
3. See Stephen White and Alex Pravda (eds), *Ideology and Soviet Politics* (London: Macmillan, 1988); and Stephen White, *Political Culture and Soviet Politics* (London: Macmillan, 1979).
4. This result of the information monopoly is well, if somewhat adventurously, treated in Michael E. Urban and John McClure, 'The folklore of state socialism: semiotics and the study of the Soviet state', *Soviet Studies*, 35 (October 1983) 471–86.
5. For two major works on the Prague Spring see H. Gordon Skilling, *Czechoslovakia's Interrupted Revolution* (Princeton: Princeton Univer-

sity Press, 1976) and Galia Golan, *The Czechoslovak Reform Movement* (Cambridge: Cambridge University Press, 1971); and for this aspect of the Solidarity episode see Neil Ascherson, *The Polish August* (Harmondsworth: Penguin, 1981) and Denis MacShane, *Solidarity: Poland's Independent Trade Union* (Nottingham: Spokesman Books, 1981).

6. H. Gordon Skilling, 'Independent Currents in Czechoslovakia', *Problems of Communism*, 34, 1 (1985); Christiane Lemke, 'New Issues in the Politics of the German Democratic Republic: A Question of Political Culture?', *The Journal of Communist Studies*, 2 (1986) 341–58.

7. Bill Lomax, '1989 in Hungary: Year of Change', *Journal of Communist Studies*, 5 (1989) 346.

8. Paul Lewis, 'Poland – Renewal Renewed', ibid, 340–2.

9. Pedro Ramet, 'Church and Peace in East Germany', *Problems of Communism*, 33 (1984) 45–7; Margaret Manale, 'L'église dans le socialisme: le cas de la République démocratique allemande', *Etudes*, 363, 6 (1985).

10. The best treatment of this evolution within Solidarity is Alexander Smolar, 'The Polish Opposition' in *The Role of Opposition: The Role of Opposition Groups on the Eve of Democratization in Poland and Hungary* (Crises in Soviet-Type Systems: Study nos. 17–18, München, n.d.)

11. Vaclav Havel, 'Anatomie d'une réticence', *Lettre Internationale*, 7 (1985) 18.

12. *Gazeta Wyborcza* of 28 May 1990 explained the apathy in the Polish local elections in part by the 'political problems within Solidarity and depression caused by the [rail] strikes'.

13. Heinz Timmermann, 'The Communist Party of the Soviet Union's Reassessment of International Social-Democracy: Dimensions and Trends', *The Journal of Communist Studies*, 5 (1989) 173–84. Bill Lomax (op. cit. p. 346) records Oleg Bogomolov's recommendation to the Hungarian HSWP that it might adopt a Swedish or Austrian style of social-democracy.

14. Judith Pataki, 'Hungarian Electoral Law Complicates Elections', *Report on Eastern Europe* (Radio Free Europe), 1, 10 (9 March 1990) 33; Michael Shafir, 'The Electoral Law', *ibid*, 1, 18 (4 May 1990) 28.

15. Radio Free Europe, RAD Cz SR/13, 1 Sep 1988, pp. 39/40 quoting *Rude Pravo)*.

16. Michael Waller, 'The Ecology Issue in Eastern Europe: Protest and Movements', *The Journal of Communist Studies*, 6 (1989) 303–28.

7 Electoral Markets and Stable States

Peter Mair

CLARIFICATIONS

This chapter begins with three clarifications. First, the markets to which it refers are electoral markets, and, within these markets, the pattern of competition with which it is concerned is inter-party competition. As is evident, parties will compete with one another when they have a market in which to compete, that is, when there are voters in competition; and the assumption which underlies the chapter, albeit guardedly so, is that the actual extent of inter-party competition, and the competitiveness of parties, is at least in part a function of the relative size of the electoral market. As the market expands, therefore, or as the number of voters in competition increases, parties are likely to become more competitive. As the market contracts, on the other hand, and as the number of voters in competition declines, parties are likely to become less competitive.

This assumption is a guarded one, however, and two qualifications are immediately necessary. The first of these is that it cannot be assumed that the competitiveness of parties is *entirely* a function of the size of the electoral market. In a perfectly balanced two-party system, for example, in which there are very few voters in competition, but where the shift of just one vote can make the difference between being a majority and being a minority, or between victory and defeat, each of the two parties is likely to prove extremely competitive. Hence intense competition can ensue even in situations of very restricted electoral availability. In contemporary Sweden, for example, the balance between the socialist and non-socialist blocs is now so finely drawn that even the relatively small Swedish electoral market can sustain quite pronounced electoral competition.

The second qualification is that it cannot be assumed that competition is *inevitable* in situations of large-scale electoral markets. In certain circumstances, for example, while large numbers of voters may be in competition, there may be few if any other rewards

119

associated with gains in electoral support, and hence the parties may not expend much effort in trying to win over the voters who are available. In Switzerland, for example, the unique formula whereby all four major parties permanently share government office means that there is little point in their competing with one another for extra votes. Hence even if the Swiss electoral market were to expand significantly it is unlikely that party competition would become more intense.

In other words, it is not just the sheer *size* of the electoral market and the extent of electoral availability which are relevant, but also the degree to which competition itself matters. That said, the emphasis must be on qualifying the initial assumption rather than on its wholesale rejection, for, other things being equal, parties are *likely* to be more competitive when there are more voters in competition and when the electoral market is more open or available. The existence of an electoral market may therefore be seen as a necessary if not a sufficient condition for party competition, in much the same way that the existence of democratic procedures themselves may be seen as a necessary but not sufficient condition for competition.[1]

The second clarification is that when parties initially confront an electoral market they have a choice of two, not necessarily exclusive strategies. In the first place, they can attempt to restrict or narrow that market, and thus engage in primarily *defensive* electoral strategies, mobilising existing adherents rather than attempting to win new supporters. Second, they may choose simply to compete in the market, and so engage in primarily *expansive* electoral strategies, constantly searching for new voters and placing relatively little emphasis on the mobilisation of existing loyalists. To the extent that the former option prevails, the market will progressively contract, and competition itself will be subdued. In the latter situation, on the other hand, the market is likely to remain quite open, and competition will be intense.

That said, it must also be recognised that it is only in exceptional circumstances that parties in a given political system will confront *a* (single) electoral market. When competition (or the absence of competition) takes place in a multi-dimensional environment, parties may confront a plurality of markets, each of which may be more or less open, and in each of which they may develop defensive or expansive strategies.[2] A religious party, for example, may find that a defensive strategy is appropriate in the electoral market which exists along the religious/secular divide, yet it may opt for an expansive strategy in the market which exists along the left/right divide. Thus while one market, or sub-market, may become quite narrow and closed, another market within the same system may remain quite open. In Belgium, for example, a relatively open market in left-right terms coincides with a remarkably closed market in linguistic terms. In Northern Ireland, there are few if any voters in competition in terms of the primary conflict between unionism and nationalism, yet electoral availability is pronounced, and competition intense, *within* each of the unionist and nationalist blocs.

The third clarification is that the size of the markets in general, and the degree of electoral availability, is largely a function of the strength and pervasiveness of relevant collective political *identities*.[3] Such collective identities may be ascriptive, and may often pre-date the emergence of political parties as such, as is the case with linguistic, cultural, ethnic or even gender identities, and, to a lesser extent, with religious identities. In other cases, these collective identities may be based on status, deriving from occupational or class distinctions, or whatever. In some circumstances, of course, while such identities exist, they may not be politically relevant,[4] and hence their impact on electoral markets may be at best indirect. In the Irish Republic, for example, while class identity is quite pronounced, class does not provide a major focus for electoral alignments. In Britain, on the other hand, class is really the only substantial collective identity which is relevant to politics, with religious and ethnic/subnational identities playing just a marginal role. Regardless of distinctions in terms of the substance and character of collective identities, however, it can be argued that the degree to which individual voters are integrated into a set of relevant collective political identities will help to determine the extent to which an electoral market exists. Where such identities are pervasive and/or pronounced, as has been the case in Austria, for example, the market for votes will be sharply restricted; where such identities are either weak or marginal, as in the United States, the market will be relatively open.

Having clarified some of these terms, the remainder of this chapter will trace some of the patterns which can be identified in electoral markets in Europe, and relate these to questions of democratic stability. The primary purpose of this exercise is to suggest that the restrictions on electoral availability which have tended to discourage competitive political strategies have largely derived from processes of organisational encapsulation. The density of organisational networks, whether based on ascriptive *or* achieved identities, has contributed substantially to the encouragement of an accommodationist political style in Europe's more plural societies and, more crucially, to the development of a consensual style among the more 'homogenous' political cultures within Scandinavia. Indeed, I shall argue that it is the relatively high organisational density which characterises so many of the small states of Western Europe, rather than the openness of their economies, which is largely responsible for their oft-noted lack of intense political competition.

In the final section of this chapter I attempt to outline some of the implications of this argument for the emerging democracies in Eastern Europe, where the absence of strong organisational networks, the weakness of stable collective identities, and the extraordinary openness of their electoral markets suggest that a highly competitive and potentially destabilising politics may well be encouraged. As Michael Waller notes in the preceding chapter, the existing power monopoly has been almost completely broken, and the scope for competition has been enhanced to a degree which has been virtually unknown in the West European experience.

DEVELOPMENTS AND CONTRASTS IN WESTERN EUROPE

At the risk of some exaggeration, and at the cost of immense generalisation, the history of the development of political parties in Western Europe can be read as a history of attempts to narrow the electoral market through the promotion and inculcation of mass political identities. This process was most clearly visible in the rise of the mass integration parties in the late nineteenth and early twentieth centuries, during the lead-up to, and in the immediate wake of the extension of voting rights to the working class and the propertyless. These parties, with their dense organisational networks, contrasted sharply with the more elitist, electorally-oriented, 'cadre' parties, or parties of individual representation, which had tended to dominate politics in the period prior to mass democracy. It was the new workers' parties in particular which offered the most striking examples of the new political strategy. Neumann has identified the contrast quite succinctly, and, while not expressed in these terms, his remarks also have a clear bearing on the different notions of party competition and electoral markets:

The first example of such a new party was presented by the continental Socialists. Their organization has been jokingly characterized as extending from the cradle to the grave, from the workers' infant-care association to the atheists' cremation society; yet such a description articulates the intrinsic difference from the liberal party of representation, with its principle of 'free recruitment' among a socially uncommitted, free-floating electorate . . . The [new] party can count on its adherents; it has taken over a good part of their social existence.[5]

That the new denominational mass parties of integration did not offer such a striking example as that provided by the class mass parties was hardly surprising. The religious parties, whether Catholic or Protestant, had less need to develop new autonomous organisational networks, since they could feed off the existing church organisations and the already strongly defined sense of religious identity. In the case of the workers' parties, however, the constituency which they were seeking to represent was itself a relatively new one, and it was only in certain cases, as in Britain for example, that the new parties were in a position to feed off a pre-existing, trade-union based organisational network.

Through mobilisation, integration, and, in Kirchheimer's terms, through 'the intellectual and moral *encadrement* of the masses',[6] the new mass integration parties therefore helped to build up and consolidate a set of collective political identities which, in turn, acted to reduce electoral availability. The result, most crucially, was a 'narrowing of the support market' and a 'freezing' of party systems in Western Europe.[7] To be sure, this freezing process was neither pervasive throughout Europe nor even throughout individual national electorates *tout court*. Organisational networks and the establishment of enduring partisan identities always remained poorly developed in France,[8] for example, and the result has been that the electoral market as a whole has remained remarkably open, with elections in France being characterised by particularly pronounced levels of electoral volatility. In yet other cases, such as Ireland, for example, the process was very uneven, with strong identities being established on the 'strong nationalist' side of the major political divide, and with weak or non-existent identities developing on the 'weak nationalist' side.[9] The result here is that while there has been a relatively restricted electoral market in terms of the competition between Fianna Fail and all other parties, the electoral market among these other parties themselves has always remained quite open.

In short, electoral markets are more restricted in certain countries than in others, and, even within individual countries, certain submarkets are more restricted than others. Moreover, since the relative degree of restriction depends, at least in part, on the depth and pervasiveness of collective political identities; and since the degree to which parties are competitive depends, also at least in part, on the openness of the electoral market; it then follows that competitiveness itself can be associated with the degree to which the polity is characterised by the presence or absence of strong collective identities. Polities which are characterised by the presence of strong identities are therefore likely to be less competitive than those in which such strong identities are absent. More precisely, polities which are so characterised will tend to be more *consensual* – at least in certain circumstances, and most obviously when no single group enjoys a clear overall majority.

ELECTORAL MARKETS AND CONSOCIATIONAL DEMOCRACY

This is not a startling conclusion. Indeed, it reflects the logic which lies behind the very notion of consociational democracy,[10] whereby strongly segmented societies (i.e. those characterised by very deeply held and quite mutually exclusive identities, based largely on language or religion) are seen to develop a stable democratic order by means of elite accommodation and a rejection of competitive behaviour. On the other hand, were such segmented societies to be characterised by competitive behaviour, it is argued that this could result in either the collapse of the polity itself, or the adoption of non-democratic means of control.

But while consociational or accommodationist solutions can develop in segmented societies, such development requires particular conditions: the society should be strongly segmented, and characterised by substantial elite authority; there should be a multiple balance of power between the different segments; the country concerned should be small; there should be at least some degree of overarching loyalty to the system in question; and there should already be a tradition of elite accommodation.[11] Surprisingly enough, little emphasis has been placed on what is the major theme of this present chapter, and that is the particular influence exerted by the size of the electoral market itself. Indeed, by taking this particular factor on board, and by recognising that the bondedness of the electorate may discourage competition and leave parties and elites with little choice but to accommodate to one another, we can then make much more sense of the reasons why elites should prove so 'willing' to abandon competitive strategies.

This has been one of the main elements addressed by Pappalardo[12] in his extensive criticisms of consociational theorists, in which he argues that much of the discussion of the preconditions of consociational democracy has mistakenly implied an immense voluntarism on the part of the accommodating elites, thus also implying that these same elites might equally have 'chosen' to be competitive. If, on the other hand, we accept, as Pappalardo does,[13] that the restrictions in the electoral market more or less 'oblige' elites to forego an expansive competitive strategy – the pervasiveness of identities meaning that there are few voters in competition and hence few rewards to be gained as a result of electoral competition – then it is not simply a matter of elite choice or elite willingness. Rather, elites, and parties, accommodate one another because they do not really have any other 'choice'; competition, in effect, is pointless: 'consociational democracy is not so much a pact among minorities in equilibrium or minorities *tout court*, as a pact among minorities who do not want and *are not in a position* to change the existing distribution of power'.[14]

Evidence of the existence of relatively restricted electoral markets in the classic consociational democracies in Western Europe certainly supports the notion that there would have been few rewards in competition, and that none of the minorities would have been in a position to change the existing balance of power. In the inter-war period, for example, at a time when Belgium, the Netherlands and Switzerland could be regarded as the paradigmatic cases of consociationalism, their mean level of electoral volatility (at 8.4) was just two-thirds that which prevailed in the non-consociational democracies of Western Europe (12.0).[15] Moreover, if we rank-order the thirteen principal West European democracies in the inter-war years in terms of their mean levels of volatility, we find that Switzerland, the Netherlands and Belgium occupy the ninth, tenth, and eleventh positions respectively, with lower levels of volatility being recorded only in Finland and Denmark.

A similar pattern prevails during the first postwar decades, from 1945 to 1965, when consociational practices also remained robust, and when Austria could be included as a fourth paradigmatic case. During this period the mean level of electoral volatility in the four consociational countries was 5.8, as against a mean level of 8.9 in the remaining non-consociational countries. In terms of the rank-order of countries, however, Belgium figures quite high on the list, coming in fifth position, with Austria in seventh, the Netherlands in eighth, and with Switzerland recording the lowest level of any country. Nevertheless, the overall pattern in both periods is undeniable. The three, and later four consociational democracies are characterised by relatively restricted electoral markets, and hence discouraged expansive competitive strategies. Here, indeed, the elites appeared to have little choice but to cooperate with one another.

To be sure, other, less palatable possibilities might be said to have existed. In Northern Ireland, for example, during the period of the Stormont regime, electoral volatility was also particularly low, the electoral market proved remarkably closed, and little competition ensued. Between 1918 and 1970, for example, almost 40 per cent of parliamentary seats in Northern Ireland remained uncontested,[16] with fewer than 20 per cent of seats being characterised by a direct nationalist *versus* unionist contest. This was a non-competitive system *par excellence*, in which, as is well known, the response of the dominant unionist elite fell considerably short of accommodationism. On the contrary, and unlike in the consociational democracies, the absence of competition in Northern Ireland led to exclusion and effective majority tyranny, which, eventually, brought about the collapse of the regime. But it is here that the other preconditions of consociationalism come into play, for, unlike Northern Ireland, the consociational democracies were *also* characterised by a multiple balance of power, with no one segment enjoying anything approaching the overwhelming majority status of the Northern Irish unionists. Moreover, there also existed an overarching commitment to system maintenance in the consociational democracies, a characteristic which, quite evidently, has always been lacking in Ulster.

SMALL STATES AND LARGE STATES

It is not just the consociational democracies which are relevant here, however. The logic goes further than this. In principle, what marks the consociational democracies off from the other West European polities is not the existence of restricted electoral markets as such.

Nor is it even the fact that this restriction derives from the pervasiveness of strong, collective and politically relevant identities. Rather, what makes these systems different is that their segmentation results from their being *plural societies*, with the segments, or pillars, being primarily defined by linguistic or religious divisions. Elsewhere in Western Europe, as Almond originally emphasised, and as Lijphart also appeared to accept, democratic stability, whether accommodationist or not, was associated with the existence of non-plural or *homogenous* political cultures which, by definition, could not be regarded as segmented.[17] Hence the logic of consociationalism could not be seen to apply to any of these other systems, and hence, most crucially, any accommodationist behaviour, and any practices which more or less approximated to consociationalism which might be observed in these homogenous political cultures would have to be explained by *other* factors.

This is precisely the task which Katzenstein[18] sets for himself in *Small States in World Markets*. For, in analysing patterns of industrial policy in Western Europe, he finds that small states *in general*, and not just the consociational democracies/plural societies, tend to develop a policy style which is quite distinctive from that developed in the larger states, and which is characterised by accommodation, compromise and cooperation between different elites and different parties. But while the degree of segmentation and the traditions of consociationalism might prove adequate to account for this pattern in Belgium, the Netherlands, Switzerland, and even arguably Austria, they are clearly inappropriate in any explanation of the similar patterns which are found in the more homogenous smaller democracies such as Denmark, Norway and Sweden. Hence Katzenstein's search for an alternative, or at least an additional explanation, and hence his primary emphasis on the fact that these small states are particularly vulnerable to the vagaries of the international economy. It is this vulnerability, he argues, and the need to ensure economic survival in a potentially hostile trading environment, which forces these smaller states to adopt a consensual rather than an adversarial style of policy-making. The argument is a reasonably convincing one, and Katzenstein builds a strong and largely plausible case in favour of the notion that the openness of a national economy may have an important impact on patterns of domestic politics. Moreover, it is an argument which does not rest exclusively on this single variable, but which also incorporates an appreciation of the influence of certain institutional characteristics (such as proportional electoral formulae), as well as that of the particular patterns of political fragmentation in these homogenous small states (such as a weak and divided right).

That said, I would also argue that Katzenstein has actually neglected one element which is of equally fundamental importance, and that is that the consensual patterns in these other small states derive almost as much from the character of their electoral markets as do the accommodationist patterns in the traditional consociational democracies. In other words, I would suggest that the absence of competitive policy styles in countries such as Denmark, Norway and Sweden may not just be because they have shared a sense of economic vulnerability with the consociational democracies; rather, it may also be because they have shared a restricted electoral market. More importantly, it can further be argued that this restriction also derives from the pervasiveness of strong, collective and politically relevant identities, and from a pattern of effective segmentation. In the case of the 'homogenous' countries, however, and unlike in the consociational democracies, this is obviously not a segmentation which is based on language or religion; rather it is one which is based on the cementing of *class* identities.

While the limited scope of this present chapter affords little opportunity to do more than simply assert such a possibility, the limited evidence which currently exists does offer some support for the argument. In the first place, there is no doubt that small states, even when not divided by language and religion, have experienced a more restricted electoral market than is the case with large states. In the inter-war years, for example, which was the period which proved most crucial in laying the foundations for the consensual practices which have since proved so characteristic of the small states,[19] the mean level of electoral volatility in Denmark, Norway and Sweden was just 7.8. In the larger and more competitive states of France, Germany and the United Kingdom, on the other hand, the mean level of electoral volatility was 14.1, almost double that in the Scandinavian states. Indeed, if one also includes the few democratic elections which were held in Italy in this period, the mean level in the larger states rises to 16.8, substantially more than double that in the smaller Scandinavian countries.

A similar contrast is evident in the early postwar years, that is, in the period 1945–65. In this case the mean level of electoral volatility in the four larger states was 11.5, which includes a remarkably low figure of just 4.6 for the then appropriately 'Butskellite' British case; without the UK, the mean level in France, West Germany and Italy,

TABLE 7.1: *Mean electoral volatility by type of state*

Period	Consociational democracies*	Small homogenous states	Large states
1918–44	8.4	7.8	16.8 (14.1)*
1945–65	5.8	6.2	11.5 (13.8)†

Notes: * Includes Austria in 1945–65 period
** Figure in brackets excludes Italy
† Figure in brackets excludes UK

SOURCE: Stefano Bartolini and Peter Mair, *Identity, Competition and Electoral Availability: the stabilisation of European electorates, 1885–1985* (Cambridge: Cambridge University Press, 1990)

which were the three most volatile electorates in Western Europe in this period, comes to 13.8. In Denmark, Norway and Sweden, by contrast, the mean level was just 6.2. These, and the earlier figures concerning the consociational democracies, are summarised in Table 7.1.

These crude aggregate figures therefore suggest that there were substantially fewer voters in competition in the smaller Scandinavian states than was the case in the larger West European democracies, and hence indicate that, as in the consociational democracies, there existed quite a restricted electoral market. Other things being equal, it was therefore also likely that the various parties and elites in these smaller states would have perceived that there was little to gain through the adoption of expansive competitive strategies: since there were relatively few voters available to be won, there would have been little point in trying to compete for them. Moreover, and unlike in Northern Ireland, the prospects for outright victory were also slim, particularly as far as socialist-bourgeois competition was concerned,[20] and hence a strategy of compromise and consensus would have seemed more appealing. In the larger democracies, on the other hand, and particularly in France, Germany and Italy during both the inter-war and early postwar years, intensive competition would have made sense. In these cases, there was a lot to gain.

But how does this relate to the question of segmentation? Quite simply, these smaller and more homogenous democracies were not only characterised by a restricted electoral market, but this restriction also appears to have derived, at least in part, from the existence of dense organisational networks which, in a manner similar to the

TABLE 7.2: *Ranking of West European democracies in terms of working-class organisational density*

	1918–44	1945–65
	High Density	
1	Austria	Sweden
2	Denmark	Austria
3	Sweden	Denmark
4	Switzerland	Norway
5	Norway	Italy
6	Belgium	Switzerland
7	Germany	Belgium
8	Netherlands	Ireland
9	United Kingdom	United Kingdom
10	Ireland	Netherlands
11	Finland	Finland
12	France	West Germany
13	na*	France
	(*Italian data not available)	
	Low Density	

Note: Ranking refers to an index summing trade union density and membership ratio of class left parties.
SOURCE: As Table 7.1.

pattern wrought by linguistic and/or religious *verzuiling* in the consociational democracies, bonded voters into a set of strong identities. In this case, however, the pattern of segmentation in Denmark, Norway and Sweden was based on *class* organisations and class identities.

As can be seen from Table 7.2, the figures here are quite revealing. Employing an index of working class organisational density which is calculated by summing levels of trade-union density and the membership ratio of class left parties,[21] it can be seen that the density of class organisational networks in Denmark, Norway and Sweden have proved particularly pronounced, especially when contrasted to that in the larger democracies. In the inter-war period, for example, these three smaller democracies ranked in second, third and fifth positions in terms of their levels of density, with Germany, the United Kingdom and France ranking in seventh, ninth, and last positions respectively. The contrast is even more marked in the early postwar period, with Sweden, Denmark and Norway occupying first, third and fourth positions respectively, as against the United Kingdom which occupies ninth position, and Germany and France, which occupy the bottom two positions.

The density of class organisational networks therefore not only tends to be much more pronounced in the smaller democracies than in the larger democracies, but also to be particularly pronounced in the more 'homogenous' of the smaller democracies. This suggests that the class 'sub-cultures' within these smaller states can play a similar restrictive role in relation to the electoral markets as that played by the primarily linguistic and religious sub-cultures in the consociational democracies (although it should be emphasised that in the case of Austria and Switzerland class organisational density is also relatively pronounced); and this, in turn, suggests that the segmentally-based incentives towards accommodationism which have existed in the consociational democracies are really not that much different to those which exist in the small and more homogenous democracies. While the *basis* of the segmentation in the consociational democracies may be distinctive, building on religion and language rather than, or as well as, class, the reality of that segmentation seems quite comparable.

The consequences are also quite comparable. Just as the segmentation along religious and linguistic lines has restricted electoral markets and discouraged expansive competition in the consociational democracies, so too has class segmentation discouraged competitive politics in the more homogenous small democracies. Indeed, Pappalardo's depiction of the electoral stalemate which has proved so influential in the consociational democracies could equally well have been applied to the cases of Denmark, Norway and Sweden, particularly insofar as socialist-bourgeois competition is concerned. Thus,

> the movement of votes among the parties is hindered by at least three closely related factors: the heavy social and organizational ties, incompatible beliefs, and the feelings of hostility and mutual diffidence of the opposing subcultural alignments; the internal homogeneity of these alignments, the members of which are seldom, if at all, exposed to crosscutting pressures and so scarcely sensitive to the appeals from other quarters; and, finally, the high level of party identification, which implies long-term loyalty of the voters to their subcultural representatives.[22]

Some concluding remarks and qualifications are necessary in this context. First, it is not my intention to suggest that the factors emphasised by Katzenstein, such as international economic vulnerability, divisions within the political right, and so on, play little or no role in the explanation of consensual political behaviour. Rather, I am simply suggesting that such an explanation neglects the fact that segmentation or *verzuiling* may also derive from class identities, and that the concept itself has a potentially much wider application than to the plural societies alone, or to divisions which are based only on religion or language.[23]

Second, by taking account of the potential for segmentation on the basis of class alignments in particular, we are then in a better position to understand not only consensual behaviour in homogenous political cultures, such as Denmark, Norway, and Sweden, but also that in the relatively exceptional Austrian case,[24] which, as we have seen (Table 7.2), is a consociational country which is also characterised by a particularly pronounced level of class organisational density.

Third, the real test of the validity of this argument, as well as the real test of Katzenstein's own explanations, may best be carried out by a closer examination of some of the cases which are neglected in both analyses. The Italian case is particularly interesting in this regard, for example, since it is a large country which has recently been characterised by quite a restricted electoral market and relatively strong organisational networks (in both class and religious terms). In addition, despite its size, Italy also appears to have been characterised by a certain degree of non-competitive accommodationism, reflected most clearly in the *compromesso storico* strategy of the Italian Communist Party, as well as in the governing agreements of the late 1970s. The Irish and Finnish cases are also particularly interesting. These are small, economically vulnerable states which, quite unusually, are also characterised by relatively low levels of class organisational density (see Table 7.2). But they also have quite contrasting patterns of electoral availability. Finland, for example, has one of the lowest mean levels of electoral volatility in Western Europe, whereas Ireland ranks among the more volatile countries. Here too, therefore, it would be interesting to test for the extent to which differential patterns of competitive politics have prevailed.

Fourth, it must also be emphasised that much of this argument derives from patterns within cross-national data in both the inter-war and early postwar periods, when the electoral markets in both the homogenous and consociational states proved particularly restricted. More recent developments, on the other hand, have not only suggested a weakening of some of the organisational networks which have sustained strong identities,[25] but they have also indicated a greater opening-up of electoral markets and an increase in electoral volatility in some of these countries, which suggests that there may now be greater incentives towards expansive competition and a greater disinclination towards accommodationism. This certainly seems to be the case in countries such as Denmark, Norway, Sweden and the Netherlands.

Finally, the qualifications with which this paper began must also be borne in mind. Competitive behaviour is more likely in a context of open electoral markets, and is less likely in the context of closed electoral markets. But this is as far as it goes, and there is no inevitability implied. The stakes are also important. In Switzerland, for example, it is not just the closure of the electoral market which is relevant, but also the fact that almost regardless of any electoral shifts which do occur, none of the four major parties is likely to be excluded from the governing cartel. In the United Kingdom, by contrast, even a very closed electoral market can prove highly competitive, in that even small swings can make the difference between governmental incumbency and opposition.

SOME IMPLICATIONS FOR THE NEW EAST EUROPEAN DEMOCRACIES

If this argument may be summarised without qualifications and caveats, it runs as follows: the prevalence of strong, collective and politically relevant identities tends to close off electoral markets; these identities, in turn, tend to derive from strong organisational networks and subcultures, whether built around language, religion, *or* class, which isolate their adherents and help cement political loyalties; in such a situation, competitive expansive electoral strategies prove unrewarding, and, other things being equal (and most particularly if there exists both a multiple balance of power and overarching systemic loyalties), democratic politics will therefore tend to be more accommodating, more consensual, and, inevitably, more stable. Finally, this pattern will be reinforced if the stakes are not too large, and if outright victory would not be seen to result in an overwhelming set of rewards.

If this is true, then it does not bode well for the future stabilisation of democracy in Eastern Europe, at least in the reasonably short term. In the first place, the stakes in the new democracies in Eastern Europe are large, with the state, in effect, being up for grabs. Whoever comes to power is not only in a position to determine that most crucial of resources, the rules of the game, but is also in a position to control the new bureaucracies and new government agencies. Given that much will now start from scratch, there are few if any legacies which will need to be accommodated. Party, inevitably, will make a difference.

Second, and even more crucially, the new electoral markets in Eastern Europe, as new markets, are particularly open, and the new electorates are almost entirely available. In one sense, of course, this situation can be seen as no different from that which prevailed in much of the rest of Europe in the early part of the century, when the suffrage was extended and when floods of newly-enfranchised and largely available voters were incorporated into the national electorates, thus raising levels of electoral volatility quite considerably.[26] In the case of the new democracies of Eastern Europe, however, it must be emphasised that these newly-enfranchised voters constitute virtually the *entire body* of the electorate, and few will have entered with pre-existing partisan loyalties.

Third, and here Michael Waller's arguments in chapter 6 are also particularly relevant, precisely because of the all-embracing nature of state power which existed prior to the revolutions of 1989, civil society in eastern Europe has remained largely underdeveloped. This too will enhance the availability of the new electorates, in that there is little in the way of an independent set of organisational networks which could promote and sustain collective identities, and thus provide channels for mass integration. Independent trade unions remain largely weak and inchoate. With some notable exceptions, religious organisations, where they exist, are also weak and undeveloped. Mass parties, in effect, are as yet non-existent. And while subnational identities are more evident and pervasive than is the case in Western Europe, their particular impact is more likely to be disintegrative than integrative.

In short, the new electoral markets in Eastern Europe are likely to be open, and the electorates likely to be available, to an extent which is almost without parallel in twentieth-century European history. And given that the stakes are so high, and given also the combination of severe economic difficulties and enhanced economic expectations, the result is likely to be an extremely competitive democratic politics which, in turn, may well hamper the stabilisation of democracy itself. Indeed, even by the summer of 1990, the signs of such competitiveness had already become apparent: the clashes between the miners and students in Romania, and the allegations of corruption and intimidation in the country's first free elections; the sit-ins in Sofia which have been organised in protest against the election of the reconstituted Communist Party in Bulgaria; the split in Solidarity in Poland; the threatened break-up of the East German coalition as the constituent parties sought to determine how the East German end of the first all-German elections was to be organised, and so on. The stakes are high, the voters are available, and hence the pressure to accommodate to one's opponents is effectively non-existent. Only time will tell whether the inculcation of stable partisan identities will prove possible, and hence whether a stable democratic order will eventually emerge.

Such few lessons as can be found in Western Europe are not wholly positive, however. In the 1970s, and in a foretaste of the transformation which recently occurred in Eastern Europe, Spain, Greece and Portugal each effected a transition to democracy. In all three cases, the stabilisation of that democracy has proved somewhat problematic, and political competition has proved intense. Most recently, in Greece, three successive general elections were required in order to find a government which could command a majority. Here too, the campaigns themselves were dominated by allegations of corruption and intimidation. In Spain, the party system has been held together only as the result of the dominance of one single party, initially the UCD, which in the space of just the three years between 1979 and 1982 witnessed its electoral support falling from 35 per cent to just 7 per cent; and later the Socialists, which now command only the narrowest of majorities. Indeed, with the exception of the Socialists, and the various but disintegrative sub-national parties, every other 'party' in Spain is largely just a loose and fragmented coalition of smaller groups, and electoral volatility remains remarkably high. In Portugal also, volatility has been particularly pronounced, with few strongly defined parties, and with a recent and possibly temporary stability being achieved only as a result of a massive swing towards the conservative Social Democrats, whose vote shot up from 30 per cent in 1985 to over 50 per cent in 1987.

These new Southern European democracies therefore continue to be characterised by very open electoral markets, enhanced electoral availability (even class organisational density remains remarkably low), and intense inter-party competition, all of which inevitably hamper the stabilisation of an enduring democratic order. That said, these particular countries have enjoyed two crucial advantages which, at least as yet, do not seem available to the more vulnerable new democracies of Eastern Europe. First, and from a more secure base, they have begun to enjoy quite substantial economic growth and increased prosperity, particularly since the mid-1980s. And second, and more importantly, they have been integrated into the European Community. In contrast, some at least of the new Eastern European democracies may well be facing quite a prolonged period of relative poverty and isolation, which, when added to the immensely competitive styles which are likely to characterise their electoral markets, may continue to leave a question mark over their ability to establish and sustain a stable democratic order.

NOTES

1. See Roberto D'Alimonte, 'Democrazia e Competizione', *Rivista Italiana di Scienza Politica* 19, 1 (1989) 115–33.
2. See Giacomo Sani and Giovanni Sartori, 'Polarization, Fragmentation and Competition in Western Democracies', in Hans Daalder and Peter Mair (eds), *Western European Party Systems: Continuity and Change* (London: Sage, 1983, pp. 307–40), and Ruud Koole and Philip van Praag, 'Electoral Competition in a Segmented Society: Campaign Strategies and the Importance of Elite Perceptions', *European Journal of Political Research* 18, 1 (1990) 51–70.
3. See Stefano Bartolini and Peter Mair, *Identity, Competition, and Electoral Availability: The Stabilization of European Electorates, 1885–1985* (Cambridge: Cambridge University Press, 1990).
4. Giovanni Sartori, 'From the Sociology of Politics to Political Sociology', in S. M. Lipset (ed), *Politics and the Social Sciences* (New York: Oxford University Press, 1969), pp. 65–100.
5. See Sigmund Neumann, 'Toward a Comparative Study of Political Parties', in Sigmund Neumann (ed.) *Modern Political Parties* (Chicago: University of Chicago Press, 1956), pp. 404–5.
6. Otto Kirchheimer, 'The Transformation of the Western European Party Systems', in Joseph LaPalombara and Myron Weiner (eds), *Political Parties and Political Development.* (Princeton: Princeton University Press, 1966), p. 184.
7. S. M. Lipset and Stein Rokkan, 'Cleavage Structures, Party Systems and Voter Alignments: an Introduction', in S. M. Lipset and Stein Rokkan (eds) *Party Systems and Voter Alignments.* (New York: The Free Press, 1967), pp. 50–1.
8. See Stefano Bartolini, 'Il Mutamento del Sistema Partitico Francese', *Il Mulino* 30 (1981) 169–219.
9. See Peter Mair, *The Changing Irish Party System: Organization, Ideology and Electoral Competition* (London: Pinter, 1987), pp. 86–9.
10. See Arend Lijphart, 'Typologies of Democratic Systems', *Comparative Politics* 1, 1 (1968) 3–44, and his *Democracy in Plural Societies: A Comparative Exploration* (New Haven: Yale University Press, 1977).
11. Lijphart, *Democracy in Plural Societies*, ch. 3; See also Hans Daalder,

'The Consociational Democracy Theme', *World Politics* 26, 4 (1974) 604–21.

12. See Adriano Pappalardo, 'The Conditions for Consociational Democracy: A Logical and Empirical Critique', *European Journal of Political Research* 9, 4 (1981) 365–90.

13. Ibid, 367–75

14. Ibid, 369, emphasis added.

15. Mean electoral volatility is calculated according to the formula proposed by Mogens Pedersen, 'The Dynamics of European Party Systems: Changing Patterns of Electoral Volatility', *European Journal of Political Research* 7, 1 (1979) 1–26, and offers a useful index of the aggregate electoral change from one election to the next, and hence also offers a useful summary indicator of the potential openness of the electoral market. The index is calculated by measuring the sum of the percentage gains of all winning parties in an election (or the sum of the losses, which is the same figure), and has a theoretical range running from 0 (all parties retain the same share of the vote as in the previous election) to 100 (all existing parties lose all their votes to wholly new parties). The figures cited in this paper are drawn from Bartolini and Mair, *Identity, Competition and Electoral Availability*.

16. See Ian McAllister, *The Northern Ireland Social and Democratic and Labour Party* (London: Macmillan, 1977), p. 16

17. See Gabriel A. Almond, 'Comparative Political Systems', *Journal of Politics* 18, 3 (1956) 391–409, and Lijphart, 'Typologies', op. cit.

18. See Peter J. Katzenstein, *Small States in World Markets: Industrial Policy in Europe* (Ithaca: Cornell University Press, 1985)

19. Ibid, ch. 4.

20. See Stefano Bartolini, 'The European Left Since World War I: Size, Composition and Electoral Development', in Daalder and Mair (eds), *Western European Party Systems: Continuity and Change*, pp. 139–76, and Adam Przeworski and John Sprague, *Paper Stones: A History of Electoral Socialism* (Chicago: University of Chicago Press, 1986). Note also the emphasis by Katzenstein, *Small States*, on the importance of proportional electoral formulae and the political fragmentation of the right.

21. Bartolini and Mair, *Identity, Competition and Electoral Availability*, pp. 231–8

22. Pappalardo, 'Consociational Democracy', p. 369

23. See also Stein Rokkan, 'Towards a Generalized Concept of *Verzuiling*', *Political Studies* 25, 4 (1977) 563–70.

24. See Katzenstein, op. cit, pp. 181–9.

25. As in the Netherlands and Denmark, for example: see Galen A. Irwin and J. J. M. van Holsteyn, 'Decline of the Structured Model of Electoral Competition', in Hans Daalder and Galen A. Irwin (eds), *Politics in the Netherlands: How Much Change?* (London: Cass, 1989), pp. 21–41, and Jan Sundberg, 'Explaining the Basis of Declining Party Membership in Denmark: a Scandinavian Comparison', *Scandinavian Political Studies* 10, 1 (1987) 17–38.

26. See Bartolini and Mair, *Identity, Competition and Electoral Availability*, pp. 147–51.

8 States and Markets in Latin America

Paul Cammack

The Latin American republics have accumulated between them, over more than a century and a half of independent political life, a wealth of experience of the relationship between states and markets. They offer examples which range from the extreme liberalism of the Murillo Toro regime in Colombia in the 1850s, which abstained from the organisation of its own military capacity, called upon its supporters to defend it if so inclined when it faced revolt, and duly fell from power, to the extreme interventionism of the pre-revolutionary regime in Cuba, which abolished the market in the dominant sugar sector, and the extreme utopianism of the Cuban revolution in its Guevarist phase, which attempted to abolish money in favour of moral incentives. With direct regard to the comparative theme to which this volume is addressed, Latin America since the Second World War has given birth to a distinctive development strategy, import-substituting industrialisation, and endowed it with a body of theory through the efforts of Raul Prebisch and other economists associated with the United Nations' Economic Commission on Latin America (ECLA).[1] One of the consequences of the deep regional economic crisis in the 1980s has been the profound questioning of this model of state-led development. In Latin America at least, the turn to the market has been as much a result of internal developments as either an imposition from outside, or a response to prevailing fashions in official international development circles.

This chapter reflects upon relations between states and markets in Latin America in the forty years after the founding of ECLA in 1949, taking attempted state-led industrialisation through import-substitution as its primary focus. It is not currently held in high regard as a development strategy. But for the greater part of the period under review, the overall record of growth in the region looks poor only in comparison with a small number of East Asian economies; only for the 1980s does it look poor on any calculation, relative or absolute. In contrast, in terms of distribution the record for the period as a whole fares badly on any comparison, ranging from inadequate to truly appalling, with the exceptions of democratic Costa Rica and revolutionary Cuba.[2]

I shall argue that it is possible to make sense of this record only through a historical analysis which integrates issues of class and international political economy through a conceptualisation of the relative autonomy of the state and its implications for capitalist development in the periphery. Although I shall draw only in a very summary fashion upon the East Asian experience, my argument is that the contrast between the two rests upon the achievement of a degree of state autonomy which furthered capitalist development in the latter case, and the failure to achieve it in Latin America. This made possible effective state intervention in East Asia, leading to rapid capitalist development along with striking gains in equity, while in Latin America state intervention was limited and ineffective in crucial areas. The relevant contrast, then, is between effective state intervention in the first case and ineffective intervention in the second, rather than reliance primarily upon the market in the first case and state intervention in the second; and this is best revealed by a Marxist analysis focused on the relative autonomy of the state in relation to class politics and issues in international political economy. As I shall argue, it follows that a turn from interventionist to market-oriented policies, even where it may appear justified by current circumstances, will bring little improvement if it is not accompanied by decisive action to remedy the weaknesses which made state intervention relatively ineffective in the first place. Without such action, market-oriented policies will have perverse effects, and reproduce the unfavourable contrast with the East Asian cases in a different form.

ANTECEDENTS

Latin America's historical experience within the international economy and the international system of states is distinctive, and stems from the unique regional experience of early independence and export-led development. By the end of the 1830s the present array of independent states was virtually in place, bar some subsequent instability in international boundaries, the continuation of Cuba under Spanish control until 1898, and Panama's latent existence as an obscure Colombian province. For some decades after independence alternative growth strategies were contested across the region, often in armed confrontations, the main contenders being a conservative strategy based upon the statist traditions of colonial rule, which generated some early attempts at protected industrialisation, and a liberal alternative based upon export-led development, with free trade as a guiding idea. The liberals were victorious almost everywhere, and by the late nineteenth century new economic, social and political orders centred on export-led development were characteristic of the region.[3] In the middle and late nineteenth century, Latin America underwent a revolution every bit as far-reaching in its effects as the industrial revolution which reshaped Europe. It was not a parallel industrial revolution, however, but a complementary revolution which made the region pre-eminent as a supplier of the mineral and agricultural commodities which Europe and the United States demanded in ever increasing amounts. Occasionally, as in Mexico under Porfirio Diaz or Venezuela under Gomez, the political counterpart of this export-led miracle of development was dictatorship; for the most part, though, as in Chile's parliamentary republic (1891–1925), Peru's 'aristocratic republic' (1895–1919), Brazil's 'Old Republic' (1889–1930), and Argentina's successive liberal and Radical republics (1881–1916, 1916–30), it was elitist democracy, dominated in the final analysis by coalitions strongly committed to export-led development. There was no lack of state intervention in this period of opening to the international market. Extensive intervention was required, here as everywhere, in order to bring 'self-regulating markets' into being, most notably the dispossession of peasant communities through 'liberal land reforms' in the 1880s in Mexico and Central America. In addition there are striking early examples to be found of state intervention in international markets: labour markets, in the case of elaborate schemes to sponsor immigration from Asia (without success) and from southern Europe (with considerable success) in the late nineteenth century, and more originally in commodity markets: witness Brazil's manipulation of the international price of coffee through successive market-smoothing operations between 1906 and 1928.[4]

Before 1930, then, substantial efforts were made across virtually the whole of Latin America, involving state action on a considerable scale, to bring regional economies into the international market. Export-led growth had its golden age between 1880 and 1914, continued under increasingly difficult domestic and international circumstances until 1930, and experienced a profound and enduring crisis as a consequence of the depression following upon the Wall Street Crash of 1929. In assessing relationships between states and markets after the Second World War, attention must be directed both to the strengths and weaknesses of export-led development before 1930, and to the economic, social and political consequences of the depression itself.

The long involvement of Latin American states with international markets in the late nineteenth and early twentieth centuries produced some dramatic successes. In the space of a couple of decades of rapid development Brazil and Cuba became the world's dominant suppliers of coffee and sugar, while Argentina's long boom after 1880 brought better standards of living than in most European countries in the same period. In Uruguay, a spectacular rate of progress brought an early experiment with welfare politics under Batlle after 1904. In this period exports per capita reached levels unequalled before or since.

However, there were three serious sources of weakness. Firstly, export-led development reinforced the social and political authority of the landed elites, while they were displaced in Europe's first industrial revolutions, to one extent or another, by new urban coalitions. There was no 'bourgeois revolution' in nineteenth-century politics in Latin America. On the contrary, landowners mobilised their rural dependants as an electoral resource, while the urban middle classes were generally tied into alliances supportive of dominant export sectors, and the urban working class was left without allies or political influence. The social question, to quote a memorable phrase attributed to Brazil's President Washington Luis (1926–30) remained 'a question for the police'. Secondly, following directly from this situation, the democracies which proliferated remained highly elitist in character, based upon a franchise which ranged from 2 to 3 per cent of the adult population in Brazil to a high of around 12 per cent in Argentina. In institutional terms, this reflected a failure on the part of competing civilian elites to develop in time the modern mass parties which Lipset and Rokkan identify as crucial to the historical foundations of democracy in Western Europe.[5] Thirdly, the oligarchical regimes proved extremely open to direct foreign control of key export sectors, particularly where minerals were concerned. Even the most optimistic analysts of the current potential for mutually beneficial relations between Third World states and multinationals are agreed that in the period before the Second War foreign investors and creditors largely dictated terms across Latin America. International bankers took over the Bolivian treasury in the 1920s, while investing corporations literally drafted investment legislation in Peru and Bolivia, and saw it passed directly into law. US interests rapidly became dominant in Cuban sugar, Chilean and Peruvian copper, and Venezuelan oil. It was only after the Second World War (with the 1938 expropriation of foreign oil interests in Mexico as a significant early example) that a general movement began to redress the balance between states and foreign investors in primary producing activities in the region.[6]

In the wake of the depression the structural consequences of these fundamental weaknesses were swiftly revealed. Against first appearances, it is the enduring legacy of export-led development, and the merely partial break with it that is represented by import-substituting industrialisation, which explains the weakness of state intervention after 1930. With the significant exception of Mexico, the depression brought down political regimes based upon export-led development before the dynamic growth processes involved and the developing social contradictions internal to them had given rise to new coalitions capable of underpinning alternative models of development. After 1930, an early return to faith in free trade and export-led development was extremely unlikely, for a number of reasons: a free trade regime was no longer available internationally; interventionist alternatives in the Soviet Union, Italy, and Germany were rightly or wrongly at the height of their appeal; and most significantly, the social and political coalitions which had underpinned such regimes in Latin America had lost their ability to command support. In 1930 alone, military intervention toppled governments in Argentina, Brazil, and Peru: while Chile and Cuba, already under dictatorships as a result of the earlier collapse of their nitrate and sugar sectors, experienced short-lived socialist and national reformist revolutions in 1932 and 1933. Either immediately, as in Peru and Brazil, or after a delaying conservative dictatorship, as in Argentina, new developmental coalitions came to power, hostile to *laissez-faire* principles, resentful of what they saw as the narrow and unpatriotic interests of traditional elites, and anxious to organise alternative bases of social support to pit against the continuing conservative alliances of landowners and peasants. As a consequence of the depression, the previously dominant elites across the region, who had been broadly committed to free trade and export-led development, lost their hegemony. They lost, in other words, their ability to govern by consent. In this part of the world at least, attitudes to the market, and to reliance upon international markets and static conceptions of comparative advantage in particular, were negative, for good reason, for a generation after 1929. However, given the 'external' origins of the shock of 1929, it was met with makeshift responses and hastily improvised alternatives.

In these circumstances, the challenge mounted by the new developmental initiatives of the post-depression period against the old regimes was far from total.[7] First of all, it relied heavily on the traditional export sectors as a source of funds for the project of state-led industrialisation. In Brazil, Vargas had to make the defence of coffee his first priority after 1930, while in Argentina Peron was forced to move alternately between squeezing the export sector for foreign exchange, and relaxing his grip in the face of falling production and shrinking surpluses for export. This was in part a consequence of the fact that the form of industrialisation attempted revolved primarily around the production of consumer goods for the domestic market: capital and intermediate goods were still imported, while no attempt was made to attain competitiveness for manufactured goods on the international market. In turn, this reflected the initially unplanned emergence of import-substituting industrialisation out of the market conditions of the 1930s: a sudden sharp drop in import capacity, and an initial response by domestic producers making more intensive use of existing stocks of machinery. It was not until after the Second World War, which gave a similar stimulus to more intensive domestic production from existing stocks of machinery which could not provide a basis for international competitiveness in normal market conditions, that elements of a conscious development strategy began to come together.

The political challenge to displaced elites was also limited, even in Argentina, which was the most dramatic case. Significantly, in no case (outside Mexico, in the 1930s) was there a challenge to the property rights of landed elites. In Brazil, Vargas defeated the landowners of the coffee state of Sao Paulo in a brief civil war in 1932, but made a point of incorporating their interests into his economic programme in the wake of it. And when he began to promote unionisation, it was strictly in the urban areas – no challenge was mounted to the social and political supremacy of landowners, although rural labourers made up the overwhelming majority of the working class. In Argentina Peron fulminated against landowners and capitalists but left their holdings intact, even assuring business elites in private meetings that he alone could stand between them and the numerically dominant urban working class, and claiming on these grounds that he was their best friend.

Latin American populism, easily the most successful political tradition associated with import-substituting industrialisation, was as concerned to control the urban working class as it was to mobilise it as a developmental counter-weight to the conservatism of traditional exporting elites. Peron crushed the Labour Party, founded in 1946 to *support* his presidential candidacy (with aspirations, as its name suggests, similar to those of its British counterpart) because he did not directly control it; Vargas systematically repressed the Communist Party, and in 1945 instigated the founding from within the Ministry of Labour of the Brazilian Labour Party (PTB), which endorsed his favoured presidential candidate (a general who had played a leading role in the out-going dictatorship) on the very day of its foundation. Finally, in both regimes state intervention in infrastructural investment and heavy industry was aimed primarily at supplementing and subsidising the efforts of domestic and foreign capital; there was no attempt to direct capital investment on a large scale, or to follow a strategic programme aimed at changing the place of the economy in the international division of labour. In retrospect, it is the *limited* character and effects of state intervention in this period that strike one most, particularly if one sets it in a broader comparative perspective.

THE LIMITS OF STATE INTERVENTION IN THE POST-WAR PERIOD

At the end of the Second World War two things stood in the way of successful state-led industrial development in Latin America: the absence of fundamental structural reform, with highly unequal distribution of land being the most prominent example; and the absence of state capacity to restructure the relationship between local economies and the world market. Both reflected the absence of a sufficient degree of autonomy on the part of the state to make possible the pursuit of policies capable of strengthening capitalist development in the longer term, at the expense in the short-term of powerful internal and external capitalist interests. As a consequence of these deficiencies import substituting industrialisation relied almost entirely on the manipulation of relative prices through tariffs and exchange rate controls, and of relative incomes through taxes on foreign trade, and officially administered wage policies. In the absence of more fundamental structural change, the redistribution achieved through these mechanisms was short-lived, and subject to reversal in periodic crises marked by inflation, trade deficits, and forced devaluation. The limitations of import substituting industrialisation as a strategy reflected precisely the limits of state autonomy across the region. A Lehmann remarks, 'ISI's weakness lay not in the inefficiencies of protectionism, but in the way both its institutional and financial resources could be controlled by dominant economic groups'.[8]

These deficiencies were greatly reinforced by two things that did not happen during and after the Second World War, and on which both East Asian and European comparisons are instructive. First of all, Latin America did not experience the structural reforms which followed upon occupation by American, or successive Japanese and American forces. As a consequence, backward landed elites retained a power of veto which they lost in much of East Asia. Peter Evans notes for the cases of Taiwan and South Korea that

The geopolitical context of American aid, combined with an absence of previous ties to traditional elites, meant that the political leverage afforded by aid was used not on behalf of traditional rural elites but on behalf of a thorough land reform in both countries. The Americans could promote land reform only because internal social structural conditions resulted in a politically weak landlord class and a degree of separation between state apparatus and landlords.[9]

In Latin America, in contrast, the United States was allied with the dominant elites, and once the Cold War got under way it tended to see their opponents as subversive. As a result, their position was strengthened rather than weakened.[10] Secondly, Latin America did not experience the largesse showered on the European economies as a result of the Marshall Plan, or throughout East Asia after the Korean War in particular. It was not for want of asking. Latin American leaders pressed the United States for economic support from the late 1940s onward, and were turned away. In part this was because Latin America still figured in global economic planning as a source of primary commodities: witness the CIA-sponsored invasion of Guatemala in 1954 when a mildly reformist regime there threatened to strip the United Fruit Company of idle lands held *in reserve* on its extensive banana plantations. In part, too, it reflected the fact that the war had brought no physical destruction to Latin America, and that Europe rather than Latin America figured as the front line in the Cold War. As a result the promotion of economic development was seen as a low priority in comparison with the urgent need to fund recovery in Europe. As a result of these combined circumstances, the United States turned a deaf ear to Latin American requests for developmental aid, and chose as their allies the very same social classes whose eradication they were pursuing with enthusiasm in East Asia.[11]

The consequences were felt at two successive moments in the post-war history of the region, the first in the immediate post-war period, the second between 1961 and 1964. On each occasion movements for reform began to gather pace across the region as a whole, only to be snuffed out by internal repression backed by the military resources of the United States. Reform was pushed off the agenda, and traditional landed elites survived. In Brazil, the Communist Party was banned in 1947; in 1948 it was banned in Chile and Costa Rica; in the same year democratic governments fell to the military in Peru and Venezuela, while the assassination of the liberal Gaitán in Colombia and the ensuing *bogotazo* (a bloody uprising in the capital, Bogotá) put an end there to a strong urban movement for reform. The populism of Vargas and Peron, and the more right-wing and less successful versions attempted by General Odria in Peru (1948–56) and General Ibañez in Chile (1952–8) were not programmes of reform, but rather alternatives to it, unable to overcome the structural constraints noted above, and hostile to democratic politics. As Bethell and Roxborough note in their incisive analysis of the character and political connotations of ISI doctrines in post-war conjuncture

> State intervention in a mixed economy, planning, support for the developing national bourgeoisie, deliberate attention to social and welfare goals, together with the (regulated) entry of foreign capital came to characterise this newly emerging body of thought. The parallels with the development of social democratic welfare ideology in Western Europe, and that region's commitment to an increasingly interventionist state are worth highlighting. Unlike the situation in Western Europe, however, *cepalista* developmental prescriptions came increasingly to be associated with authoritarian statism as the links between economic development, social reform and democracy became ever more tenuous.[12]

Latin American populism and developmentalism were respectively political and economic second-best options for previously dominant elites who had lost their capacity to rule directly on their own behalf as a result of the depression and the new internal balance of power and international economy to which it and the Second World War gave rise. Rather than a dramatic break with the past, they represented a partial accommodation with it. If they did not lead to sustained economic development it was because of the limited and ineffective character of state intervention, rather than because intervention was taken too far.

When reformist currents briefly emerged in the 1960s, the feeble basis for reform was again swiftly revealed. In Peru, Chile, and Brazil, reformism emerged as a progressive alternative to populism, but in each case it failed to clear the first hurdle in the way of the development of 'self-regulating markets' at a national level – the achievement of substantial land reform. In all three countries, land reform was seen by pro-capitalist modernisers, more or less progressive from case to case, as an essential precondition for the creation of dynamic markets in land and labour, and for the expansion of the domestic market for manufactures. But in all three cases, conservative alliances were able to limit or block even fairly modest proposals for reform. And in all three cases, the weakening or defeat of proposals for land reform was the prelude to the radicalisation of politics, the collapse of democracy, and the introduction of long-term military rule. In Brazil, Goulart (1961–4) broke with the indigenous tradition of populism to which he was heir to call in 1963 and early 1964 for substantial structural reforms, with land reform at the top of the list. He was deserted as a result by conservatives in his own governing coalition, and ousted by a military coup within a fortnight of issuing a public call for reform. In Peru, Belaunde came to power in 1963 on a promise of reform, including land reform, but found his proposals blocked by an alliance between Odria's UNO party and the now conservative Apristas; here a reform-minded military removed him in 1968, and introduced their own reform in 1969. And in Chile, the original proposals for sweeping land reform came not from the Socialist-Communist coalition which brought Allende to power in 1970, but from Frei's Christian Democrats, originally a breakaway from the Chilean Conservative party, and elected in 1964, partly thanks to $20m from the CIA to cover electoral expenses, on the promise of a 'Revolution in Liberty'. Frei's reform bill, like that of Belaunde in Peru, was weakened by opposition not only from the right, but also from within the Christian Democratic party itself, and the ensuing radicalisation of political debate over rural issues was responsible for splits in the Christian Democratic party, and the election of Allende on a more radical but ultimately unsustainable programme.

Again, as in the post-war period, the internal balance of class forces and the lack of state autonomy played a large part in explaining the failure of reform, but were overlaid by the decision of the United States, in the wake of the Cuban revolution, to side with reaction. After a brief flirtation with reform in the early period of the Alliance for Progress, the United States threw in its lot with military establishments across the region. The first evidence of this came with the toppling in early 1962 of the reformist junta of October 1961 in El Salvador, soon followed by support for the overthrow of Goulart in Brazil, and the 1965 invasion of the Dominican Republic by 20,000 US Marines. To summarise, reform was blocked at two successive moments, the first after the Second World War and the second after the Cuban Revolution. In the wake of the first of these came developmental populism, with the limitations and contradictions noted above; in the wake of the second came a wave of long-lasting military regimes, for the most part frankly reactionary in their politics. There has been substantial debate over the issue of whether explanations for this general turn of events across the region should give priority to US imperialism, or to indigenous reaction. But the crucial point is that the two reinforced each other, however the mix may have varied from place to place. The Cuban Revolution prolonged the alliance between the United States and the most conservative elements of Latin American society, and further hindered long overdue social and economic reform. In the paradigmatic case, that of El Salvador, landed elites constructed a durable alliance with an internally-focussed military in the late nineteenth century. Brief episodes of reform, never surviving for more than a matter of months, were experienced in 1931, 1944, 1960–1 and 1979–80, only to be obliterated by a repressive re-imposition of the status quo through armed force and preventive mass murder.

The implications of all this for the relationship between states and markets in Latin America after the Second World War are perfectly clear. States generally lacked the degree of autonomy from dominant classes to be able to overcome their resistance to policies that would have brought more effective and equitable markets into being. In those circumstances, the second best policies they were able to pursue soon ran into the difficulties which have been noted by critics of import-substituting industrialisation as pursued in the region.[13]

Similar conclusions can be derived from an examination of relationships between Latin American states and foreign capital in the same period. In comparative terms, the most striking characteristic of Latin American industrialisation since the Second World War is the dominant role that has been played by foreign capital both in terms of direct investment by multi-national corporations (MNCs), and in terms of inflows of commercial loan capital. The contrast with East Asia is summarised as follows by Evans:

> In Latin America bureaucratic authoritarian state apparatuses emerged in societies already thoroughly penetrated by direct foreign investment. In East Asia, by contrast, bureaucratic authoritarian regimes were already in command by the time foreign investors began to take a real interest. Consequently the state was from the beginning in a much better position to determine what role transnational capital would play in the industrial division of labor.[14]

A brief review of the extensive literature on relations between states and foreign capital in Latin America confirms the accuracy of the Latin American half of this contrast. At worst, as in the case of Peru, efforts to re-orient relations between the national economy and international markets have proved entirely fruitless. Stepan's description of the attempts of the national-reformist military regime of General Velasco between 1968 and 1975 reveals a record of failure at virtually every level, while Becker's account of its efforts to bring new investment in copper, despite the anti-dependency gloss which Becker seeks to give it, entirely confirms the dependence of the Peruvian state on foreign capital and technology, and its need to reshape its own state apparatus to fit the needs and logic of international capitalism.[15] Lacking the ability to direct or extract resources from its own dominant classes, or to persuade foreign investors to enter the country, the Peruvian military regime was driven to large-scale borrowing on the international market in the easy conditions which prevailed in the immediate aftermath of the oil price rises of 1973, and thus Peru became the first Latin American country to experience the debt crisis which spread across the region after 1982. In the best cases, those of Mexico and Brazil, rapid industrial development was achieved by taking full advantage of the changing character of the international economy and the international division of labour, but without challenging either its priorities or its logic. In both cases the outcome has been extremely high levels of foreign control of key sectors, a strong bias in production towards luxury goods, a reinforcement of highly unequal patterns of distribution of wealth and income, an extreme degree of reliance on foreign loans, and generally a subservience on the part of the state to the demands of private capital, and of foreign capital in particular. In Peru, as in Chile under Allende, an attempt to challenge domestic elites and foreign capital ended in defeat. In Brazil and Mexico, in contrast, state intervention has largely been at the service of long-term capitalist development in which foreign capital has played a central role. In each case the state has been successful in that it has maximised the local benefits available within the logic of the developing international division of labour; but it has not been able to challenge that logic in the way that first Japan and latterly the East Asian economies have been able to do as a consequence of their substantially greater autonomy from both local dominant classes and foreign capital.[16] Gordon White and Robert Wade are quite right to argue that

> whereas the liberal analysis says that Latin American governments intervened too much in the market and that is why their countries performed less well than East Asia, we find that state intervention in the latter has been both stronger and more selective than in the former, not only at the national boundary but also in key parts of domestic industry.[17]

As they point out in relation to Taiwan and South Korea

> Both governments have been centrally concerned to prevent emerging groups from acquiring autonomy from the state, to prevent independent channels of interest aggregation from forming. The result is that in both countries the central state managers have had unusual autonomy (in a capitalist context) to define national goals, and unusual power to get those goals accomplished, without having to enter into the bargaining and shifting alliances such as have characterised the policy process even in the more authoritarian regimes of Latin America.[18]

There is one Latin American country for which this comparison does not entirely hold, as White and Wade note in passing, and it is the exception which proves the rule. In Mexico, the outcome of the 1910–17 revolution was the subordination of the landed elites of the period of export-led development to a highly autonomous developmental state which was able to implement a sweeping land reform in the 1930s, and which launched a sustained process of capitalist development while enjoying considerable organised support from workers and peasants incorporated into the regime by Cardenas (1934–40). A further indication of the degree of autonomy achieved was the petroleum nationalisation of 1938, and the prosecution of an independent foreign policy throughout the post-war period, in particular defiance of US demands that the region should close ranks against the Cuban revolution and communist subversion in Central America. As a result of the revolution, Mexico avoided the crisis of elite political capacity that hit the rest of the region in 1929. The successful post-revolutionary construction of a relatively autonomous capitalist state confirms the theoretical significance of the considerations advanced above in relation to the rest of Latin America.[19] Even here, though, the relative autonomy of the state was gradually eroded during the 1960s and 1970s, as the legitimating institutions of the regime entered upon a process of decay. Central executive positions came to be dominated by technocrats well versed in the demands and priorities of international finance, but less attentive to the need to renew the popular base of the regime, and preserve the representative character of the ruling Institutional Party of the Revolution (PRI). The regime embarked at the same time on a process of 'liberalisation' which was a matter of form rather than substance, concerning as it did the opening up to democratic contestation of areas which were increasingly marginalised from decision-making processes. In the end, the process of liberalisation developed a dynamic of its own which ran beyond the limited goals of the regime, and set in motion a genuine process of democratisation.[20]

CONCLUSION: THE STATE AND THE MARKET IN CONTEMPORARY LATIN AMERICA

The current global trend towards privatisation and the rolling back of the state is being felt as strongly in Latin America as it is elsewhere. In the early 1990s, substantial programmes to move state-owned enterprises into the private sector were under way in the three leading Latin American economies of Argentina, Brazil, and Mexico. At the same time, the incoming regime in newly democratic

Chile committed itself to accepting the greatly reduced state role in the economy which was one of the legacies of the Pinochet period, while independent conservative candidate Mario Vargas Llosa in Peru made privatisation the centre-piece of his liberal platform in his eventually unsuccessful bid to win the presidency away from APRA's Alan Garcia. Unusually, these issues were being debated in Central and South America in the context of a regional process of movement towards democracy, launched in 1979 with the transition from military rule in Ecuador, and subsequently bringing the departure of every military regime which was in power at that time. This combination of circumstances gives a stamp of individuality to the renegotiation of relationships between states and markets in the region. In the light of the foregoing analysis, I shall suggest that there are few grounds for expecting a commitment to market-oriented strategies of development to lead to rapid economic recovery and sustained development.

As we have seen, the adoption of market-oriented capitalist development strategies in East Asia was preceded by substantial reforms imposed either by strongly interventionist states or external forces, and by successful state intervention to create the conditions for international competitiveness. Thus when the shift to liberal policies came, it was made from a position of strength. In Latin America, in contrast, the shift is being made from a position of weakness. Fundamental reforms are still awaited in the region, and on the current evidence there is little to suggest that they are being advocated and pursued.[21] On the contrary, both land reform and fiscal reform have generally been avoided, and academic commentators have generally advocated the postponement of social and economic reform, including measures for the redistribution of income.[22] The historical analysis offered here strongly confirms Rhys Jenkins' recent argument, made on the basis of a comprehensive comparison of recent industrial policy in East Asia and Latin America, that the crucial difference between the two is not the precise strategy adopted, but rather 'the ability of the state to direct the accumulation process in the direction which is required by capitalist development at particular points in time'.[23] Three conclusions follow, each with significant consequences.

The first is that it is misleading to depict free market and 'interventionist' policies as making low and high demands respectively upon the state: a capacity for effective intervention on the part of the state is as much a requirement for the pursuit of liberal economic policies as it is for intervention aimed at resisting the pressure of market forces. The evidence suggests that Latin American states have generally lacked the capacity to pursue policies of either type effectively. Where a policy of active intervention has been abandoned as a failure, this has not led to a process of reform which has strengthened the capacity of the state to promote alternative liberal policies any more effectively. Even if a more liberal policy orientation should now be thought appropriate, then, there is little evidence to suggest that Latin American states are equipped to pursue it. The argument, common in some quarters, that the market should be given its head because of the inability of the state to conduct an interventionist policy overlooks this point. On this view, state intervention might be desirable in principle, but regrettably to be foregone in practice.[24] I would argue, against it, that Latin American states will find national development no easier to achieve through market-oriented strategies than through intervention. Relative autonomy from domestic and international capitalist forces is a necessary though not sufficient condition for both, and it is generally lacking across the region. Those who urge caution on new rulers in Latin America, suggesting the postponement into the distant future of social and economic reform, and call upon the impoverished majority of re-enfranchised citizens to be content with feeding on the rule of law, only confirm this diagnosis. They implicitly accept that democratic rulers in the region do not have the authority over privileged minorities to embark on needed reforms without fear of overthrow.

The second conclusion is that even if capitalist development is seen as the goal, it is wrong to advocate either liberalism or intervention as a universally appropriate means to this end, in abstraction from specific historical and structural circumstances, and specific conjunctures. State intervention in Latin America after the depression and after the Second World War was not wrong-headed, but ineffective. It may be less realistic than ever to suppose that it is a viable option, but at the same time successful economic development may still be impossible without it.

The third and final conclusion relates to the current process of democratisation. Harsh authoritarian rule has been a central feature of successful economic development in East Asia, although the propagandists for the market in the region have not generally dwelt on this fact. In contrast, democracy, like economic liberalism, has come to Latin America not as a triumphant conquest, but as a result of the temporary exhaustion of the alternative, in this case as a consequence of the comprehensive failure of authoritarian rule. One does not need to subscribe to the view that economic development in the Third World is possible only under authoritarian rule, to accept that in contemporary Latin America, weakly institutionalised regimes face strong and contradictory pressures.[25] The crucial point here is not so much that the majority of these democracies are recently established, but that they appear to be established on an extremely precarious basis. It is true, and remarkable, that not one democratic regime has been overthrown in Latin America since the first of the new democracies was established in Ecuador in 1979. However, it is equally the case that there is as yet not a single case among them of a democratically elected government securing re-election. In every single election held in the new democracies in the 1980s, the opposition came to power. While this provides strong evidence of a genuine competitiveness that has been lacking in the past, it speaks equally badly of popular appraisals of policy performance. In addition, the weakness of parties has been a conspicuous feature of the period. Not only have particular parties all but disintegrated as a consequence of transition from opposition to government (most notably APRA and Accion Popular in Peru, and the PMDB in Brazil), but there has been a general regional trend towards personalism, again reflected most notoriously in the cases of Collor in Brazil, and Vargas Llosa and Fujimori in Peru, along with Menem in Argentina. Whatever the merits of general contrasts between authoritarian and democratic regimes, the new democracies in Latin America appear both electorally and institutionally fragile. It is difficult to avoid the conclusion that it would be unwise to expect the early development of a capacity to address the fundamental changes required if a sound basis is to be provided for the pursuit of *either* interventionist *or* market-oriented programmes of economic recovery and development.

NOTES

1. For an accessible account, see Joseph Love, 'Raul Prebisch and the Origins of the Doctrine of Unequal Exchange', *Latin American Research Review*, 15, 3 (1980) 45–72.
2. For a brief account of some of the consequences, see William Dixon, 'Progress in the Provision of Basic Human Needs: Latin America, 1960–1980', *Journal of Developing Areas*, 21, 2 (1987) 129–40.
3. For a valuable discussion see Frank Safford, 'Politics, Ideology and

Society in Post-independence Spanish America', *Cambridge History of Latin America*, vol. III (Cambridge: Cambridge University Press, 1985), ch. 9.

4. See Stephen Krasner, 'Manipulating International Commodity Markets: Brazilian Coffee Policy 1906 to 1962', *Public Policy*, 21, 4 (1973) 493–523. More generally, see Steven Topik, *The Political Economy of the Brazilian State, 1889–1930* (Austin: University of Texas Press, 1986).

5. Seymour Martin Lipset and Stein Rokkan, 'Cleavage Structures, Party Systems, and Voter Alignments: An Introduction', in S. Lipset and S. Rokkan (eds), *Party Systems and Voter Alignments: Cross-National Perspectives* (Glencoe, NY: Free Press, 1967).

6. The classic study here is Theodore Moran, *Multinational Corporations and the Politics of Dependence: Copper in Chile* (Princeton, NJ: Princeton University Press, 1974).

7. The best comparative discussion on the issues discussed briefly in the following paragraphs is John Sheahan, *Patterns of Development in Latin America* (Princeton, NJ: Princeton University Press, 1987).

8. See David Lehmann, *Democracy and Development in Latin America* (London: Polity Press, 1990), pp. 36–7.

9. Peter Evans, 'Class, State, and Dependence in East Asia: lessons for Latin Americanists', in F. Deyo (ed.) *The Political Economy of the New Asian Industrialism* (Ithaca, NY: Cornell University Press, 1987), p. 210.

10. As should be clear, the contrast proposed is structural, rather than merely geographic. The logic of the argument is reinforced by the case of the Philippines, where traditional elites were similarly kept in power. As a consequence, a 'Latin American' pattern of development ensued, leading in the end to the creation of a 'hyper-autonomous' state under Marcos. For an illuminating study, see Gary Hawes, *The Philippine State and the Marcos Regime: The Politics of Export* (Ithaca, NY: Cornell University Press, 1987).

11. For an account of the resentment this attitude caused in Brazil, see Stanley Hilton, 'The Armed Forces and Industrialists in Modern Brazil: The Drive for Military Autonomy (1889–1954)', *Hispanic American Historical Review*, 62, 4 (1982) 629–73.

12. Leslie Bethell and Ian Roxborough, 'Latin America between the Second World War and the Cold War: Some Reflections on the 1945–8 Conjuncture', *Journal of Latin American Studies*, 20, 1 (1988) (167–89), 176–7.

13. For a similar argument, applied to the case of Turkey in the 1970s, see Henri Barkey, 'State Autonomy and the Crisis of Import Substitution', *Comparative Political Studies*, 22, 3 (1989) 291–314.

14. Evans, 'Class, State, and Dependence in East Asia', p. 215.

15. See Alfred Stepan, *State and Society: Peru in Comparative Perspective* (Princeton, NJ: Princeton University Press, 1978); and David Becker, *The New Bourgeoisie and the Limits of Dependency: Mining, Class and Power in "Revolutionary" Peru* (Princeton, NJ: Princeton University Press, 1983).

16. For a persuasive case study, see Douglas Bennett and Kenneth Sharpe, 'Agenda Setting and Bargaining Power: The Mexican State versus Transnational Automobile Corporations', in R. Kronish and K. Mericle (eds)

The Political Economy of the Latin American Motor Vehicle Industry, (Cambridge, Mass.: MIT Press, 1984).

17. Gordon White and Robert Wade, 'Developmental States and Markets in East Asia: An Introduction', in G. White (ed.) *Developmental States in East Asia*, (London: Macmillan, 1988) p. 9.

18. *Ibid.*, p. 10.

19. See Nora Hamilton, *The Limits of State Autonomy: Post-Revolutionary Mexico* (Princeton, NJ: Princeton University Press, 1982). For a brief comparison of Mexico and El Salvador which follows the logic suggested here, see Enrique Baloyra, *El Salvador in Transition* (Chapel Hill, NC: University of North Carolina Press, 1982), pp. 18–22.

20. Paul Cammack, 'The Brazilianization of Mexico?', *Government and Opposition*, 23, 3 (1988) 304–20.

21. The clear exception to this general situation is Nicaragua, where the Sandinista regime did pursue fundamental reform between 1979 and 1990, in defiance of extreme military and economic hostility from the United States. It follows that the prospects for the long-term consolidation of democracy (and the eventual re-election of the Sandinistas) are much brighter than elsewhere. Unfortunately, the ability of reactionary forces in Nicaragua and outside to resist democracy *with* social and economic reform remains high.

22. See G. O'Donnell and P. Schmitter, 'Tentative Conclusions About Uncertain Democracies', in G. O'Donnell, P. Schmitter and L. Whitehead, eds, *Transitions from Authoritarian Rule* (Baltimore: Johns Hopkins University Press, 1986), vol. IV, and J. Malloy, 'The Politics of Transition in Latin America', in J. Malloy and M. Seligson (eds) *Authoritarians and Democrats: Regime Transition in Latin America* (Pittsburgh: University of Pittsburgh Press, 1987). For my critique, see P. Cammack, 'The Politics of Democratization', in B. Galjart and P. Silva (eds) *Democratization and the State in the Southern Cone: Essays on South American Politics* (Amsterdam: CEDLA, 1989).

23. Rhys Jenkins, 'The Political Economy of Industrialization: A Comparison of Latin American and East Asian Newly Industrialising Countries', revised version of paper originally presented to 46th International Congress of Americanists (Amsterdam, 1988), mimeo, 1990, p. 51.

24. This view has recently been forcefully advocated by Joel Migdal, *Strong Societies and Weak States: State-Society Relations and State Capabilities in the Third World* (Princeton, NJ: Princeton University Press, 1988).

25. A recent review of this perennial topic is Karen Remmer, 'Democracy and Economic Crisis: The Latin American Experience', *World Politics*, 42, 3 (April 1990) 315–35. Her optimistic conclusion is weakened by two issues which she does not address, the first that the comparison she makes is between out-going authoritarian regimes and established or in-coming democratic regimes, the second that whatever can be said of the comparisons between these regime types, the overall performance regardless of regime type has been poor.

9 States and Markets in Africa

Ralph A. Young

PRIVATISATION AND MARKETS

The debate over the role and significance of privatisation in Africa has assumed increasing importance in Africa over the last decade. As its dimensions have come into sharper focus, privatisation has helped occasion a wider-ranging debate over the role of the African state in the management of economic change and development – a debate, that is, about the nature of the relationship between states and private sectors in Africa, and of the proper boundaries between them.

Privatisation is not a straightforward concept. Narrowly defined, privatisation can be viewed as involving the transfer of productive activities or services currently being undertaken by the public sector to the private sector – as a strategy intended to 'recalibrate the scales of control and ownership' between the two.[1] Such transfers in turn can be effected in a number of ways, including the direct sale of assets or the sale of part or all of the equity, leasing, management contracts, or the contracting out of functions; various additional techniques exist.[2] But privatisation can also be seen in much broader terms. It can be defined as a process by which efforts are made to circumscribe the role of the state within the economy while at the same time enlarging the scope for market forces. The measures appropriate for achieving this might include policies redefining the scope of the state's role (for example, by relaxing state monopolies), requiring public enterprises to perform according to private sector criteria of efficiency and profitability, or in other ways reducing the impact of governmental regulations upon the workings of the market economy.

To appreciate the significance of privatisation as a mechanism of economic and political change in the current era, it is this broader definition that should provide the point of departure. One survey of the British experience of privatisation identified seven separate strands in the privatisation strategy pursued by the first two Thatcher governments after 1979.[3] Taken individually, examples of nearly all could be found in the policies of successive British governments since the early 1950s. What emerges from this account is the presence of five ingredients which together have given privatisation in the 1980s its distinctive character as a strategy of state reform: (a) the wide range of public activities now considered suitable for this option; (b) the array of methods available for the achievement of such aims; (c) the harnessing of the separate strands of the privatisation programme into a package of mutually supporting components; (d) the existence of a coherent conception of goals and methods underpinned by partisan and ideological attachments supplying a critical element of political will; and, (e) the emergence of significant political constituencies which have provided a reservoir of active support for reform programmes of so radical a nature.

In the case of less developed countries (LDCs), the available literature has tended to address the issue of privatisation primarily in terms of the narrower formulation; that is, debate has tended to focus on the possibilities and problems encountered in efforts at the divestiture of state-owned enterprises in Third World settings. Moreover, despite the widespread interest shown by LDC governments in privatisation, many analysts have suggested that in practice its impact is likely to be limited for the following reasons:[4]

– Divestiture is technically a difficult process, and may prove beyond the administrative capacity of many Third World states.

– The economic setting in many LDCs – not least the lack or under developed nature of capital markets – may well impose major constraints on efforts to transfer public sector activities to the private sector.

– The economic objectives of Third World public enterprises are often intertwined with non-economic (or equity) objectives, making private sector alternatives unattractive to policy makers.

– The economic and budgetary benefits of privatisation may not be straightforward, denying the privatisation case of one of its most compelling arguments.

– Opposition from vested interests may well raise the likely costs of divestiture beyond levels that prudent governments would wish to pay.

A 1987 World Bank study by Elliot Berg and Mary Shirley was able to identify some twenty-six LDCs which had by mid-1985 placed privatisation on their public agendas.[5] Only seventeen had undertaken actual transfers of equity in public enterprises by that stage and, apart from Chile and Bangladesh, the number of enterprises undergoing privatisation had been modest – eighty-five in all (thirty of them African).[6] The relatively limited significance of this activity was merely underlined when the value of assets transferred or the employees involved were considered.

While this stress on the narrower conception of privatisation is understandable – and indeed will be reflected in the following examination of the Sub-Saharan African case – it is also evident that the broader conception may be important for delineating the context in which public enterprise divestiture has been occurring. Certainly this has been so for Africa, where economic adversity and escalating debt problems since the later 1970s have exposed many governments to pressures from both multilateral financial institutions and Western bilateral aid agencies to initiate a substantial redefinition of the state's role within the economy. It has been against such a backdrop (though not only for such reasons) that divestiture within Sub-Saharan Africa has become widespread over the decade, and especially during the second half. Whereas Berg and Shirley identified fourteen African states which had placed privatisation on their public agendas by 1985, the number had climbed to forty, or 85 per cent of the total, by 1990.[7] On the other hand, it should be noted that whatever the increase in its geographical spread, the setting for privatisation in many African states remains far from propitious. Its implementation has often been cautious and selective, while its longer-term prospects as a mechanism for state reform are difficult to gauge. Of the five ingredients cited earlier as giving coherence to the British experience of privatisation in the 1980s, all can be identified as features of the privatisation process in Sub-Saharan Africa; only the first two, however, have any significance.

PRIVATISATION AND AFRICA

Africa's experience of privatisation can be traced back three decades – though these early instances, lacking any shared context, differed greatly in their origin, scope and consequences. Thus as Zaire gained its independence in 1960 the Belgian authorities hastily dissolved two public companies to prevent their investments in various private sector undertakings – including a majority stake in the mining conglomerate Union Minière du Haut-Katanga – from falling into the hands of the incoming black regime.[8] Following the army coup which overthrew the radical Nkrumah regime in Ghana in 1966, the new military rulers sought to privatise a considerable number of the enterprises created under Nkrumah in the 1960s to assist the state-guided drive to industrialisation.[9] The sweeping measures introduced in Zaire in 1973 and 1974 to terminate the dominance of foreign capital in major sectors of the economy – resulting in the state acquiring some 120 industrial concerns and the transfer of many hundreds of other enterprises to members of the Zairian political class or politically connected entrepreneurs – had to be substantially reversed in 1976 and 1977.[10] The socialist regime in Tanzania reprivatised the butchery trade in the capital Dar es Salaam in 1977 because of its unsatisfactory performance under state control.[11] Since the early 1970s a significant process of privatising urban services (such as water supply and transport) has been documented in at least nine states – sometimes under formal contract but sometimes not – as urban populations have expanded beyond the resources of public agencies.[12]

Yet such legacies have had only limited bearing on the current privatisation debate in Africa. Rather there has been what Cook and Kirkpatrick term a convergence of factors which have come into common focus since the later 1970s and early 1980s.[13] One of these was external to Africa. The problems of economic adjustment and adaptation which many Western economies had experienced following the first oil shock in the early 1970s gave additional impetus to an ongoing debate about the proper balance to be sought in advanced industrial economies between market forces and the economically interventionist state. The debate was to provide important ammunition to the conservative regimes which acquired office at the decade's close in two Western powers of key significance to Africa – Britain and the United States. The former after 1979 was a pacesetter in advancing privatisation. In the American case, though divesting public enterprises or services was less pivotal, the Reagan administration made support for private enterprise an important part of its package of policies directed at the Third World. By the middle 1980s, if there was any one organisation acting as an evangelist for privatisation in Africa, it was the United States Agency for International Development.[14]

The debate over the role of the state in the advanced economies was to be paralleled by a separate, though related, debate concerning the interventionist role of the Third World state – and especially the states in Sub-Saharan Africa. In the 1960s and 1970s, the first generation of independence for most African countries, a considerable expansion occurred in the size and scale of many African states – reflecting widespread assumptions regarding the centrality of the state's role in engineering economic development in the face of weakly developed indigenous private sectors and an often substantial foreign economic presence. Significant domestic constituencies gave their support, were acquiescent, or lacked the leverage to resist. By the later 1950s and early 1960s, Western aid agencies had accommodated themselves to (and indeed come to underwrite) this expanded role, including its encouragement of economic planning and the use of public enterprises for a variety of purposes: (a) to establish essential infrastructure; (b) to create strategic industries whose capital or technological requirements might exceed existing private sector capabilities; (c) to otherwise undertake economic roles for which the private sector lacked either resources or profit incentives; (d) to generate investible surpluses to counterbalance the absence or underdeveloped nature of local capital markets; (e) to boost employment or enhance access to goods and services among regions or social classes; and (f) to provide an instrument by which the state could gain control over the economy's 'commanding heights' – particularly heights previously occupied by foreign firms or resident alien entrepreneurs unlikely to share the government's priorities for national development.[15]

Though significant public sectors had frequently been handed down as one of the legacies of the colonial era, after independence public enterprises in African states commonly underwent rapid expansion in numbers and size.[16] They spread into a wide range of productive and commercial activities. They accounted for shares of gross domestic product often substantially above the average for other regions. Their role in formal sector employment was prominent and sometimes predominant. Their impact on domestic credit markets risked creating serious 'crowding out' problems. Though total numbers remain uncertain, one recent survey identified 2,959 public enterprises among just thirty African states.[17]

By the end of the 1970s experience was serving to undermine earlier expectations regarding the state's beneficial role in development. The rapid expansion of the public enterprise sector had in particular produced a lengthy catalogue of problems.[18] Significant numbers of African public enterprises had become habitual loss-makers, and could only survive through government subsidies. Inadequate preparatory studies frequently saddled them with excess capacity. There was insufficient managerial and technical manpower, while serious overstaffing occurred at lower grades. Sheer numbers of public enterprises made parastatal activities hard to co-ordinate. Their financial operations proved difficult to monitor, in turn facilitating corruption. The monopoly position they often occupied encouraged inefficiency. The conflicting goals assigned to them posed obstacles to profitable performance. Governments frequently regulated prices for their goods and services on other than economic grounds. Though nominally autonomous, public enterprises were sometimes heavily encumbered by 'bureaucratic' controls, and were also prone to political interference over the siting of facilities, staff management, the award of contracts, and even routine operational decisions.[19] The fact that public enterprises were often undercapitalised and had difficulties in financing operations from their own resources fostered a propensity to borrow, adding to domestic inflationary pressures, external debt and balance of payments problems.[20]

If recognition of the failings of public enterprise sectors was widespread within Africa itself,[21] the issue of public sector reform was actually put onto public agendas by an array of economic difficulties causing growth rates to falter after 1974. By 1980 real income per capita was in general decline. The oil shocks of 1973–4 and 1979–80 dramatically increased energy costs while also depressing Western demand for Africa's raw materials. The debt burdens accumulated during the 1970s assumed critical proportions when interest rates rose in the early 1980s; as a percentage of GDP, Africa's debt soon exceeded that of other regions.[22] Escalating debt in turn underlined the shortcomings of the industrialisation strategies being followed by many African states: the import-substitution formula on which these were based often entailed heavy import dependence (for equipment and raw materials); overprotection of infant industries had failed to stimulate improved efficiency. Declining agricultural exports and rising food imports, though partly attributable to recurring droughts, were also traceable to official policies that maintained overvalued exchange rates, or squeezed surplus capital from agriculture to support other sectors (especially industry).

Given the centrality of the African state's role, a crisis originally of largely economic dimensions necessarily became a crisis of the state itself. This circumstance in turn received recognition by several regimes: for example, in the Ivory Coast after 1977, Senegal after

1978, Kenya and Togo from 1979, Nigeria by 1983 and South Africa by 1985.[23] In each case reform options were developed internally for the public sector, including the possibility of divestiture.[24]

A more far-reaching reassessment of the role of the state as development manager, however, was taking place externally, and notably within the World Bank.[25] The Bank had long been a key supplier of development capital and technical expertise to African states and hence a major underwriter of public sector expansion. That its views were shifting from established developmental paradigms was underscored by the publication in 1981 of the Berg Report and also by the 1983 edition of the Bank's annual *World Development Report*, which incorporated a special review of the role of public management in development.[26] These documents argued that development performance (particularly in Africa) had been distorted by inappropriate policies, that the role of many LDC states had in any case become over-extended in relation to their administrative and financial capabilities, and that ways of scaling back this role to manageable terms had to be identified in the interests of macroeconomic efficiency – not least to create space for the greater play of market forces to underpin and sustain this efficiency.

As one observer has noted, such views were actually 'eminently in conformity with the original principles and rules programmed' into the Bank at its inception in 1945, and had found periodic expression in Bank reports despite its extensive involvement in state-led development efforts after the later 1950s. Yet a range of new factors now helped shape the Bank's posture, including pressures exerted by the more ideologically conservative Western governments (especially the United States), the escalating seriousness of the debt crisis, and the cumulative effects of its own experience with Third World states in the development field.[27]

By the later 1970s both the World Bank and the International Monetary Fund were devising innovative mechanisms for channelling finance to LDC debtor countries, and for the Bank these were to entail an important shift from the project loans which had traditionally been its principal operational device. By 1979 new 'structural' and 'sectoral' adjustment facilities were in place. These were designed to assist recipient economies over the medium term to undergo restructuring to stimulate those economic sectors with (especially export) growth potential while reducing sources of macro-economic inefficiency elsewhere.[28] Along with the IMF, which formally concentrated on short-term stabilisation assistance for countries with balance of payments problems but which in 1986 also introduced a 'structural adjustment facility', the World Bank deployed the mechanism of conditionalities – that is, of making loan capital available only if recipient governments committed themselves to carrying through agreed economic policy reforms. The two multilateral financial institutions proved markedly successful in persuading other Western aid agencies to make additional funding contingent on compliance with the reform programmes they were pursuing.

Against a background of widespread economic recession in Africa, the role of external agencies in promoting privatisation has been considerable. This has been especially true of the World Bank, but also of the IMF, USAID and more recently the United Kingdom's Overseas Development Administration.[29] World Bank reports and staff papers, despite the disillusionment they register concerning the role of LDC public enterprises, stress that pragmatic considerations have guided Bank recommendations to particular countries; that divestitures typically occur as part of broader parastatal reform programmes; and that privatisation should be seen as neither a panacea nor an easy alternative.[30] The separate analyses undertaken by Mosley and Babai of structural adjustment loans made to LDCs between 1980 and 1986 both conclude that while public enterprise reform was a frequent condition of Bank lending, divestiture itself remained relatively uncommon.[31] Yet even then African states were being more frequently targeted for divestiture than were those elsewhere.[32] This targeting has since become more marked, especially if consideration is taken not just of loan conditionality measures but of the promotional effects of funds and technical assistance made available to encourage adoption of privatisation programmes. By the later 1980s a majority of the roughly thirty LDC governments which had received Bank assistance over privatisation programmes were African; of eighteen francophone African recipients of Bank structural adjustment assistance, more than two-thirds had public enterprise reform programmes in place or under preparation, all containing a privatisation component.[33] Such initiatives, whether supported by incentives or conditionalities, inevitably tread a fine line regarding the capacity of recipient governments to retain scope for autonomous political choice.[34]

THE PATTERN OF PRIVATISATION

Certainly whatever the stimulus, by the later 1980s Africa was proving a seemingly fertile field for divestiture activities. Of the 1,343 privatisations planned, underway or completed worldwide of which the World Bank by 1988 had record, African states accounted for around 35 per cent.[35] African states also accounted for the highest share of completed divestitures (29.4 per cent, with Western Europe coming second at 26.4 per cent), and of planned divestitures (46.5 per cent, with Asia next at 20.2 per cent). They came second – to Latin America and the Caribbean – only among divestitures underway (22.8 per cent, as against 50.2 per cent). On the other hand, within Africa divestiture activity has been unevenly spread. As of early 1988 four states – Guinea, the Ivory Coast, Niger and Uganda – accounted for 56 per cent of the divestitures either completed or underway; three-quarters of the divestitures still at the planning stage were in Ghana, Nigeria, Senegal and Togo.[36] Overall West Africa has had a greater range of privatisation programmes than other parts of the subcontinent. Again, despite Britain's own lead in this field, anglophone African states proved noticeably slower than francophone states to show serious interest in privatisation. Given the circumstances under which it has emerged, the impact of the divestiture issue has transcended ideological boundaries between the capitalist and socialist states; yet differences remain discernible in the degree of willingness evident among the latter to grasp the privatisation nettle.

The privatisation programmes that have taken shape have thus differed greatly in focus and scale. Some have been limited in scope or centred on particular public enterprises (as in Malawi, Rwanda, Somalia and Swaziland). For twelve states, divestiture commitments appear potentially considerable, if fully pursued and especially if linked to macro-economic policy shifts towards greater liberalisation.[37] In two further cases they are likely to entail a fundamental reshaping of the economic role of their public sectors. Thus in Nigeria, the military regime of General Ibrahim Babangida, having ordered the liquidation of all agricultural commodity marketing boards in April 1986, launched an ambitious scheme to restructure Nigeria's public enterprise sector in January 1988 that entailed the divesting of ninety-eight federal and state enterprises and the full or partial commercialisation of more than three dozen others.[38] In the South African case, the significance of the privatisation programme that took shape after

1985 derived particularly from the size and strategic importance of the enterprises involved. With the oil-from-coal producer SASOL privatised earlier in the decade, the corporations now targeted for privatisation included those responsible for iron and steel production, electricity supply, post and telecommunications, and South Africa's transport infrastructure.[39]

Divestiture programmes often require comprehensive (and lengthy) reviews of existing public sectors to establish regime priorities, though Togo and the Ivory Coast have initiated numerous privatisations without formal master plans.[40] Establishing an effective administrative machinery to manage such programmes has proved difficult. Rather than being delegated to sector ministries, privatisation activities have frequently been made the responsibility of separate administrative units – sometimes with ministerial status but often headed by senior civil servants (and occasionally by figures recruited from the private sector).[41] In some settings, however, presidential patronage interests have clearly outweighed more technocratic concerns.[42]

The actual patterns of privatisation have been varied. In Table 9–1, privatisations by economic sector as of early 1988 are shown for a sample of twenty-six African states – both for divestitures actually completed or underway and for those being planned.[43] The dominance of manufacturing enterprises under both headings is not unexpected, though the secondary significance of commercial and service enterprises perhaps is. The impact that privatisation programmes have been making on the institutional fabric linking the African state with the rural sector – in direct production, marketing or agroindustrial roles – is worth underlining. It has proved impossible to assemble accompanying data on the value of assets disposed of through privatisation. Certainly the more than $1.1bn earned by the South African government through the public flotation of the iron and steel corporation ISCOR in November 1989 has had no close competitors,[44] and there is some evidence to suggest generally modest cash returns to African states from individual divestitures occurring thus far.[45]

An indication of the range of techniques utilised in completed divestitures among the same group of states is provided in Table 9.2, though the source used does not provide full coverage for liquidations, the relaxation of state monopolies and the contracting-out of services.[46] With the commencement of the Nigerian divestiture programme in January 1989, the figure for public flotations has been rendered obsolete, though it nonetheless underlines the manner in

TABLE 9.1: *Divestiture in Africa by Sector (1988)*

A: Divestitures underway or completed

	%	No.
General Manufacturing	32.2	(75)
Rural Development	26.2	(61)
Food/Refreshments	9.0	(21)
Tourism	8.6	(20)
Commerce/Services	7.7	(18)
Transport/Communications	5.1	(12)
Oil/Gas Refining/Distribution	4.3	(10)
Banking/Financial Services	3.9	(9)
Mining	1.7	(4)
Utilities	1.3	(3)
	100.0	(233)

B: Divestitures planned

	%	No.
General Manufacturing	27.6	(64)
Rural Development	24.1	(56)
Banking/Financial Services	12.9	(30)
Commerce/Services	12.5	(29)
Food/Refreshments	8.2	(19)
Tourism	6.9	(16)
Transport/Communications	3.4	(8)
Utilities	2.2	(5)
Oil/Gas Refining/Distribution	1.7	(4)
Mining	.4	(1)
	99.9	(232)

SOURCE: Calculated from R. Candoy-Sekse with A. R. Palmer, *Techniques of Privatization of State-Owned Enterprises: Inventory of Country Experience and Reference Materials*, vol. III (Washington, D.C.: IBRD, 1988).

which the menu of available divestiture options has been shaped not just by the varying difficulty of the techniques themselves but by the underdeveloped nature of African capital markets. Established stock exchanges exist in Abidjan (Ivory Coast), Lagos (Nigeria), Nairobi (Kenya), Harare (Zimbabwe) and Johannesburg (South Africa); a bourse was recently opened in St Louis (Mauritius), and one is promised in Zambia. The Lagos exchange has played a vital part in the initial phase of Nigeria's privatisation programme, while the Johannesburg exchange is expected to be the primary vehicle for

TABLE 9.2: *Techniques of privatisation in Africa (1988)*

Private Sales	93
Management Contracts	47
Sale of Assets	29
Liquidations	20
Leases	15
Management/Employee Buyouts	7
Public Offerings	3
Insufficient Data	4
	218

SOURCE: Calculated from R. Candoy-Sekse, with A. R. Palmer, *Techniques of Privatization of State-Owned Enterprises; Inventory of Country Experience and Reference Materials*, vol. III (Washington, D.C.: IBRD, 1988).

divesting South Africa's public corporations. Yet the other exchanges have had marginal roles in this sphere – in Kenya and Zimbabwe because of the resistance the governments have shown to privatisation, and in the Ivory Coast because of the close personal control President Félix Houphouet-Boigny has exercised over the divestiture programme.

The array of techniques used in privatisation in Africa has also been influenced, though less visibly, by the limited capital resources and relative lack of production (as opposed to commercial) experience of indigenous entrepreneurial strata, and by the shortcomings of local banking sectors. Gaps in available data make difficult any precise calculation of the role of foreign capital in African privatisations, but it has clearly been substantial.[47]

While the privatisation phenomenon has already had significant impact in Sub-Saharan Africa, its impact has nonetheless remained uneven, the obstacles formidable, the levels of domestic support limited, and the future prospects uncertain. Divestiture programmes have typically been introduced into public enterprise sectors in a financially unhealthy condition, with individual enterprises losing money, heavily indebted, operating with inadequate records or accounts, or substantially overmanned (and frequently exhibiting all these problems). Where enterprises are profitable, governments are understandably reluctant to privatise. The timetables to which governments find themselves committed may be unrealistic. Moreover in the African case existing legal frameworks or investment codes may prove unfavourable. Divestiture is a technically demanding exercise even in advanced economies. With the necessary skilled personnel unavailable locally, divestiture programmes in Africa have been commonly dependent on technical assistance or financial aid provided by external agencies, notably the World Bank and USAID, which in turn have sometimes utilised staff provided by Western merchant banks or consultancy firms.[48]

In contrast to the experience of developed countries, where the wave of privatisation activities in the 1980s occurred under relatively propitious economic circumstances, privatisation has entered African political agendas under widely-generalised recessionary conditions that have inevitably had a dampening effect on domestic and external investment confidence. In addition, the structural constraints present in many African economies such as the limited size of domestic markets, the disadvantages of geographical location (for landlocked states) or unevenly developed internal communications networks, and the thinness of local private capital might tend to inhibit an expanded private sector role displacing that of the state. They also point to potential difficulties in encouraging the element of market competition essential for 'capturing' macro-economic efficiency gains where privatisation occurs. Indeed where governments are forced to offer tax, monopoly status or asset valuation concessions to attract private sector interest, the likelihood not just of longer term macro-economic benefits to the economy but of short-term financial gains to the treasury may be considerably diminished.[49]

While the constraints on privatisation arising from either the economic setting or a state's administrative capacity may be formidable, it is political concerns which frequently have overriding significance. Whatever its economic rationale, privatisation in practice entails the redistribution of resources within society and hence is inherently political in the manner in which it impinges upon the existing structure of social and political interests. In the African context, the likelihood that in the short term there will be fewer winners than losers as a consequence of privatisation greatly expands the potential for conflict over the issue, and enhances its sensitivity for African regimes.[50] As a privatisation consultant working in Malawi was able to observe: 'It has been nowhere near as easy as we thought . . . We've realised privatisation is more of a political exercise than a financial one. It's basically about re-allocating power – and that's tricky.'[51] Even within governments showing strong pro-market inclinations, there is likely to be opposition to privatisation from vested interests with a stake in a large state sector – ministries unwilling to surrender their parastatal empires, enterprise managers with emoluments and prerogatives to protect, or business interests dependent on public sector contracts.[52] But public enterprises may also offer strategic bases for the extraction of 'bureaucratic rents', and often function within networks of political patronage that may be linked to the very centres of state power – points underlined by a senior Madagascar official who told a visiting journalist:

> We must not delude ourselves. Socialism, especially when it fails, is a godsend. And the return to a market economy will not go unopposed, without depriving a number of those elected, civil servants and business people [of their] brazen privileges.[53]

Hardly less potent are the redistributive issues which arise with regard to society at large. Though the political leverage of African trade union movements is generally not high, regimes have frequently been required to remain attentive to union objections over job losses associated with privatisation, given the volatility of urban constituencies at a time of increasing unemployment and rising pressures on lower-class living standards.[54] Other criticisms which unions have articulated – that privatisation might concentrate domestic economic power or transfer important sectors to foreign control – have also found echo in middle class opinion networks. Measures that might open host economies to foreign 'recolonisation' may be as sensitive an issue for indigenous entrepreneurs as for university-trained professionals and the radical intelligentsia. In Nigeria the decision by General Babangida's government to place privatisation on its priority agenda in 1986 provoked such concerns while also rekindling deep-seated regional and class divisions over the likely distribution of benefits between the Lagos-based entrepreneurial elite and other parts of the country (especially the less developed northern states).[55] The Kenyan government, having launched preparations for a divestiture programme in 1983, had let momentum ebb by 1985, as it became clear that privatisation was likely to concentrate gains on the economically powerful but politically sensitive Kikuyu and Asian communities.[56] In South Africa the ISCOR flotation aroused black opinion over the privatisation issue. It was seen as an attempt by the white political establishment to protect bastions of white job privilege from the reach of a future black-dominated government. Nelson Mandela and other senior African National Congress leaders have strongly opposed privatisation on these grounds.[57]

PROBLEMS AND PROSPECTS

As a mechanism for state reform, privatisation was much commoner in Africa by the end of the 1980s than had seemed reasonable to anticipate even half a decade ago. The novelty of Africa's privatisation experience however, makes its significance difficult to assess. Moreover, though some patterns are discernible between regions, between francophone and anglophone states, and between clusters of regimes adhering either to capitalist or socialist development models, the impact of privatisation activity has been variable across all these categories, complicating the identification of explanatory factors. What is clear is that in the African case the privatisation phenomenon did not have its origins in any basic shifts over the past decade in the nature of African regimes or the social forces on which they are based. It derived its initial impetus from the increasingly adverse economic circumstances which beset most African states after the later 1970s, from a significant policy reorientation regarding the economic role of the state occurring in the case of influential Western powers, and from shifts in the priorities guiding major Western aid and multilateral financial institutions. In addition, Africa's socialist states have narrowing space for manoeuvre through the reduction of Cold War tensions and the declining involvement by Russia and other Eastern bloc states in continental affairs after the middle 1980s. Yet it is also evident that such 'external' pressures have been only one strand in a complex setting within which African states themselves have remained central actors, with the shortcomings of their public enterprise sectors widely recognised. The domestic political dynamics and economic circumstances of individual countries ensured that factors like 'political will' and 'political capacity' were key variables in the divestiture calculus.

Privatisation has acquired significance in Africa within the context of a more broadly-focused movement towards public sector restructuring, economic liberalisation and other policy reforms that point to a substantial recasting of the state's role in the economic sphere. Though the divestiture of public enterprise has frequently not figured among the most central of the 'reform' options associated with this process of policy change, privatisation may well prove a key marker as to the extent to which it will lead to substantial alterations in the boundaries between states and markets. An answer to such a question is complicated by the close association of privatisation with other economic liberalisation measures; the impact of the former is hard to isolate from the latter. Nonetheless developments over the decade have brought a shift in the political centre of gravity. 'Privatisation' has entered African policy discourse in a manner unimaginable in the early 1980s. Whatever the limitations on the actual implementation of divestiture programmes, the formal commitment to them indicates a changing balance of power between governments and private sectors. Though Africa offers few ideologically infused cases comparable with the Chilean divestiture programme launched in 1973, public comments by African leaders suggest that altered attitudes towards the state's role are widespread. The earlier impetus for public sector expansion has been eroded; few significant political movements remain committed to extending the state's economic power. Under the impact of unfavourable circumstances, socialist programmes have everywhere undergone major retrenchment; some have been effectively abandoned. At the same time there has been a measurable opening of space for capitalist development – perhaps more so, as Sklar suggests, than at any time since the pre-independence period.[58]

Yet current divestiture efforts are likely to leave substantial public sectors in place nearly everywhere; the divestitures of which the World Bank had record in early 1988 might well account for little more than 10 per cent of Africa's public enterprises. Moreover, the major privatisation programmes have been concentrated in perhaps a third of the states. While formal privatisation commitments have sometimes crystallised following a change in a regime's top leadership, the fact that these have often also emerged against a backdrop of regime continuity would caution against expectations that many fundamental conversions have occurred on the road to a 'free market' Damascus. Nor will the reform process be necessarily irreversible should there be a marked improvement in Africa's economic prospects – or a severe economic downturn.[59] Again, should structural adjustment efforts fail to produce beneficial results, or should the economic needs of Eastern Europe seriously reduce the aid or foreign investment available, there could also be renewed pressures for substantial state intervention in the economic sphere. The recent emergence of democratic reform movements in Africa – triggered by events in Eastern Europe and by sympathetic signals from several Western powers – is unlikely to produce a secure 'democratic opening' to which a liberal economic regime could be anchored, given the years of economic adversity which many African states have experienced.

NOTES

1. *West Africa*, 3,731 (20–6 February 1989), 260.
2. See R. Hemming and A. M. Mansoor, *Privatization and Public Enterprises* (Washington, D.C.: International Monetary Fund, 1988), pp. 6–7.
3. S. Young, 'The Nature of Privatisation in Britain, 1979–85', *West European Politics*, 9 (April 1986), 235–52.
4. See, for example, P. Cook and C. Kirkpatrick, 'Privatisation in Less Developed Countries: An Overview', in P. Cook and C. Kirkpatrick (eds), *Privatisation in Less Developed Countries* (Brighton: Wheatsheaf Books, 1988), pp. 31–3; R. Hemming and A. M. Mansoor, 'Is Privatization the Answer?' *Finance and Development*, 25 (September 1988) 32–3; T. Killick and S. Commander, 'State Divestiture as a Policy Instrument in Developing Countries', *World Development* 16 (December 1988) 1,473–5, 1,477; and E. J. Wilson III, 'Privatization in Africa: Domestic Origins, Current Status and Future Scenarios', *Issue*, 16, 2 (1988), 24.
5. E. Berg and M. M. Shirley, *Divestiture in Developing Countries* (Washington, D.C.: International Bank for Reconstruction and Development, 1987). (Hereafter cited as IBRD.)
6. *Ibid.*, Table 2, p. 22.
7. Individual countries have been counted under the 'privatization' heading either because such activity has already occurred or because there has been a formal public commitment to divestiture. In four instances, no evidence of privatisation over the past decade has been located: Botswana, Burkina Faso, Comoros Islands and Djibouti. In three others – Cape Verde, Lesotho and Namibia (before independence) – the evidence is suggestive but not sufficiently detailed to allow inclusion.

   The best general survey of the African experience with privatisation remains T. M. Callaghy and E. J. Wilson III, 'Africa: Policy, Reality or Ritual?' in R. Vernon (ed.), *The Promise of Privatization: A Challenge for U.S. Policy* (New York: Council on Foreign Relations, 1988), pp. 179–230. For a valuable compendium of information on the privatisation programmes of eighty-three countries – sixty-six of them LDCs and twenty-six of the latter African – see R. Candoy-Sekse with A. R. Palmer, *Techniques of Privatization of State-Owned Enterprises: Inventory of Country Experience and Reference Materials*, vol. III (Washington, D.C.: IBRD, 1988).
8. C. Young and T. Turner, *The Rise and Decline of the Zairian State* (Madison, Wisc.: University of Wisconsin Press, 1985), pp. 281–6.
9. See T. Killick, *Development Economics in Action: A Study of Economic Policies in Ghana* (New York: St Martin's Press, 1978), pp. 311, 313–4, 320–2; and E. Hutchful (ed.) *The IMF and Ghana: The Confidential Record* (London: Zed Books, 1987), pp. 20–2, 27–36, 143–216.
10. Young and Turner, *Zairian State*, pp. 326–62.
11. *Africa Research Bulletin*, Economic, Financial and Technical Series, 14 (31 August 1977), p. 4,367. (Hereafter cited as ARB/ES.)
12. See R. E. Stren, 'Urban Services in Africa: Public Management or Privatisation?' in *Privatisation in Less Developed Countries*, pp. 217–47;

and M. A. Cohen, 'Francophone Africa', in D. C. Rowat (ed.), *International Handbook on Local Government Reorganization* (Westport, Conn.: Greenwood Press, 1980), pp. 418–20.

13. See Cook and Kirkpatrick, 'Privatisation in Less Developed Countries', pp. 4ff.

14. See T. Killick, 'Twenty-Five Years in Development: The Rise and Impending Decline of Market Solutions', *Development Policy Review*, 4 (June 1986) 101–2; P. Young, *The Enterprise Imperative: Promoting Growth in Developing Countries* (London: Adam Smith Institute, 1988), pp. 8–15; and *West Africa*, No. 3,610 (10 November 1986), p. 2,369.

15. See S. Kagwe, 'Some Organization Factors Affecting the Performance of Public Enterprises in Africa', in African Association for Public Administration and Management, *Public Enterprises Performance and the Privatization Debate: A Review of Options for Africa* (New Delhi: Vikas, 1987), pp. 51–3, 58–9; and J. R. Nellis, *Public Enterprises in Sub-Saharan Africa* (Washington, D.C.: IBRD, 1986), pp. 12–17.

16. See E. J. Wilson III, 'Contested Terrain: A Comparative and Theoretical Reassessment of State-Owned Enterprise in Africa', *Journal of Commonwealth and Comparative Politics*, 22 (March 1984) 4–27; and also IBRD, *World Development Report 1983* (Washington, D.C., 1983), pp. 48–51.

17. Nellis, *Public Enterprises in Sub-Saharan Africa*, pp. 4–5. An ideologically diverse group of eight countries accounted for over half the total cases: Ethiopia, Ivory Coast, Kenya, Madagascar, Senegal, Sudan, Tanzania and Zaire. The 2,959 figure marginally overstates the total for the countries surveyed, since the 'base point' year selected in several cases would ignore subsequent divestitures. On the other hand, the overall African total for public enterprises must be considerably higher; among countries for which adequate data was not available were several known to have substantial public sectors.

18. Nellis, *Public Enterprises in Sub-Saharan Africa*, pp. 17–41; and Callaghy and Wilson, 'Africa: Policy, Reality or Ritual?', pp. 191–222 *passim*. See also M. M. Shirley, *Managing State-Owned Enterprises* (Washington, D.C.: IBRD, 1983); Y. Haile-Mariam and B. Mengistu, 'Public Enterprises and the Privatisation Thesis in the Third World', *Third World Quarterly*, 10 (October 1988), 1,576–8; and J. Nellis and S. Kikeri, 'Public Enterprise Reform: Privatization and the World Bank', *World Development*, 17 (May 1989) 660–3.

19. Some writers caution against ignoring the functional significance of such activities within the context of the patrimonial authority patterns tending to typify politics in postcolonial African states. See Callaghy and Wilson, 'Africa: Policy, Reality or Ritual?', pp. 179–80; and R. Sandbrook, 'Patrimonialism and the Failing of Parastatals: Africa in Comparative Perspective', in *Privatisation in Less Developed Countries*, pp. 174–5.

20. Nellis, *Public Enterprises in Sub-Saharan Africa*, pp. 23–4; and Shirley, *Managing State-Owned Enterprises*, p. 15.

21. And not least at official level; see E. J. Wilson, 'The Public-Private Debate', *Africa Report*, 31 (July/August 1986) 93.

22. Between 1980 and 1988 twenty-five African states underwent no fewer

than ninety-nine debt reschedulings; E. V. K. Jaycox, 'Structural Adjustment in Sub-Saharan Africa: The World Bank's Perspective', *Issue*, 18, 1 (1989) 38. See also T. W. Parfitt and S. P. Riley, *The African Debt Crisis* (London: Routledge, 1989), pp. 14–26.

23. For the Ivory Coast and Kenya, see Callaghy and Wilson, 'Africa: Policy, Reality or Ritual?' pp. 203–4 and 192–3 respectively. For Nigeria, see T. Falola and J. Ihonvbere, *The Rise and Fall of Nigeria's Second Republic, 1979–84* (London: Zed Books, 1985), pp. 164–5; and *Guardian*, 7 November 1983, p. 15. For Senegal, see J. P. Lewis, 'Aid, Structural Adjustment, and Senegalese Agriculture', in M. Gersovitz and J. Waterbury (eds), *The Political Economy of Risk and Choice in Senegal* (London: Frank Cass, 1987), pp. 296–302, 304–7. For Togo, see K. Djondo, 'Anatomy of a Privatisation Scheme: The Togo Example', *African Business*, 114 (February 1988) 16. For South Africa, see V. Padayachee, 'Private International Banks, the Debt Crisis and the Apartheid State, 1982–1985', *African Affairs*, 87 (July 1988) 361–76; T. Young, 'Restructuring the State in South Africa: New Strategies of Incorporation and Control', *Political Studies*, 37 (March, 1989) 69–70, 76–7; and *ARB/ES*, 22 (30 November 1985), p. 7,958.

24. These different reform options followed varying trajectories, both in terms of exact origins and eventual outcomes. In the Nigerian and Senegalese cases internal reform initiatives were quickly to become subsumed within aid packages being negotiated externally with multilateral financial institutions.

25. Though also elsewhere; for the French case see Lewis, 'Aid, Structural Adjustment, and Senegalese Agriculture' pp. 300–1.

26. *World Development Report 1983*, pp. 41–127; the Berg Report was formally published as *Accelerated Development in Sub-Saharan Africa: An Agenda for Action* (Washington, D.C.: IBRD, 1981). See also D. Babai, 'The World Bank and the IMF: Rolling Back the State or Backing Its Role?' in *Promise of Privatization*, pp. 254–85; and 'The World Bank', *Economist*, 300 (27 September 1986).

27. Babai, 'World Bank and the IMF', pp. 264, 275.

28. The Bank's policy-based (as opposed to project) lending increased from 6 to around 20 per cent of funding disbursed between 1979 and 1986; by 1988 this proportion within the Bank's African funding stood at 40 per cent. Paul Mosley, 'Privatisation, Policy-Based Lending and World Bank Behaviour', in *Privatisation in Less Developed Countries*, p. 129; and Jaycox, 'Structural Adjustment in Sub-Saharan Africa', p. 40.

29. While IMF and World Bank views on the shortcomings of LDC public sectors have been similar, the former has remained primarily concerned with their impact on governmental budgetary deficits, external indebtedness, and balance of payments problems; because the actual budgetary benefits of divestiture might prove elusive, it has tended to favour liquidations over privatisations and, until recently, over public enterprise reform. Babai, 'World Bank and the IMF', pp. 262–3, 266–7, 272–4.

30. See, for example, M. Shirley, 'The Experience with Privatization', *Finance and Development*, 25 (September 1988) 35; M. Alexander, 'Privatisation in Africa', in V. V. Ramanadham (ed.), *Privatisation in*

Developing Countries (London: Routledge, 1989), pp. 323–47; and Nellis and Kikeri, 'Public Enterprise Reform', pp. 664–5. See also *World Development Report 1983*, pp. 85–7; and IBRD, *World Development Report 1987* (Washington D.C., 1987), p. 68.

31. Mosley, 'Privatization, Policy-Based Lending and World Bank Behaviour', pp. 129–39; and Babai, 'World Bank and the IMF', pp. 267–71, 276–81.

32. As Babai observes, 'privatisation – and, more generally, the reform of state firms – is still mainly an affair of the poor in Bank lending'; 'World Bank and the IMF', p. 270.

33. Nellis and Kikeri, 'Public Enterprise Reform', p. 665; and Alexander, 'Privatisation in Africa', p. 347.

34. See, for example, P. Mosley, 'The Politics of Economic Liberalization: USAID and the World Bank in Kenya, 1980–4', *African Affairs*, 85 (January 1986), pp. 107–19; Dan Baum, 'The Wayward Siblings', *Africa Report*, 34 (January/February 1989), p. 50; C. L. Morna, 'Ghana: The Privatization Drive', *Africa Report*, 33 (November/December 1988) 62; and Callaghy and Wilson, 'Africa: Policy, Reality or Ritual?' pp. 185–6.

35. These figures are calculated from C. Vuylsteke, *Techniques of Privatization of State-Owned Enterprises: Methods and Implementation*, vol. I (Washington, D.C.: IBRD, 1988), Table 3, pp. 177–80. Table 3 includes data on twenty-six African countries, and appears to omit liquidations.

36. Candoy-Sekse, *Techniques of Privatization*, vol. III.

37. Benin, Cameroon, Gambia, Ghana, Guinea, Guinea-Bissau, Ivory Coast, Mali, Niger, Senegal, Togo and Uganda.

38. ARB/ES, 23 (31 May 1986), pp. 8,198–9; and 25 (29 February 1988), p. 8,996.

39. ARB/ES, 25 (29 February 1988), pp. 8,996–7; and *Financial Mail*, 26 February 1988, pp. 36–8.

40. On the Ivory Coast, see Callaghy and Wilson, 'Africa: Policy, Reality or Ritual?', pp. 203–7. On Togo, see Djondo, 'Anatomy of a Privatisation Scheme', pp. 16–7; P. M. Hirschoff, 'The Privatization Drive', *Africa Report*, 31 (July/August 1986) 89–92; and H. Nankani, *Techniques of Privatization of State-Owned Enterprises: Selected Country Case Studies*, vol. II (Washington, D.C.: IBRD, 1988), pp. 137–46.

41. Noting the vested interests potentially threatened by parastatal reform or privatisation, Mosley observes: 'It has been the [World Bank's] hope that there would exist technocrats within the governments with whom it deals who would be persuaded by the offer of concessional finance to confront those . . . interests.' Mosley, 'Privatisation, Policy-Based Lending and World Bank Behaviour', p. 135.

42. The Ivory Coast is ably analysed in this regard in Callaghy and Wilson, 'Africa: Policy, Reality or Ritual?', pp. 204–5, 206–7. On Madagascar, see Baum, 'Wayward Siblings', p. 50.

43. The list comprises Benin, Cameroon, Central African Republic, Equatorial Guinea, Gabon, Gambia, Ghana, Guinea, Ivory Coast, Kenya, Liberia, Malawi, Mali, Mauretania, Mozambique, Niger, Nigeria, Rwanda, Sao Tome e Principe, Senegal, Sierra Leone, Somalia, Togo, Uganda, Zaire, and Zambia.

44. *Focus on South Africa* (Cape Town), November 1989, p. 14, and December 1989, p. 4.
45. In the Guinea case, for example, the amount received from sales of fourteen public enterprises to the private sector averaged around $770,000; such a figure is unlikely to closely reflect the original value of the assets involved. Calculated from Candoy-Sekse, *Techniques of Privatization*, vol. III, pp. 25–6.
46. Other sources would suggest considerably more numerous formal liquidations than recorded here; if informal closures of enterprises are included, the total would certainly exceed that for private sales; see, for example, Nellis, *Public Enterprises in Sub-Saharan Africa*, p. 45. Of the two latter categories, the relaxation of state monopolies has been the more significant – especially in the sphere of agricultural marketing and the distribution or retailing of food and domestic goods.
47. Though more so in francophone than in anglophone African states; see Alexander 'Privatization in Africa', pp. 349, 350; and Candoy-Sekse, *Techniques of Privatization*, vol. III.
48. Nellis and Kikeri, 'Public Enterprise Reform', pp. 665–7; Callaghy and Wilson, 'Africa: Policy, Reality or Ritual?', p. 187; Alexander, 'Privatization in Africa', pp. 345–6; Young, *Enterprise Imperative*, pp. 28–30; and *West Africa*, No. 3,731 (20–26 February 1989), pp. 260, 261–2.
49. For the Togo case see Berg and Shirley, *Divestiture in Developing Countries*, p. 9; and Nankani, *Techniques of Privatization*, vol. II, p. 145.
50. Wilson, 'Privatization in Africa', pp. 28–9.
51. *Financial Times*, 30 August 1989, p. 6.
52. On the role of public sector lobbies over the privatisation, see Callaghy and Wilson, 'Africa: Policy, Reality or Ritual?', pp. 194 (Tanzania) and 199–200 (Nigeria); Shirley, 'Experience with Privatization', p. 34; and P. Cook and M. Minogue, 'Towards a Political Economy of Privatization in Less Developed Countries' (International Development Centre, University of Manchester, 1989, mimeo).
53. ARB/ES, 23 (31 July 1986), p. 8,196. See also Cook and Minogue, 'Towards a Political Economy of Privatisation', p. 12; and Sandbrook, 'Patrimonialism and the Failing of Parastatals', pp. 173–4.
54. See, for instance, the remarks of the Malian prime minister, ARB/ES, 25 (31 May 1988), p. 9,101; and those of the head of Ghana's Divestiture Implementation Committee in Morna, 'Privatization Drive', p. 62.
55. The strategy the government resolved upon – an emphasis on stock market flotations of public enterprises, with limits on individual share purchases and a vigorous campaign to spread share-buying throughout the federation – largely defused these issues; but continued heavy reliance on the Lagos stock exchange for divestitures appeared unfeasible as of early 1990 because of the risk of 'crowding out' private sector share sales; *Financial Times*, 19 March 1990, Survey on Nigeria, p. IV.
56. Callaghy and Wilson, 'Africa: Policy, Reality or Ritual?', p. 193; and Mosley, 'Privatisation, Policy-Based Lending and World Bank Behaviour', p. 139, n4.
57. *Guardian*, 10 May 1990, p. 16; ARB/ES, 27 (28 February 1990), pp.

9,831–2; and *Focus on South Africa*, March 1990, p. 16, and June 1990, p. 4.

58. R. L. Sklar, 'Beyond Capitalism and Socialism in Africa', *Journal of Modern African Studies*, 26 (March 1988) 11–12.

59. See Wilson, 'Privatization in Africa', pp. 26–8; and H. Bienen and J. Waterbury, 'The Political Economy of Privatization in Developing Countries', *World Development*, 17 (May 1989) 629.

10 The Inevitability of Symbiosis: States, Markets and R&D

Roger Williams

The performance of research and development (R&D) on an organised and large-scale basis constitutes one of the major benchmarks of history. That is a large claim but the situation warrants no less. Britain led the way in the Industrial Revolution by entrepreneurship which successfully exploited the products of invention: thereafter a more deliberate process of innovation gradually established itself as the central dynamo of change. In the twentieth century, and especially since the Second World War, R&D-led technological innovation has become the source of an unending stream of products of critical importance for economic growth, military potential, and social development.[1] As a result, in the forty-five post-war years, companies within the industrial states, and therefore these states themselves, have been in competition with each other as never before as regards their ability to profit successfully from technological innovation, a point not nearly widely enough appreciated.[2] The ending of the Cold War can be expected to lead gradually to the erosion of the one major factor which has distorted this competition, the concentration by some states on defence technology. Much of this latter technology, though of increasingly high cost, and certainly 'advanced', tends to be relatively sterile in its overall economic significance, a point taken up below.

It is important to realise that R&D, far from being a category apart, has now become pervasive to almost all economic activity. Its link with manufacturing industry is most obvious, but it has become fundamental in cases like energy and transport too, and even in such service sectors as education and finance. It was consequently inevitable that governments would become heavily involved with R&D, whether by providing funds or incentives for others to do the work, or by themselves establishing the requisite facilities and personnel. However, to demonstrate that every responsible government must

179

now give a high priority to the support of R&D is one thing, to show how that support should best be offered and what its scale should be is quite another.

Before trying to make progress on this question, there is one further preliminary point which deserves to be made. Precisely because a country's R&D position is now critical to so many policy areas, governments cannot abdicate from substantial responsibility in regard to the formation and calibre of the national scientific and engineering workforce. Studies have repeatedly suggested that the general educational level of workforces, the depth of their vocational training, and the proportion of qualified scientists and engineers in senior managerial positions, are all prime indicators of a country's total industrial standing.[3] Important as this point is, space prevents it being pursued in more detail here.

This chapter has three main objectives. First, it attempts to make clear the issues which arise in regard to the need for state support with the various types of R&D. Second, it briefly draws attention to the post-war R&D records of four countries, and to the general importance of comparative international figures on R&D performance. And third, it tries to identify some of the more significant current trends. Underlying the whole is a central conviction: the activities encompassed by the term R&D are now without equal as the touchstone of success for the modern state.

TYPES OF R&D

It is convenient to think of R&D as comprising a spectrum of activities, as follows:

Basic (or pure or fundamental) research – undertaken to increase scientific knowledge, curiosity-driven and with no particular application in mind;

Strategic research – carried out with some eventual application in mind even when this cannot be precisely specified, therefore stimulated by technological need and given a sense of relevance by that need;

Applied research – pursued with a specific goal in mind, normally improving an existing product or process or creating a new one;

Development – systematic work drawing on existing knowledge and bridging a gap between research and production, but still containing the essence of novelty.

These definitions do not map perfectly onto the terms 'science' and 'technology', but broadly science is to be equated with knowledge, technology with application.

In using these terms at least three caveats need to be noted. First, there is nothing absolute about such definitions, so that, for example, strategic research, now sometimes regarded as a sub-category of applied research, was in less utilitarian times commonly thought of as objective basic research: it follows that there is an inevitable element of subjectivity in classifying a given piece of work. Second, although the idea of a spectrum is useful for explanatory purposes, it is a mistake to think only linearly, that is, to try to assign a given project uniquely to one category: what happens typically is that such a project will involve aspects of each of several of the categories. And third, there is much activity which follows development but precedes or accompanies production: this work may itself be designated as development but such a description can be confusing and misrepresent the true position, above all if no element of novelty is involved.

A first question which the above definitions pose for government concerns the support of basic research. It has been suggested that since basic research is 'an essential part of cultural development', then 'every civilised country should accept some commitment to its furtherance'.[4] Basic research is not only the training-ground for those who will continue to work in this area, but also for many of those who will subsequently work in strategic and applied research, in development and indeed in management. In addition, although the world stock of basic research is in principle available to all in the open literature, to access it, and even more to take full advantage of technology emerging elsewhere, for example via licences, a given state must itself sustain a high indigenous level of technical competence.

There is a difficulty here in that during the 1950s and 1960s, when Japan was deriving great benefit from licensing foreign technology, its support of basic research was low. In effect what Japan did then was to perform applied R&D on the technology which it licensed from abroad to generate a stream of technological products, the successful commercial exploitation of which then gave the country spectacular economic growth. This example is important to those who would prefer to limit government support of basic research, since it allows them to suggest that such support is not essential to commercial success but should in many ways properly be compared with, say, the support of the arts, something which government funds because it chooses to rather than because it must. However, the situation facing a country in the 1990s and henceforth may well differ substantially from that which faced Japan in the 1950s, in that accessing foreign technology almost certainly now requires more domestic know-how in the first place.[5] This point, practically and intellectually interesting though it is, cannot be considered further here, at least directly. What is apparent is that in all countries the public purse is likely to provide most of the funds for basic research indefinitely. Philanthropists and foundations might help at the margin but there is next to no scope here for the market, since nothing immediately marketable is sought in carrying out basic research.

A second key question, at the other end as it were of the R&D spectrum referred to above, concerns the distortion, also mentioned above, introduced by government support of R&D for defence purposes. This is not the only non-commercial reason for which government supports applied R&D, but in most countries it dwarfs in significance support arising out of regulatory or other legislative requirements. Clearly, since a state can have no more paramount concern than the preservation of its own security, it would be fair to claim that the R&D necessary to underpin the artefacts needed for that security must have first call on national R&D resources. Of course, the R&D needed in this sense is a matter of judgement, and therefore of controversy, but there is also another and severe problem which arises from the pre-emption of national R&D resources by the demands of national security. This is that the commercial contribution from military technology, directly via sales of military equipment and indirectly via spin-off to the civil sector, seems even in the most favourable circumstances (those of the United States) to be unable fully to offset commercial opportunities foregone precisely because of the concentration on military technology. This is what was meant above by the suggestion that defence technology tended to be sterile. Economies where the defence distortion is large risk losing competitive edge. To put it colloquially, while a society may elect for guns rather than butter in the short to medium term, in the long term such a choice may come to mean neither guns nor butter. This is to put the matter in an extreme form, but the increasing technical complexity and correspondingly increasing cost of military technology during recent decades, together with the specialisation of that technology, leaves no doubt that the phenomenon is real enough, a consideration which has certainly influenced Mr Gorbachev. This point too, though even more pressing than that made above in respect of basic research, will also not be taken further here except in so far as it bears directly upon the central theme of the chapter, the changing balance between state and market in the support of R&D.

It has already been noted that the market is likely to fund only a negligible amount of basic research, but is the situation so very different in respect of much of strategic research? Application here is probably both uncertain and long-term, and while large companies will no doubt invest in some such research they will be likely to limit their involvement to their identified future needs, and smaller firms, one can be sure, will avoid this sort of work altogether.

In complete contrast, few quarrel with the argument that civil applied research and development should in principle be funded by industry, and that expenditure on it should reflect both market and technical assessment of a kind which industry itself can best make. However, even here there can be cases where defects in the market mechanism mean that selective government support for industrial technology can produce national economic benefit. There is also the incontrovertible fact that most countries support their own companies' R&D efforts, though there are as many mechanisms as countries and the exact levels of support may in any particular case be quite impossible to disentangle. It follows that any country which elects not to subsidise its industrial R&D may risk handicapping its industry in international competition.

There are also more indirect measures open to government to stimulate private sector R&D, for instance tax incentives – an approach tried by both the conservative Reagan administration in the United States and the Hawke Labour government in Australia. Or there is the prospect of legislation requiring firms to disclose their R&D expenditure, the aim being to shame poor performers into doing more. There is also a wide variety of schemes inviting some form of matching support from industry, as with the UK Alvey programme in information technology, for example.

THE R&D HISTORY OF FOUR STATES[6]

What one might call the 'R&D history' of the major industrial states during the post-war era is instructive. There is room to consider here only four cases, and those briefly – the USA, Japan, the UK and the USSR.

The USA

In 1945 there was no doubt of the technological hegemony of the United States, and little expectation that this dominance could be quickly eroded. Indeed, 'technological can-doism' was uniquely identified as American, with relations between government, industry and academia producing there an historically unprecedented synergy. In 1945 the nuclear weapon above all symbolised the capability of the American way, and after a brief period of uncertainty in the late 1950s, when it appeared that leadership in space exploration might have passed to the USSR, the conviction of American technological superiority was renewed by the success of the Apollo programme in 1969. A decade after that, however, and the Carter administration found itself fearful that without federal support, at least for generic technologies and what was called re-industrialisation, the US might be overtaken by the more buoyant economies of West Germany and Japan. Reagan's accession was meant to quell such doubts and his Strategic Defence Initiative was a re-assertion of American self-confidence in its R&D capacity. But the argument about the American need for an industrial policy designed to maintain and enhance the country's industrial base continues – the removal of the Head of the Defence Advanced Projects Agency in the Pentagon in April 1990 was occasioned, it seems, by his decision to offer federal assistance to a Californian microchip company which lacked a clear defence connection.[7] The American ethic, it appears, remains that federal R&D support of firms in the defence field is appropriate, but such support must not be offered more generally.[8] Or in other words, America's industrial policy is its defence policy. The resulting sym-biosis between firms and the state has long been known as the military industrial complex: it has generated a truly huge literature, and prompted perhaps the most famous of all presidential farewell addresses – that of Eisenhower. The consequent blend of private economic power and public political power has persisted in the

United States now for half a century, as one writer has put it, a 'form of private socialism', and it may well take more than the ending of the Cold War to undermine it seriously.

Japan

In complete contrast, Japan began the post-war period defeated, its industry mostly destroyed, its technological base severely damaged. But the country quickly acquired a genuine overriding goal – to catch up with the West – as the only way to expunge the shame of military failure. It was a ridiculous goal, incapable as it seemed in 1945 of attainment. Political scientists will no doubt long continue the argument as to how precisely Japan is governed, what exactly are the respective roles of the Liberal Democratic Party (LDP), the bureaucracy and industry. What is not in serious dispute is the paramountcy for all these elements of the central techno-industrial aim. In 1990 that aim stands largely fulfilled, though it has not been accomplished without significant social costs. It is in fact a decade since the *Economist* described the LDP government as plausibly the most successful government in all history.[9]

The R&D formula has remained almost the same throughout: mostly neglect basic research; encourage co-operation between Japanese firms on strategic research; move to the competitive mode for applied research and development; provide government guidance, above all via controlled access to foreign licenses, but only limited governmental funds; emphasise quality, first through product reliability, later through innovative design; ensure that the education system is focussed to back up these policies. Japan still faces problems but many of them are genuinely those of success. In the R&D field, for instance, a rich country can afford to worry about its poor performance in winning Nobel Prizes and can devote more funds to basic research. It can ask whether its education system is too intensive. It can face the new challenge of environmentalism with the margin provided by wealth. The Japanese model works outstandingly, for Japan. In modified form it appears to be working elsewhere in South-East Asia. And the present outreach of Japanese firms means that their methods as well as products are now being exported to Europe, to East Asia, and to the United States. This is a space well worth the watching.

Britain

Britain partly emulated the United States, that is, defence technologies and the R&D required to sustain them were unquestioningly underwritten by the state. But British governments also had few inhibitions about underwriting non-defence technologies as well. Over the years, and between the parties, a bewildering array of policies was tried. Labour intervened more than the Conservatives but both were enthusiastic. There were some spectacular distortions, most notoriously in the case of nuclear energy. Industry meanwhile tended to take the view that if government was going to spend generously on R&D, then there was little point in committing private money to an activity with unavoidably high risk levels and long payback periods. The Stock Exchange concurred. Too many industrialists failed to spot the increasing sophistication and internationalisation of markets. The education system and the career, reward and status structures in society continued to transmit dubious, if not downright misleading, signals. The downward drift of the economy became remorseless, yet international-class basic research continued to thrive.

When finally in 1979 a government was elected which was determined to reverse national decline, its departure from past practices and the underlying consensus were, except for the matter of funding university research, perhaps less clear cut in the R&D field than in most. A turnround was said to have been managed by the late 1980s, and UK industry was certainly more capable by then of standing on its own feet than it had been a decade earlier, but there had been no comprehensive miracle and in 1990 the United Kingdom was still not a society fired with excitement by the profits to be made from technology. A country which had once led the world with an industrial revolution based on invention was still finding the requirements of sustained innovation a very different matter, and possibly not even very congruent with the essential style of British life.

In line with the Thatcher governments' ideological outlook, the R&D objectives of the UK Department of Trade and Industry (DTI) were formally changed in 1988, and, while it would be inappropriate in this chapter to go into too great detail in regard to the R&D policies of any one country, consideration of this particular change brings out an extremely important practical and philosophical point. The main conclusion of the DTI's review of its R&D in January 1988 was said to be that 'the balance of existing policies should be changed in order to move away from near-market R&D support'.[10] The justification given for this was that firms were best placed to assess markets and to balance the risks and rewards of financing R&D and associated innovation. Government, it was stated, 'should not take on responsibilities which are primarily those of industry. The closer to the market place that innovation is taking place, the more fundamental this should be as a guiding principle of policy'. A related consideration, though not specifically mentioned in the White Paper on the DTI, is that of additionality, in the sense of the requirement for the output from a policy to be greater than that which would have occurred without government intervention.

Now the logic of government's wishing to avoid paying for near-market R&D, and seeking additionality, is irresistible. The problem comes in reliably determining how near to the market R&D is, and in knowing with confidence what would occur without government support. Two further complications which can arise are that while government may eschew the near market so far as funding R&D is concerned, market conditions are determined at least in part by the other policies of government which bear upon commercial behaviour; and second, as already noted, that the market in the case of internationally traded goods is invariably shaped in part by what other governments do in terms of R&D support and in respect of such other policies as public procurement and export guarantees.

One could multiply examples, but in the West generalisations taking note of the experiences of these three countries will not be found greatly in error. Specifically, with respect to market forces it is readily seen that insistence on a state/market dichotomy is not especially helpful in the R&D field. In some sectors, such as chemicals, market factors have always dominated. In others (above all defence) they probably never will. Granted, the UK government in the 1980s, in this as in other fields, emphasised market discipline; and granted too that the privatisation of the electricity industry in the UK was the development which eventually smoked out the incompatibility between R&D-driven nuclear power and the market. The fact remains that in the US and Japan, and even in large measure in the UK, underlying styles in the state/market R&D relationship have tended to persist even when the actual level of state support has shifted substantially.

The USSR

The case of the USSR is of exceptional interest. The distortion introduced into Western economies by defence spending, though serious, has been mitigated by the fact that the balance of these economies, and much of the activity even of defence firms, have been subject to more or less free market forces. And even when governments in the West were intent on picking winners in the non-defence field, there was still an abundance of commercial activity in their economies which remained exposed to market forces. In the Soviet Union matters were otherwise. There state planning aimed to be total, market signals had no place, and even negative feedback loops were discouraged. *Glasnost* and *perestroika* between them have now permitted us to see the scale of the failure perpetrated by the world's greatest social science experiment. Quite naturally, analysts contrast the economic disaster on view in the USSR with the economic growth which the West has come to take for granted. And the situation has been if anything even worse in the USSR's satellites, for each of them suffered not only the same deadening forces as were at work in the USSR itself, but also the requirement that their economies, and therefore their R&D, broadly conform to the pattern established by the USSR and the Soviet bloc as a whole.

Soviet bloc performances would not have compared well even had the performances of Western economies continued along the lines they were following when the Soviet system was first set up. But since then Western economies have embarked on headlong R&D-based technological innovation. And the inescapable fact is that the requirements of central planning and successful technological innovation are completely at odds with each other. Innovation needs a spontaneity and flexibility of response, it needs to be informed by reliable market awareness, it calls for individuals at all levels to be prepared to take responsibility, and it works best when sustained by co-operative teamwork. Ideally R&D needs to be driven by the career interests of those who are engaged in it, and pulled forward by the prospect of profit. Practitioners need up-to-date access, via literature and travel, to related work going on elsewhere, and in the area of commercial products they also need industrial intelligence to give them a view on the options available to competitors. R&D activities are highly dynamic, but someone also has to incorporate R&D results into industrial production, debug them as necessary, and improve the specification steadily thereafter. The social context of innovation in the Soviet Union has amounted almost to the antithesis of all these requirements.

Set free by the events of 1989, there is every reason to believe that the countries of Eastern Europe, and perhaps in due course even some of the Soviet Union's own republics, will find appropriate paths to modern economies. But those paths will differ and among the differences will be the R&D choices these states make. They will also, as is already evident, move at different speeds along their chosen paths. Comparison of them with the least developed of the world's countries also brings out that they, unlike the latter, have always possessed most of the infrastructure and orientation they need to join the successful Western countries. Formerly the misuse of that infrastructure was their particular tragedy, now its proper use is their greatest hope.

A final note: the contrast between the USSR and Japan could in fact hardly be more instructive. The R&D results of others were available to both via licensing (and reverse engineering) – albeit with some security constraints denying certain technologies in the Soviet case, though the latter do not much change the argument. What happened was that Japan proved capable of benefiting from this: the USSR did not.

INTERNATIONAL COMPARISON

This chapter has argued that in the post-war period commercial competition between states has become substantially more intense and a dominant feature of the international scene; that successful technological innovation is the key to such competition; and that R&D is a central aspect of technological innovation. It follows that great interest attaches to international comparisons of R&D expenditure. Successful technological innovation, however, is about much more than R&D. It includes, in particular, such elements as market research and marketing, good design, efficient manufacturing with high quality control, and effective after-sales service. There are also broader economic aspects to be taken into account, such as the investment climate, patent, tax and regulatory provisions, and work-force characteristics. High R&D spending will avail little if the wrong overall goals are selected or these other factors are not conducive to innovation. But because R&D can be quantified, despite complications of the kind alluded to below, whereas most of these other elements can be described only qualitatively, there has been a tendency for R&D to receive disproportionate attention. It is also the most glamorous element in innovation.

A simple example will illustrate the resultant dangers. Government is a supplier of substantial volumes of R&D funds, but the public sector is also itself a considerable user of the fruits of technological innovation. If government expects to influence the quality and quantity of innovation by its expenditure on R&D, then it is scarcely less reasonable for it to expect to do so also through intelligent public sector purchasing, attempting to 'pull' innovation, as it were, from in front rather than 'pushing' it from behind. Yet except for a flurry of interest in the late 1960s under a Labour government and another brief flurry in the early 1980s under a Conservative one, in the UK public purchasing has never received the attention given to the much more exciting issues arising in respect of R&D. Governments elsewhere too cannot be said wholly to have avoided this trap, though some of them do appear to have put R&D into better overall perspective.

Despite this reservation in regard to the significance of other elements in innovation, comparative R&D expenditures are important. In particular, they are now regularly quoted in parliamentary debates, Congressional inquiries and so on. Indeed, a recent House of Lords report takes to task the selective quotation of R&D statistics by UK government ministers up to and including the Prime Minister in defence of policy positions.[11]

If R&D expenditure is one measure of a state's investment in its own future, how close can one get to reliable international comparisons? The essential problem is that although in principle the OECD countries at least collect R&D statistics as laid down by the Frascati manual,[12] in practice there is great scope for interpretation and therefore national variation, and it can therefore be extremely difficult to compare like with like. The basis of international comparison is normally the expression of gross (that is public and private) expenditure on R&D (GERD) as a percentage of GDP. The problems arise when the GERD/GDP ratio is broken down to reflect the public/private and civil/defence splits. Further, in examining trends in the GERD/GDP ratio it is important to realise that changes in the denominator can be more important than those in the numerator, and a better indicator would therefore be the comparison of growth in GERD against growth in GDP. OECD have also suggested that it is useful to compare GERD with a country's gross fixed capital formation, on the grounds that this provides a measure of the capacity to turn R&D into technological progress. Whatever the limitations of this last proposal, at least it brings out that expenditure on R&D should not be seen in isolation from investments which allow the results of that R&D to be exploited. Even allowing for the great difficulty in comparing like with like in international R&D statistics, some conclusions stand out. They are illustrated in the following tables,[13] which relate to the six highest spending Western countries – comparable, and reliable, figures for the USSR and Eastern European countries are not yet available.

Table 10.1 shows that, in volume terms, the United States is in a league of its own, with Japan in a second division and the FRG top of a third which also includes Britain and France. However, Table 10.4 shows that the USA and the UK, and to a lesser extent France, are heavily biased towards defence R&D. Table 10.2 demonstrates that the Japanese government funds only about half as much of the country's GERD as do most of the other countries, though with the FRG also distinctly lower than the USA, UK and France. And Table

TABLE 10.1: *The absolute levels of GERD (1985 figures)*

	(£ billion)
USA	63.5
Japan	21.2
FRG	11.2
France	8.3
UK	8.1
Italy	4.0

TABLE 10.2: *Percentage of GERD financed from public sources (1983 figures)*

France	54.0
Italy	52.4
UK	50.2
USA	49.2
FRG	39.4
Japan	24.0

SOURCE: for Tables 10.1 and 10.2: Cabinet Office, *Annual Review of Government Funded Research and Development* (London: HMSO, 1988 and 1989).

TABLE 10.3: *Percentage of R&D performed in the business enterprise sector and financed by industry (1983 figures)*

Japan	98.1
FRG	82.2
Italy	77.6
France	73.0
USA	67.6
UK	63.0

TABLE 10.4: *Government funding of defence R&D as a percentage of GDP (1985 figures)*

USA	.854
UK	.679
France	.460
FRG	.136
Italy	.077
Japan	.014

SOURCE: for Tables 10.3 and 10.4: Cabinet Office, *Annual Review of Government Funded Research and Development* (London: HMSO, 1988 and 1989).

10.3 reveals that industry funds virtually all the R&D in the business sector in Japan, compared with only about two-thirds to four-fifths in the other countries. The differences between countries as brought out in these tables, and there is no reason to suppose great variation later in the decade, are too large not to reflect an important underlying reality.

CURRENT TRENDS

Among the more significant trends currently affecting the international pattern of R&D expenditure are collaboration, privatisation, the impact of environmentalism, and expectations of a 'peace dividend', only the last of these being really new. There are also of course fashions in R&D funding – for instance, civil nuclear R&D enjoyed this status in the 1950s, electronics and computers in the 1960s, micro-electronics in the 1970s, and biotechnology in the 1980s. Threats (for example, the greenhouse effect or AIDS) and opportunities (for example, the research potential of the electron microscope or the laser) can also be expected regularly to occur and to shift the character and scale of public and private R&D support. However, collaboration, privatisation, environmentalism and a projected peace dividend seem more far-reaching than any of these.

International collaboration in R&D[13] has in fact become a remarkable phenomenon in recent decades. It has gone furthest in Europe, both within the EEC and outside it. Initially the EEC's achievements were meagre, the Euratom initiative an embarrassment, but with the series of Framework Programmes of recent years this is steadily changing. Outside the EEC there have been many bi- and multi-lateral projects, with a particular concentration in the defence field. But the heavily R&D based Airbus programme now seems set to become one of Europe's major civil industrial successes, and the EUREKA programme of co-operative R&D was conceived by France as a non-defence response to the American Strategic Defence Initiative ('Star Wars'). In big science (e.g. CERN), collaboration has become the only means of maintaining involvement in the relevant research area. In technological areas collaboration is for governments a mechanism for gearing up the national R&D effort while also spreading risks and possibly enlarging final markets. For firms too collaboration has become now a strategy of choice. Inevitably, collaboration also brings problems. It puts up costs even though those to each partner should be lower. It can be inflexible. Balancing equity and efficiency is a perennial difficulty, *juste retour* normally a democratic necessity but usually a managerial complication. Deciding intellectual property rights can be a lasting irritation. Nevertheless, it is generally believed that collaboration will increasingly be the way of the future. It makes sense for electorally-oriented governments and market-oriented firms: it blurs the distinction between the responsibilities of states and the disciplines imposed by markets.

International projects can certainly take on a life of their own, the states which sponsored them finding their room for manoeuvre subsequently constrained by a project's own dynamics. But states can also use collaboration to further national ends. This is the more easily accomplished when states are themselves supporting parallel national programmes, a point whose force France especially has appreciated, above all in the space field. To sum up: collaboration offers a distinctively new blend of state and market forces. It is highly appealing as an approach for the medium-sized countries of Europe, an awkward issue for the hitherto self-sufficient United States, feasible on a significant scale for Japan only if that country can overcome the suspicions of its prospective partners, and attractive, or it may even be essential, for countries like Canada and Australia.

Privatisation, which the British had tended to think in the early 1980s a national obsession of the Thatcher government, by the late 1980s was a clear trend internationally, as the chapters by Cammack and Young demonstrate. The basic idea is both simple and persuasive: put economic activity back in the private sector which is its natural home and where distortions introduced by government will be minimised. However, in regard to R&D at least, while privatisation may help, it cannot wholly solve the problem of the respective responsibilities of the public and private purses. To illustrate this, consider as an example the UK energy sector. Here gas has been privatised, electricity (in late 1990) is about to be privatised, and the case for privatisation of coal is foreshadowed. After privatisation it becomes a matter for each industry to decide for itself what R&D it would be justified in funding. But this still leaves the government with the decision of whether, and to what extent, to underwrite research which would not be done without government support, for example on alternative energy sources, and on fusion and fission power. In short, like it or not, government cannot (even in a thoroughly privatised sector), escape the role of being the R&D funder of last resort.

By the 1980s environmentalism had become a serious political force, and one certain to bear increasingly on R&D profiles. Increased questioning of the shape and scale of both public and private R&D was implicit in 1970s titles like *The Limits to Growth*, *Only One Earth* and *Small is Beautiful*.[14] But here was a force neither of the market nor yet of the state, rather of the participating public. Environmentalism's modern origins lie with late 1960s America, politicised by the unfolding Vietnam trauma, and its central 1970s target became nuclear power. An unending series of local and regional environmental insults through the 1980s stoked the fires. And at the end of that decade the discovery of the threat posed by chlorofluorocarbons to the ozone layer, and possibly by carbon dioxide and other gases to the earth's climate regime, brought home the global character of the planet's environmental problems.

Some have seen environmentalism as another check on market freedom, a further excuse for the dead hand of state regulation. That in effect was President Reagan's view. Environmentalism does undoubtedly challenge old ways of doing things, and it does require the authority of the state if significant and permanent changes are to be made. But it is not unequivocally inimical to economic efficiency predicated upon market forces. The only requirement – but it is a substantial one – is that environmental costs be included in market pricing. Traditional economic analysis takes both sources and sinks as essentially infinite, and what environmentalism has shown is that the latter at least must be treated as finite – that is, there are limits to the pollution which the planet as a whole, and particular parts of it such as rivers and seas, can absorb. The problem here is that action by individual governments is often of only limited value, the situation requires genuinely collective action. One then runs into the familiar complications of the commons, in this case the 'global commons' as they have come to be called, where there is benefit for the individual state in ignoring, where it can, collective agreements designed to maximise benefits for all. The political arrival of environmentalism means a new role for states acting in concert: it need not mean the abandonment of market discipline. It is bound to mean changes in the pattern of R&D activity: indeed, this has already begun to occur. What is in prospect is a switch, no doubt gradual, from environmentally indifferent technologies to so-called environmentally friendly ones. The implications of such a switch will be profound: the R&D necessary to underpin it massive.

Finally, there are the hopes entertained for a peace dividend as the frozen positions of the Cold War are dismantled. In 1990 this was the subject of much speculation, both academic and journalistic.[15] Real action here, however, was still for the future, longstanding funding commitments being hard to change fundamentally, as realisation of a worthwhile dividend would certainly require. Confident assessment was also complicated in autumn 1990 by the implications of the Gulf Crisis. The central questions were easy enough to discern: to what extent would defence R&D budgets be cut and how far would cuts be taken up by increased expenditure on civil R&D? How far, and how fast, could defence R&D facilities be converted into civil ones?

FINAL CONSIDERATIONS

That science was the key to national prosperity was a universal, and virtually unquestioned, assumption for a quarter of a century after the war. The motion was enshrined, for example, in *Science The Endless Frontier*, which Dr Vannevar Bush produced for President

Roosevelt and which successfully argued the case for federal funding of research, basic as well as applied.[16] The same idea was seized upon by de Gaulle to usher in what Gilpin later called *France in the Age of the Scientific State*.[17] And, notoriously, it was the core assumption of the series of speeches by Harold Wilson in the run-up to the 1964 General Election.[18] After all this, even without the renewed emphasis on the market which came to characterise the 1980s, one might have expected increased questioning of the shape and scale of government R&D support. Indeed, to an extent, the environmental movement of the 1970s began this task.

However, it was the market-oriented ethic of the 1980s which led to the most direct interrogation of R&D budgets. As the taskforce on science policy of the House Committee on Science and Technology put it: Can federal funding for science be viewed as an investment and be measured in a way comparable to other forms of economic investment? Elsewhere the question might not be put as directly as this, but the matter was one which occupied many governments in the early 1980s. These governments found themselves faced with, in the scientific community, a highly articulate interest grown comfortably plump largely on public funds. The possibilities for doing good science seemed to be growing without limit. And, despite all, there existed a continuing conviction that economic growth was dependent upon healthy science. Taking these considerations together, this was always a policy sector where appeals to market discipline were going ultimately to be limited.

As to questions of the type put by the House Committee, they received perhaps their fullest answer in a study which the US Congressional Office of Technology Assessment (OTA) undertook in the mid-1980s.[19] That study concluded that while economists had been able to demonstrate a strong positive correlation between R&D spending and economic growth, with private returns in excess of 20 per cent per annum and social returns in excess of 40 per cent on private R&D expenditures, they had '*not* been able to show comparable returns, and at times been unable to show *any* returns' on federal R&D expenditures. Among the reasons given for this was, quite naturally that 'most government expenditures, including R&D expenditures, are for so-called 'public goods' whose market value is, by definition, extremely difficult to measure in economic terms'. In fact, the OTA study went further, concluding that 'using economic returns to measure the value of specific or general federal research expenditure is an inherently flawed approach'. But the situation was even worse than this, the OTA thought, for 'even if some economic or financial model can be devised' there would have been no way of ensuring its 'uniform application across all research fields and budgets'. The OTA's final summing-up was that the factors which should bear on R&D expenditure were 'too complex and subjective', the pay-offs 'too diverse and incommensurable', and the institutional barriers 'too formidable' for there to be any prospect of allowing 'quantitative models to take the place of mature, informed judgement'. Beyond this all OTA could point to was the desirability of improved communication between the parties responsible for planning, performing and utilising R&D.

This was an American review and, to repeat, the most comprehensive of its kind ever produced anywhere, but there can be little doubt that a similar conclusion would have had to be reached in whatever country the analysis had been performed. The most significant implication of the study for present purposes is that it tacitly limited the application of market forces in the R&D context. Even in its consideration of US industry the OTA study found 'limited practical utility of quantitative techniques for research decision making . . . and the reliance on subjective judgement and good communication between R&D, management and marketing . . .'.

Now it may be objected that it is a mistake to equate quantitative methods with market forces, and mature judgement with state intervention, particularly if industrial firms themselves depend more upon judgement than quantitative techniques. However, to the extent that OTA's findings apply, what is being said is that the signals which the market can give are insufficient to determine the optimum public spend on R&D: that remains very largely a matter of judgement, judgement informed no doubt on point of detail by market assessment, but nevertheless judgement based on much wider criteria.

There is certainly some validity in distinguishing between states in terms of the roles they allot respectively to themselves and to the market in settling the national R&D pattern. But this is equally certainly not the only important dichotomy. Thus Pavitt and Patel recommend instead a division between national systems which are technologically dynamic and others they describe as technologically myopic, the difference being that the former 'recognise the cumulative, irreversible and uncertain nature of technological activities, whereas the latter do not'.[20] In particular, myopic systems are said to evaluate technological activities 'like an ordinary investment, namely, on the basis of their prospective rate of return in responding to an existing and precise market demand'. Of the six characteristics Pavitt and Patel list for dynamic systems, only two could be said to be sensitive to the state/market division (higher level of industry-funded R&D, and decreasing specialisation in technologies oriented to national as against international opportunities). Pavitt and Patel's classification of states contains no surprise: they talk of the 'dynamism of Japan', the 'vulnerability of the USA', the 'variety of Europe', with the Federal Republic of Germany the 'dominant technological power' and the UK having the lowest real rate of R&D expenditure by industry. Of course, Japan is not dynamic across the whole field of R&D, or the UK myopic, but the labels are not unreasonable and their political implications are real enough.

The essential conclusion would seem to be that how R&D tasks are divided between the state and the market seems on the evidence to matter much less than that they are performed properly by one or the other, or best of all, by the two in a flexible symbiosis. Above all, what governments in the industrial states must do is realise that R&D-led interstate industrial competition has now become a dominant theme of international relations. It is a welcome relief that this has replaced military rivalry to the extent that it already has, but it would be foolish to suppose that as a result history has somehow ended. On the contrary, the R&D challenges ahead can be expected to be demanding ones and wise governments will give unremitting attention to meeting them, fully encouraging the application of market forces, but also monitoring them, quietly aware that there is a place for both co-operation and competition, and for government support as well as private initiative.

NOTES

1. Felicity Henwood with Graham Thomas, *Science, Technology and Innovation. A Research Bibliography* (Brighton: Wheatsheaf Books, 1984).
2. Michael E. Porter, *The Competitive Advantage of Nations* (London: Macmillan, 1990).
3. National Science Foundation, *International Science and Technology Data Update 1988* (Washington: 1988).
4. House of Lords Select Committee on Science and Technology, *Civil Research and Development*, Session 1986–87, 1st Report, HL 20–II (London: HMSO, 1986), p. 218.
5. Leonard Lynn, 'Japanese, Research and Technology Policy', *Science*, 233(1986) 296–304.

6. Leonard L. Lederman, Rolf Lehming and Jennifer S. Bond, 'Research Administration: Research Policies and Strategies in Six Countries: A Comparative Analysis', *Science and Public Policy*, 13(1986) 67–76. See also: Harry Atkinson, Philippa Rogers and Richard Bond, *Research in the United Kingdom, France and West Germany: A Comparison*, vol. 1, Science and Engineering Research Council, July 1990.
7. *The Financial Times*, 24 April 1990.
8. Suzanne Berger, Michael L. Dertouzos, Richard K. Lester, Robert M. Solow and Lester C. Thurow, 'Toward a New Industrial America', *Scientific American*, 260(1989) 21–9. The quotation at the close of this paragraph is from Walter Adams, 'The Military Industrial Complex and the New Industrial State', *American Economic Review*, LVIII, 2 (May 1968) 654–60.
9. *The Economist*, 24 May 1980.
10. Department of Trade and Industry, *DTI – the department of Enterprise*, CM 278 (London: HMSO, 1988), para. 8.2.
11. House of Lords Select Committee on Science and Technology, *Definitions of R&D*, Session 1989–90, 3rd Report, HL 44 (London: HMSO, 1990), pp. 16–19.
12. Organisation for Economic Co-operation and Development, *The Measurement of Scientific and Technical Activities "Frascati Manual", 1980* (Paris: 1981).
13. Cf. Roger Williams, *European Technology, The Politics of Collaboration* (London: Croom Helm, 1973), and Margaret Sharp and Claire Shearman, *European Technological Collaboration* (London: Routledge and Kegan Paul for the Royal Institute of International Affairs, Chatham House Papers 36, 1987).
14. D. H. Meadows and the MIT Project Team, *The Limits to Growth*. A Report for the Club of Rome (1972); Barbara Ward and Rene Dubos, *Only One Earth: The Care and Maintenance of a Small Planet* (London: Deutsch, 1972); E. F. Schumacher, *Small is Beautiful: A Study of Economics as if People Mattered* (London: Blond and Briggs, 1973).
15. Philip Gummett and Judith Reppy, 'Military Industrial Networks and Technical Change', *Government and Opposition*, 25(1990), 287–303.
16. Vannevar Bush, *Science the Endless Frontier: A Report to the President* (Washington, DC: US Government Printing Office, July 1945).
17. Robert Gilpin, *France in the Age of the Scientific State* (Princeton, NJ: Princeton University Press, 1968).
18. Sir Alan Cottrell, 'The Rise and Fall of Science Policy', *New Scientist*, 14 October 1976, 80–2. Also Richard Clarke, 'Mintech in Retrospect – I', *Omega*, 1(1973), 25–38.
19. Office of Technology Assessment, *Research Funding as an Investment: Can We Measure the Returns? – A Technical Memorandum* (Washington, DC: US Congress, OTA-TM-SET36, April 1986).
20. Keith Pavitt and Pari Patel, 'The International Distribution and Determinants of Technological Activities', *Oxford Review of Economic Policy*, 4(1988) 35–55.

11 Political Structures and Broadcasting Marketisation: a Comparison of Britain and West Germany

Peter Humphreys

Until recently broadcasting policy in Britain and West Germany has been characterised by a longstanding commitment to public-service monopoly or duopoly service provision: commercial competition has not been a feature of either system (although private broadcasters have been allowed in Britain since 1955). However, in both countries neo-liberal party or coalition governments have come to power with very similar ideological convictions, aiming to break up these structures and replace them with more commercial and competitive ones. This 'marketisation' of the broadcasting sector has been propelled by commonly experienced technological and market pressures, and actively engineered by almost identical coalitions of domestic political actors pushing for regulatory change. Despite all these pressures for sectoral, cross-national policy *convergence*, a significant variation has occurred in policy-making 'style' between these two countries, pointing towards an important element of *divergence* of policy outcomes (the policy process is not quite complete in the British case at the time of writing).

This chapter examines the pressures for convergence, then subjects the policy process to a (necessarily fairly general) empirical inquiry, before arriving at a conclusion which, following the 'new institutionalism', suggests that the dynamics of the policy process have to be seen in terms of important institutional differences in the British and West German political systems, particularly their constitutional profiles. In turn, these differences have to be understood in terms of the countries' very different historico-cultural contexts. The institutional characteristics of the 'macro' level of politics will be shown to be partly reproduced at, and otherwise to have had a significant impact on, the sectoral level, at least in the case of broadcasting.

A 'CONVERGENT' PARADIGM CHANGE IN WEST EUROPEAN BROADCASTING: TOWARDS MARKETISATION

The 1980s have seen a paradigmatic transition in European broadcasting from a predominantly public service model to an industry in which commercial pressures are increasingly being freed from traditional regulatory restraints. In West Germany, the public service monopoly has recently been broken with the launch of two large, and a number of smaller, new commercial television channels, all of which are increasingly available on local terrestrial frequencies. In Britain, legislation is currently being enacted to replace the public service BBC/ITV duopoly with a much less regulated framework for three commercial channels (channels 3, 4 and 5) possibly followed by a sixth channel in the 1990s, again with the promise of a proliferation of local broadcasting. This paradigm change has been driven by a combination of technological and market imperatives which are commonly experienced and point towards a *convergence* of policy making across Western Europe in the direction of 'marketisation'.[1]

By marketisation is meant a combination of deregulation, privatisation and competition. Of these closely interrelated components, deregulation alone evades easy definition. Deregulation is far more than the simple removal or loosening of certain rules and regulations. While important, a simple focus on the latter would be too formalistic and would ignore the fundamental philosophical transformation which underpins it. Thus deregulation is perhaps best understood in terms of a transformation of the regulatory climate from a general commitment to the principle of broadcasting as a universally provided public good (entertainment, education and information in equal measure), towards the concept of broadcasting as 'electronic publishing' with the emphasis on consumer sovereignty (implying an almost certain shift of priorities towards the entertainment function).[2]

The Policy Networks in Favour of 'Marketisation'

In the age of transfrontier satellite broadcasting deregulation is also very much about the new possibilities for the circumvention of over-restrictive national regulations. Low-powered communications satellites have provided the means for new broadcasting entrepreneurs to access a rapidly expanding West European cable market. Medium- and high-powered satellites have brought the possibility of direct broadcasting by satellite (DBS). Yet, satellite technology is merely the most dramatic arbiter of regulatory change. The other 'new media' of cable and video cassette recorders have also combined with important technical developments in the management of the spectrum, the latter releasing new frequencies for terrestrial broadcasting (especially at the local level), to vastly expand the possibilities for the launch of new broadcasting services and thereby to undermine the 'scarcity of frequencies' rationale for a continued strict regulation of the sector.

During the late 1970s and early 1980s, government interest in the promotion of information technology (IT), was reflected in a number of government commissions and reports (such as the British Information Technology Advisory Panel's *Cable Systems*; and a whole series of similar reports in West Germany). An interesting feature of these commissions and their reports was that they already reflected the formation of networks between representatives of the concerned industrial interests and official policy makers. The mark of the former interests was quite evident in the recommendations produced. Therefore, it is hardly surprising that they gave an important stimulus to the search for new, much looser and more flexible regulatory frameworks which would be conducive to the most rapid introduction and commercialisation of the 'new media'.[3]

In turn, this supplied powerful encouragement to those commercial interests seeking to diversify into broadcasting operations. The latter sought to exploit the issue of technological change in order to delegitimise the public-service monopoly, and to gain entrance to the sector; and, have enacted new rules of the game better in tune with their own commercial ambitions and no longer geared towards former goals of universal public-service provision. They too succeeded in gaining privileged access to policy makers, forming distinct policy networks, for instance with national telecommunications administrations and/or industry ministries. The latter (the West German Bundespost and DTI) themselves had a keen technocratic and organisational-political interest in developing the new media. In both countries, grand national cable plans (state-led in West Germany and market-led in Britain) were quickly embarked upon and in West Germany ambitious prestige broadcasting satellite projects were also developed and launched. British Telecom was even an active diversifier into the commercial operation of new cable and satellite ventures (for instance renting transponders on the Luxembourg Astra satellite and then awarding several to Rupert Murdoch).[4]

Service providers, such as independent producers, film and video companies and, importantly, the publishers of the press, have all attacked the public service monopoly (or duopoly) broadcasters and exploited the technological openings in order to gain entrance to the industry. Faced with the expansion of the audiovisual sector under the impact of the new technologies, publishing interests (e.g. Murdoch and Maxwell in Britain, Springer and Bertelsmann in West Germany) have awoken to the powerful competitive challenge to their position in the information and advertising markets. The advertisers' lobby has also been a vocal advocate of deregulation. Compared with the US and Japan, Western European broadcasting represents an undeveloped advertising market with a very dramatic growth potential (especially in West Germany where broadcast advertising restrictions have been very strict in the past). Advertisers have an additional motive: namely, that competition among broadcasters for advertising revenue will bid down the inflated costs which they have until now incurred in gaining access to public service monopoly broadcasting outlets. Equipment manufacturers have detected attractive new prospects in the development of the 'new media', including new reception and decoding equipment.[5]

Political parties, for their part, saw the 'new media' as a new opportunity to gain partisan political benefits. Thus, in both Britain and West Germany, governments (Thatcher's Conservatives in 1979; Kohl's conservative-liberal coalition in 1982), coming to power after fairly long periods in opposition, embarked upon these ambitious programmes for cable and satellite television at least in part motivated by their concern to outflank public service monopolies which they perceived as having been consistently biased against them. Perhaps more importantly, in both countries these new governments subscribed to neo-liberal programmes, advocating a drastic reduction of state intervention and regulation. They were similarly committed to the rejuvenation of their national economies by a liberation of market forces. Hence, in the broadcasting sector, both governments saw marketisation as a device to reduce the perceived bureaucratic inefficiencies and alleged financial profligacy of the monopoly/duopoly broadcasters. They also saw marketisation as a policy to establish consumer sovereignty, founded upon the belief that public-service regulation restricted the citizen's freedom of choice, a state of affairs which could no longer be justified in the new technological era of broadcasting. Therefore they sought to open up the monopoly/ duopoly structures of their respective broadcasting systems to competition and new private commercial entrants. They also believed that domestic marketisation was the only realistic response to the imperatives of increasingly internationalised and competitive broadcasting markets, the only policy consistent with gaining benefits from inward investment and shaking up lethargic domestic actors.[6]

Thus, in both countries the established policy community in the broadcasting sector has been destabilised in recent years by a combination of *convergent* forces. The issue of how to adapt to technological change provided a new opportunity for new actors to gain market entrance and provide new services; these new actors, in turn, formed policy networks with government departments (in West Germany, at both federal and state level) committed to the promotion of these new technologies and to the exploitation of their economic growth potential. After the accession to power of ideologically similar central governments, these networks were strengthened by the presence of policy makers highly sympathetic to business interests and also motivated by their own narrow party political interests in deregulation and marketisation. As the result, long-established public-service broadcasting policy communities dissolved into new and looser networks for and against marketisation.

The fact that there was no significant cross-national variation in the composition of these networks means that this, at least, can be held as a constant for the purposes of analysis. Very conveniently, both the nature of distributional coalitions and the complexion of the party-governments in the two cases can be dismissed straightaway as explanatory variables for any divergence of policy outcomes. This is not to suggest, however, that the manner of interaction within, or between, these policy networks might not vary according to different institutional factors or procedural norms shaping the policy process in each case. It is precisely to an examination of the latter variables that this chapter now turns.

FACTORS FOR DIVERGENCE

When the analytical focus switches to the policy process itself, significant *divergence* becomes apparent. During this stage, governments are prone to become embroiled in the practical politics of trade-offs between conflicting interests. Here there are essentially two questions to be addressed. To what extent have governments been compelled to adapt their earlier 'heroic' or technological/market 'rational' approaches to the more 'humdrum' exigencies of 'partisan mutual adjustment'? Secondly, how to explain this divergence? In attempting to explain this latter question, use will be made of Lijphart's (1982) distinction between 'majoritarian' and 'consensus' patterns of government. While Lijphart's distinction was intended to provide an analytical classification of types of liberal democracies, it can be usefully applied in the cause of comparative policy analysis. It is an institutionalist approach *par excellence*.[7]

The Patterns of 'Brokerage'

Britain

Traditionally, major innovations in the field of British broadcasting have resulted from a lengthy process of deliberation and elite consultation, accompanied by a limited measure of public discussion. In this respect, the field of broadcasting has followed an allegedly traditional British policy style. For example, Jordan and Richardson, writing *at the beginning* of the Thatcher period, characterised the 'dominant', or 'preferred', British policy style as reflecting ' . . . normative values, . . . to avoid electoral politics and public conflict in order to reach consensus or "accommodation" in [a] labyrinth of consultative machinery'.[8] They pointed to the 'normal' pattern as being one of 'bureaucratic accommodation': policy-making is typically 'reactive' and leads to 'institutionalised consensus. . . . The stress on negotiation . . . inhibits radical change'.[9] In similar terms, Jack Hayward, *writing in the mid-1970s*, described the British 'policy style' as 'incremental' or 'humdrum': a 'continuous process of mutual adjustment between a plurality of autonomous policy-makers operating in the context of a highly fragmented multiple flow of influence'.[10] In fact, ' . . . there is a well-developed body of literature describing the predilection for consultation and the strong desire to avoid action that might challenge well-entrenched interests' [such as, we might suggest, the 'duopoly'].[11]

Indeed, in the broadcasting sector, decisions like the introduction of commercial broadcasting (1954), BBC2 (1964) and a fourth television channel (1981) had resulted from a lengthy elite-consultative, bureaucratic and incrementalist policy-making cycle. Tunstall has pointed out that, in the television sector, typically 'policy cycles' had lasted on average twelve years and have been accompanied by Royal Commissions and independent committees to ensure a pragmatic and evolutionary approach.[12] In the 1980s, however, the Conservative government departed from this incrementalist or 'humdrum' policy style, and instead acted with uncommon boldness, or 'heroism', in order to radically reform the structures of television.

In 1981 the government established the Hunt Committee to consider the regulatory issues surrounding the introduction of cable television. In 1982, after only six weeks of opinion canvassing and deliberation, the Hunt Report was produced. Evidence and submissions had been received from a wide range of organisations and individuals. Despite the quickness, the latter point might appear to suggest a consultative policy style. However, the Hunt Report clearly adhered to a very limited agenda. Moreover, it was an uncustomarily thin document (compared with the usual weighty volumes). It had been supposed to consider the question of whether and how the existing broadcasting services were to be protected: it merely proposed a large measure of deregulation for the new sector. Again within months, it was followed by a White Paper which echoed its deregulatory message. This too indicated the government's undignified 'haste in boldly pushing through an ambitious and heroic project without any deep consideration for complex procedures of accommodation of interests or negotiation'.[13]

Moreover, the government's contempt for the incrementalist British policy style was most dramatically illustrated when, before the legislative process was more than half completed, it actually issued the first eleven cable television franchises! In 1984, there duly followed the Cable and Broadcasting Act. This legislation marked a first sharp break with the tradition of public-service broadcasting. Most notably, it established a new regulatory authority, the Cable Authority, the explicit task of which was to promote the growth of a new market-oriented sector of broadcasting by 'light touch' regulation, in other words to act both as player and referee.[14]

While these radical policies for the new media were being enacted, the campaign to reform the traditional broadcasters also gained momentum. During 1985, the licence fee became the subject of public controversy (not least as a result of editorials in Rupert Murdoch's *Times* attacking the BBC). On 27 March 1985, the government established another, strikingly small committee, this time packed with experts with various degrees of enthusiasm for liberalisation, and chaired by a leading free-market economist, Professor Alan Peacock. Its brief was to review alternative or supplementary methods of financing the BBC: in particular, the question of whether the BBC should be allowed to run advertising. In June 1986 the Peacock Committee published its report, rejecting the introduction of advertising. However, it did seriously advocate the establishment of a system of 'pay-as-you-view' (subscription/or pay TV). More importantly though, the Peacock Report made a number of other very radical recommendations, including the awarding of ITV franchises by competitive tendering ('auctioning') and the floating free of Channel Four from its ITV/IBA connection (its re-establishment as a commercial channel).[15]

Finally, in November 1988, the government produced a very radical White Paper entitled *Broadcasting in the 1990s: Competition, Choice and Quality*.[16] This document expressed the government's aims of increasing the range of services available to the consumer, introducing greatly increased competition into broadcasting and increasing the 'efficiency' of broadcasting operators. The White Paper caused very considerable controversy, yet once again within a very short period its recommendations were adopted more or less in their entirety in a Broadcasting Bill, which began its passage through Parliament in the autumn of the following year.

Despite extensive amendment of the 'small print' at the committee stage, the broad thrust of the Bill remains very radical. Competition is to be greatly increased by several main instruments. Following the recommendation of the free market-oriented Peacock Committee, the ITV franchises, now called Channel Three, are to be allocated in future as the result of competitive bidding (blind bids), albeit after the applicants satisfied a notional, but largely unspecified, 'quality threshhold'. 'Quality' considerations might allow for lower bids to be accepted, but exactly how this will work remains unclear. The franchises are to be awarded and supervised by a new 'light touch' regulatory body, to be called the Independent Television Commission (ITC) which will replace the IBA and the Cable Authority. Significantly, there will no longer be any barriers to take-overs, albeit after two years has elapsed, between franchise rounds. There are only fairly liberal limits on cross-ownership between the press and broadcasting. Moreover, it looks very likely that Rupert Murdoch's Sky Television services will escape such restrictions by dint of their being broadcast from the Luxembourg-based Astra satellite. Also following the recommendations of the Peacock Report, Channel Four is to be floated free of the ITV companies to sell its own airtime, although it is intended that it retain its public-service remit to provide minority interest programming. However, it is difficult to see precisely how this expectation might be fulfilled when the company has to survive in open competition and is no longer protected by its former cosy relationship with the ITV/IBA nexus. Moreover, competition will be further increased by the introduction of a fifth national commercial channel, called Channel Five (with the later possibility of a sixth channel) and the open supply of satellite television. The Bill also contains provision for the deregulation and expansion of independent radio, under the light touch regulation of a new Radio Authority. Finally, competition is to be promoted by the privatisation of the IBA's transmission function.

Although these measures will mainly have the effect of truly 'marketising' all services apart from the BBC, the latter organisation certainly does not emerge unscathed. It will continue to be funded by the licence fee in the short term, probably until its present Charter expires in 1996. However, the indexing of its licence fee to the retail price index is set to end in April 1991. Since broadcasting costs rise significantly faster than the general rate of inflation, this latter measure can be expected to increase still further the financial squeeze which the BBC has been suffering for some years now. Another significant change, originally signalled by the White Paper, is the government's intention to give all television services, 'including those of the BBC', freedom to raise finance through subscription and sponsorship. Moreover, the White Paper stated ominously that the Government 'looks forward to the eventual replacement of the licence fee'.[17] In one important respect alone does the government appear to place a continuing high premium on regulation. The Broadcasting Bill gives a legislative basis to the Broadcasting Standards Council (already actually established in 1987) with the duty of reinforcing standards on 'taste and decency and the portrayal of sex and violence' (about which nearly all agree).

In short, the policy cycle has been very short and intense and characterised by a marked absence of unprejudiced consultation and brokerage between concerned interests.

West Germany

As in the pre-Thatcher literature about the British policy style, policy analysts of West German public policy have stressed the typically consensual style of German policy-making. Analysts have pointed to such factors as: the German political parties' non-ideological nature and their hugging of the middle ground; a traditional German inclination towards the depoliticisation of potentially conflictual questions (i.e. the preference for consensus-building, which is partly a reaction against the doctrinal politics of the Weimar Republic); and, as Dyson has stressed, a notionally 'Germanic' respect for 'rationality' (*Sachlichkeit*) in policy-making.[18] Katzenstein, too, has emphasised the essential 'incrementalist rationality' of the German policy style. However, the latter explains it in terms of institutional factors, such as the need for mutual accommodation arising from a federal system; and the important role of parapublic institutions (eg. the 'corporatistic' style of broadcasting regulation by representatives of the 'socially significant groups').[19] Others have stressed the important role of law in politics and the need to conform to constitutional and legal provisions. To a significant degree these reflect an institutionalised normative commitment to 'public-service' principles, formalised in the idea of the *Sozialstaat* (a state whose goals are social justice, representation and pluralism).[20]

Indeed, broadcasting is an excellent example of a policy sector which has hitherto functioned well due to an institutionalised consensus, which arose from co-operative federalism and was bounded by constitutional-legalism, notably several key interventions of the Federal Constitutional Court during the post-war period which have underpinned the public-service monopoly nature of the post-war broadcasting system (in the face of earlier attempts to introduce commercial television).[21]

However, the recent debate about the 'new media' and the future of broadcasting led to a near-collapse of cooperative federalism and, as a result, produced a grave and for a long time seemingly intractable policy deadlock. This arose because, in West Germany's federal system, it is the *Länder* which are assigned exclusive responsibility for media policy. In order to gain a regulatory framework for the new media, the FRG therefore had to wait for the CDU/CSU- and SPD-controlled *Länder* governments to agree amongst themselves. However, due to political polarisation over the issues of the 'new media' and the future of public-service broadcasting, the *Länder* were unable to agree. As a result, a degree of uncertainty was created for the German media and electronics sectors. In contrast with Britain, the whole policy process for the introduction of the 'new media' both began significantly earlier and has been a very lengthy, indeed laborious, affair that bears all the features of a characteristically bargained and incrementalist process and outcome.

During the social-liberal (SPD-FDP) government between 1969–82, the important economic and industrial stakes consequent upon the technological changes affecting telecommunications and broadcasting were becoming increasingly apparent to policy makers. In accordance with the German 'policy style', the SPD-FDP government established as early as 1974 a corporatistically composed government expert commission (the first of several) to look into the policy implications. Reflecting a characteristic concern to maintain a consensus among its fairly diverse members (compare with the Peacock Committee), the commission very cautiously recommended the establishment of four pilot projects to experiment with the applications of cable, in particular cable television. However, as suggested, in Germany broadcasting policy is the legal jurisdiction of the *Länder*. The SPD *Länder*, following national party policy, were against any deregulation and liberalisation of the 'public-service monopoly' of broadcasting. They feared that cable television would be the 'hole in the dyke' for the introduction of private commercial broadcasting. Therefore, during the period of the SPD-FDP government there was no general programme for the cabling of Germany – in fact, there occurred what the then conservative opposition called a 'cable blockade'.

Unlike broadcasting, telecommunications was a federal jurisdiction. Yet so long as the SPD-led Bonn government remained in power, and therefore also in control of the telecommunications ministry (the Bundespost Ministry), it was able to limit cabling to the four cable pilot-projects suggested by the government commission. These experiments took place against a background of mounting political polarisation over the new media and the future of broadcasting. Local electoral victories enabled the conservative parties to preside over no fewer than three of the four pilot-projects, and they used them to introduce a new 'market-model' of broadcasting at least at the local level. However, although this gave an important foothold to the policy network pushing for marketisation, the established public-service broadcasting policy community remained largely intact and indeed dominant during this period of SPD rule in Bonn.

In 1982, however, the SPD-FDP coalition was suddenly replaced by a conservative-liberal coalition (CDU/CSU/FDP) in Bonn. The new government determined to use the 'new media' as the instrument for achieving its aforementioned goal of a radical deregulation and commercialisation of the entire broadcasting sector. Despite the fact that broadcasting regulation lay beyond the competence of central government, the decisive new factor was the entrance of the Bundespost into the established policy community. The Bundespost, now controlled by the CDU, could exert a wholly new measure of political leverage by virtue of its command of the new technological resources. Accordingly, in 1983 it launched a massive national cable plan, financed to the tune of DM one billion per annum rising in 1986 to one-and-a-half billion. It also rented a number of satellite broadcasting channels on ECS and Intelsat communications satellites to feed the cable networks, and accelerated West Germany's own satellite construction programme. Pressure was now put on SPD *Länder* to enact deregulatory broadcasting laws to permit private commercial broadcasting. In this latter goal, the CDU/CSU were able to use Bundespost investment as a potent instrument of political blackmail.

With the Bundespost now playing a key role, the policy network pushing for marketisation could at last seize the initiative. The CDU/CSU *Länder* quickly drew on the technological resources released by the Bundespost to expand their cable systems, sponsored various commercial broadcasting operations, including several new satellite channels, and introduced their own deregulatory broadcasting laws to break the public-service monopoly. Generally, the new CDU/CSU laws adopted the principle that, since pluralism would be likely to be achieved quasi-automatically by virtue of the simple multiplication of channels, there would be no longer any need for stringent public-service regulation. At this point, however, the remnants of the former public-service broadcasting community (better described now as a competing network) were able to mount a spirited defensive operation. In this, they were able to draw upon resources derived from the nature of the West German political system (and of a kind which were simply unavailable in the British case).

Committed to maintain public-service safeguards, the SPD parliamentary party in Bonn now took a specimen deregulatory law by a CDU-governed *Land* (Lower Saxony) to the Federal Constitutional Court (*Bundesverfassungsgericht*) in Karlsruhe, complaining that the law did not fully respect the public-service commitments enshrined in previous broadcasting laws (and derived from earlier Court rulings). In taking this step, the SPD was exploiting a characteristic avenue of oppositional behaviour in the West German political system, namely legalistic opposition – the 'well-trodden road to Karlsruhe'.[22]

Another resource was the federal system, more particularly the Conference of Prime Ministers of the *Länder* (the *Ministerpräsidentenkonferenz*).

While the Court was involved in its lengthy deliberations, the policy process became bogged down by the need for laborious negotiations between the prime ministers (*Ministerpräsidenten*) of the *Länder*. The reason was quite simply that the passage of the customary individual broadcasting laws by the *Länder* was no longer a sufficient basis for a regulatory framework for broadcasting in the age of satellite television. Since by its very nature satellite television, especially DBS, amounted to 'national' broadcasting in that it could be received by the whole country, franchising and regulatory decisions made in individual *Länder* would necessarily have a national impact. Therefore, the *Ministerpräsidenten*, including those of the SPD, were faced with the increasingly urgent necessity of making some collective decisions about the entire national broadcasting system.[23]

In order to arrive at an arrangement for such matters that commonly affected all *Länder* alike, the traditional practice of West German broadcasting policy making suggested that negotiation of an inter-state treaty on broadcasting (a *Staatsvertrag*) would be necessary. Such a process, however, implied a degree of consensus among the *Ministerpräsidenten*. At first, in view of the polarised debate between the parties and interest groups the basis for such a consensus did not appear to exist. The alternative, however, was the possible imminent disintegration of the Federal Republic's broadcasting landscape. As one West German broadcaster put it, the country could easily face a situation resembling a '. . . mosaic of individual media territories, a truly paradoxical situation in the day and age of satellites'.[24]

The negotiations were hard and bitter. In order to blackmail the SPD *Ministerpräsidenten*, the CDU/CSU *Ministerpräsidenten* threatened to go so far as to withdraw their support for the ARD (the public-service broadcasting sector). They also hinted darkly that SPD intransigence would meet with their refusal to support the raising of the television licence-fee, upon which the public-service broadcasters depended, when it next came up for renegotiation. For their part, the SPD *Länder* were inclined to deny access to satellite channels sponsored by the CDU/CSU *Länder*. Since much of the population lived in SPD-controlled *Länder*, this was a potent counter-threat. In short, over the period 1983–86, agreement was repeatedly blocked by the obdurate refusal of one party or another to compromise. The established broadcasting policy community had apparently dissolved into two competing networks – one pro-market, the other pro-public-service – but, unlike Britain, each seemed to command enough resources to neutralise the other.

The Federal Constitutional Court came to the rescue when, in 1986, it made a historic ruling as a result of having considered the SPD complaint against the Lower Saxony law. The Court did not merely rule against certain features of this single law, thereby upholding the SPD's most serious reservations about CDU/CSU deregulation. It went much further: it established a number of parameters within which deregulation had to be constrained. In fact, it suggested that a 'dual broadcasting system' should be established. This would involve a private commercial sector benefiting from a significant measure of deregulation. At the same time, it established important guarantees for the future of the 'public-service' sector, including a firm commitment to the licence fee and its periodic revision to ensure adequate financing for the public-service sector. Moreover, it placed some significant public-service obligations on the new private commercial sector, confirming the principle of corporatistic regulation by the 'socially significant groups', albeit within a new looser framework than had applied to the public-service broadcasters. This authoritative ruling broke the two-year old policy deadlock between the *Ministerpräsidenten* of the *Länder*. In 1987 the combined SPD and CDU/CSU *Ministerpräsidenten* were able to produce an agreed *Staatsvertrag* for the future of the West German broadcasting system more or less exactly along the lines of the 'dual model' suggested by the Constitutional Court.[25]

Thus, the policy outcome was a classic West German compromise solution. In stark contrast to the British case, broadcasting reform in West Germany can, therefore, be seen as both incremental and moderate. Public-service broadcasting has an assured future in West Germany. What has happened is that a regulated private commercial sector has at last been introduced, some thirty years after the same occurred in Britain.

The importance of the institutional factor

How, then, are we to interpret the preceding empirical examination of the policy process? There were, after all, very powerful convergent pressures at work in the broadcasting sector in each case. The combination of technological, market and ideological pressures for marketisation were commonly experienced. Moreover, the configurations of policy communities and networks were so similar as to reinforce the expectation of convergence. However, to leave the matter here would be to disregard an important element of analysis. The *dynamics* of policy networks depend on the *resources* possessed and exchanged by the different members of those networks.[26] The latter depend, in turn, on 'rules of the game', involving informal and formal procedural norms and organisational factors which set constraints on the actors' discretionary behaviour. Now it can be argued that the 'rules of the game' are themselves dependent, to an important extent, upon the institutional framework within which they operate. Indeed, it has become very clear that, in the broadcasting sector at least, the different regime characteristics of the British and West German political systems have produced a considerable variation of degree of constraint on the policy process.

Different institutional frameworks are rooted in very different historical experiences. Like the political system in which it is embedded, British television's regulatory arrangements could be said to have been fashioned by Britain's 'liberal establishment'. Historically speaking, the evolution of British television reflected the unbroken – liberal and democratic – relationship between government, national traditions and Britain's political culture. With one or two notable exceptions (e.g. the General Strike of 1926; or Suez in 1956), there had never been any serious question of the state capturing broadcasting. Indeed, a 'gentleman's agreement' had been established in the early days of British broadcasting about the independent, public-service nature of the system.

By contrast, in Germany, the impact of the historical/cultural factor is stark. The wholesale capture and misuse of broadcasting by the National Socialists during the Third Reich had served to underpin the need for much stricter and very much more formalised democratic safeguards than had ever been required in the British case. Accordingly, the formative years of the post-dictatorship broadcasting system had been dominated by a common concern among elites, of all persuasions, to secure it as a force for democracy. Unsurprisingly, against the background of this historic conjuncture, both the Allied occupiers and the early post-war German elites considered 'gentleman's agreement', 'elite consensus' and liberal political culture (notably absent) to be exceedingly inadequate guarantees for the public-service model which they held, at that time, to be a necessary innovation to ensure the democratic functioning of the reestablished broadcasting system. Indeed, in the West German case, the new regulations and structures of television reflected a powerful normative constitutional imperative to actively regulate for pluralism, balance and diversity in broadcasting. As with the political system more widely, in the West German case the historical lesson was the need for reliance on firm institutional and constitutional safeguards.[27]

Quite evidently, in Britain recent broadcasting policy-making has been influenced by that country's variant of what Lijphart has called the 'majoritarian' model of democracy.[28] Most notably, the concentration and dominance of executive power, the absence of constraints on the latter which would flow from federalism and a strong system of judicial review, and the reliance upon convention ('gentleman's agreement') rather than a written constitution, have all combined to present the opportunity to a radical political executive, based on a decisive parliamentary majority, to carry through a radical package of regulatory reform with very little effective opposition – notwithstanding the country's traditional 'consensual' policy style. By contrast, within the West German political system there exist important countervailing powers to the will of the political executive. The checks and balances of its more 'consensual' model of democracy[29] have prevented the radical reformers from carrying through such a wholesale deregulation and marketisation of West German television.

Firstly, the Federal Constitutional Court: the 'guardian of the Constitution' has ensured that a manifestly incremental and cautious deregulatory approach has been taken to the introduction of a new private commercial broadcasting sector. Secondly, the federal nature of the political system has meant that policy-making, for instance within the *Ministerpräsidentenkonferenz*, has had to respect the principle of cooperative federalism, another important factor for an incrementalist approach. Drawing upon these political resources, the SPD policy makers were able to achieve a very significant measure of success in establishing important guarantees for the future of the public-service broadcasting sector. Thirdly, the institutional norm of consensus had been operative right from the outset of the policy process, as indicated by the respect for corporatistic representation in the commission which began policy formulation, and indeed the latter's recommendation of preliminary pilot-projects rather than (as in the British case) a voluntaristic launch into a cable programme.

Hence, the public-service broadcasters have been able to face the future of a more competitive television system with increasing confidence about their guaranteed role within it. Most illustratively, unlike in Britain, there has been no question of the abolition of the television licence fee that underpins the public-service mode of operation. The greatest irony of all is that West Germany inherits the duopoly model, while Britain, whose public-service television system provided so much inspiration for the West Germans during the occupation and early post-war years, would appear to be racing towards a fully-blown American-style commercial model of television, and might well end up with a rump and increasingly 'ghetto-ised' public-service.

These case studies have demonstrated that political structures are of primary importance in explaining why convergent pressures towards deregulation and marketisation have produced significantly divergent policy processes and outcomes. The distinct institutional characteristics of the two political systems have provided the respective policy actors with very different political resources and scope for manoeuvre. In short, institutional variance has defined very different boundaries of public action. This would seem to suggest that a focus on institutions should stand at the very centre of comparative policy analysis. In so much as the policy process, even at the sectoral and sub-sectoral (issue-specific) levels, cannot remain unaffected by the nature of the 'macro' political system, the dynamics of interaction between policy communities and networks have to be examined in these terms.

Moreover, in the words of a leading 'new institutionalist', namely Peter Hall,[30] different 'complexes of institutions' and 'routines and rationalities' depend very much upon 'historical conjunctures'. This, the chapter has suggested, is clearly an important factor in explaining significant institutional variation of the two cases of broadcasting sector examined. Indeed, the West German case clearly points to the important effect of 'traumatic historical experiences and processes of learning from political catastrophes . . . on the institutional apparatus and on the timing and substance of public policy'.[31]

NOTES

1. K. Dyson and P. Humphreys, *Broadcasting and New Media Policies in Western Europe* (London: Routledge, 1988).
2. K. Dyson and P. Humphreys, 'Deregulating Broadcasting: the West European Experience', *European Journal of Political Research*, 17 (1989) 137–54.
3. See, for example, W. Hoffmann-Riem, 'New Media in West Germany: the Politics of Legitimation', in K. Dyson and P. Humphreys, *The*

Political Economy of Communications (London: Routledge 1990) pp. 171–97.

4. Dyson and Humphreys. *Broadcasting and New Media Policies*.
5. Ibid.
6. Ibid.
7. A. Lijphart, *Democracies: Patterns of Majoritarian and Consensus Government in Twenty-One Countries* (New Haven, Conn. and London: Yale University Press, 1984).
8. G. Jordan and J. Richardson, 'The British Policy Style or the Logic of Negotiation', in J. Richardson (ed.), *Policy Styles in Western Europe* (London: Allen and Unwin, 1982), pp. 80–110.
9. Ibid., p. 80–1.
10. J. Hayward, 'National Aptitudes for Planning in Britain, France and Italy', *Government and Opposition*, 9, 4 (1974) 397–410, 398–9.
11. J. Richardson et al, 'The Concept of Policy Style', in J. Richardson, *Policy Styles in Western Europe*, p. 1.
12. J. Tunstall, 'Media Policy Dilemmas and Indecisions', *Parliamentary Affairs*, 37, 3 (1984) 310.
13. J. Dyson and P. Humphreys, 'The New Media in Britain and France', *Rundfunk und Fernsehen*, 33:3–4 (1985) 366.
14. Ibid.; also, *Cable and Broadcasting Act*, London: HMSO, 1984.
15. R. Negrine, 'British Television in an Age of Change', in Dyson and Humphreys, *The Political Economy of Communications*, pp. 148–170, p. 156.
16. Ibid., pp. 157–8.
17. More recent statements made by ministers would seem to confirm this intention. Moreover, Alan Peacock has recently reaffirmed his views on this matter.
18. K. Dyson, 'West Germany: the Search for a Rationalist Consensus', in Richardson, *Policy Styles in Western Europe*, pp. 17–46.
19. P. Katzenstein, *Policy and Politics in West Germany. The Growth of a Semi-Sovereign State* (Philadelphia: Temple University Press, 1987).
20. For example, S. Bulmer and P. Humphreys, 'Kohl, Corporatism and Congruence: the West German Model under Challenge', the 'Conclusion' in Bulmer, *The Changing Agenda of West German Public Policy* (Aldershot: Gower) pp. 177–97, p. 193.
21. P. Humphreys, *Media and Media Policy in West Germany* (Oxford: Berg, 1990) ch. 4, pp. 155–92.
22. G. Smith, *Democracy in West Germany* (London: Heinemann, 1979), p. 190.
23. Humphreys, *Media and Media Policy in West Germany*, pp. 257–8.
24. W. Konrad quoted in ibid., p. 258.
25. Ibid., pp. 270–80. For the Court's ruling see: 'Urteil des Bundesverfassungsgerichts vom 4. November 1986 – IBvF 1/1984', *Media Perspektiven Dokumentation*, IV/1986, pp. 213–47. An evaluation of this law, in English, is contained in K. Berg, 'The Fourth TV Judgement of the Federal Constitutional Court', *EBU Review*, 38, 3 (May 1987) 37–43. For the inter-state treaty see: 'Staatsvertrag zur Neuordnung des Rundfunkwesens vom 12. März 1987', *Media Perspektiven. Dokumentation*, 2 (1987) 81–8. For a very useful discussion of this treaty, in English, see:

K. Berg, 'The Inter-State Treaty on the Reform of the Broadcasting System in the FRG', *EBU Review*, 39, 2 (March 1988) 40–9.

26. S. Wilks and M. Wright, 'Policy Community, Policy Network and Comparative Industrial Policies', the 'Conclusion' in S. Wilks and M. Wright (eds), *Comparative Government-Industry Relations; Western Europe, the United States and Japan* (Oxford: Clarendon Press, 1987), pp. 274–313; and M. Wright, 'Policy Community, Policy Network and Comparative Industrial Policies', *Political Studies*, 36 (1988) 593–612.

27. Humphreys, *Media and Media Policy in West Germany*, ch. 3 pp. 124–54.

28. Lijphart, *Democracies*.

29. Ibid.

30. P. Hall, *Governing the Economy: the Politics of State Intervention in Britain and France* (Cambridge: Polity Press, 1986), pp. 8–9.

31. M. Schmidt, 'Learning from Catastrophes: West Germany's Public Policy', in F. Castles, *The Comparative History of Public Policy*, (Cambridge: Polity Press, 1989) pp. 56–99, p. 90.

12 The State and the World Steel Market: Industrial Policy, Trade Regulation and the GATT Uruguay Round[1]

Martin Rhodes

On 27 July 1989, President Bush fulfilled a hastily-made campaign promise and approved a renewal, for two and a half years, of the protectionist system of 'voluntary restraint agreements' (VRAs) which had sheltered the US steel industry since the early 1980s. He had little choice: despite the predominance of free trade sentiments within his own administration, and regardless of a revival in the fortunes of the steel sector, the proponents of an aggressive, 'strategic trade policy' were in the ascendant.

In steel, a powerful coalition spanning the large integrated steel companies, their smaller 'mini-mill' counterparts, the United Steelworkers union and the influential 150-member Congressional 'steel caucus', was calling in unison for further import restrictions. In the background, US trade policy was being shaped by a strongly protectionist Congress. 1988 saw the passage of the Omnibus Trade and Competitiveness Act (known to some as the 'Ominous Trade Act'[2]) which legitimised a greater unilateral definition of US trading rights. The following year saw some of its principles put into practice: the deployment of the Act's so-called 'Super-301' provisions (which have recently allowed Japan, Brazil and India to be castigated as 'unfair traders') and the attack on Japan under the Structural Impediments Initiative (SSI). Both contravened the multilateral spirit of the General Agreement on Tariffs and Trade (GATT).

By mid-January 1990, Carla Hills, the US Trade Representative in President Bush's cabinet, was congratulating herself on the successful conclusion of bilateral steel pacts with the largest importers into the US market, the European Community (EC), Japan, South Korea,

Brazil and Mexico. All had subscribed to a new 'consensus' on government support: in return for continued access to the US market under VRAs until March 1992, and the promised return to free trade from that date, they agreed to phase out subsidies and liberalise their own domestic markets.

The significance of the steel pacts is twofold. In policy terms, they represented a triple triumph for Carla Hills and the Bush Administration. The form of the VRA renewal itself enshrined an artful compromise between the more extreme demands of the steel lobby (ranging from calls for a five-year VRA extension to proposals for a more draconian replacement, involving binding agreements and financial damages against violators) and the free trade lobby of domestic steel consumers and foreign exporters. Second, the terms of the 'steel consensus' represented the first successful attempt during the Uruguay Round of GATT negotiations to use the US market as leverage in changing the domestic policies of foreign states. But they were also something of a diplomatic victory. For while the bilateral pacts would allow the US to act both as judge and jury in defining 'trade distorting practices', the multilateral rhetoric of the so-called 'consensus' would help to mask this fact and, with any luck, placate both its trading partners and the GATT secretariat.[3]

In terms of the wider debate on trade regulation, and the role of states in international markets, the steel case has much wider implications. Alongside certain other major sectors such as textiles and agriculture, steel is not subject specifically to a code within GATT. But current US attempts to create a 'level playing field' in the steel market bear directly on the central issue of the Uruguay Round – how best to avert unilateral regulation and reduce the global level of protection through negotiated, multilateral, adjustment. For these reasons, steel provides a litmus test of current US trade policy. It is also an illuminating case study of comparative industrial policy and protection since these are the targets of current US actions. The following discussion begins with a comparison, examining steel market management in the US, the EC and Japan. The impact of market management on competitiveness is assessed; the steel pacts are then examined in detail, and their implications for international trade assessed. In conclusion, the broader strategic agenda of US trade policy is considered.

MARKET MANAGEMENT AND THE STATE

Free markets have been likened to infinity: they can be approached, but they can never be reached. To extend the analogy, steel markets have rarely gone much beyond zero. For the history of steel is also one of cartels, market management, and massive state intervention. Why? First, there is its almost natural proclivity for protection. It is a high-risk industry. Steel works have always been expensive to build and operate, and in the twentieth century set-up costs have soared in line with the achievement of higher economies of scale, boosting the minimum size of efficient operation. All this makes profits sensitive to even marginal fluctuations in demand. Protection and cartels have been the natural, defensive, response.

Then there is the state. In the developed world, steel has always had a close, if not always productive, relationship with governments. It has always been central to industrial growth and weapons manufacture, and therefore of key strategic importance. It has also been a major employer. Thus, whether under private or public control, steel has bequeathed political power, even after its economic heyday. In the newly industrialised countries (NICs), steel has typically been given 'infant industry' treatment, initially to help provide for infrastructure and import-substitution, and then, in the most ambitious and competitive NICs, to make the first forays into lucrative foreign markets.

Nevertheless, while subsidies were rife, and non-tariff barriers extensive, steel trade was fairly free until the late 1960s. Since then, domestic production and international trade have become highly politicised. For the US and the European Community, a number of factors made protection irresistible: the recessionary impact of the twin oil shocks in the early 1970s, the declining importance of manufacturing in the OECD economies, and the spread of lighter, more sophisticated substitutes for steel across a wide range of products. To this was added a new competitive challenge, first from Japan (which became the largest exporting nation after 1965) and then from the NIC newcomers – the South Koreans, the Brazilians and more recently the Taiwanese. In the face of attack, the most attractive strategy was retreat, behind a steadily rising protectionist wall. For producers and politicians, the imperative was clear: to create 'competitive breathing space' for their steel firms. In the process, the architecture of protection became increasingly complex. By the 1980s, it covered the greater part of the global steel market.

The United States: the protected market

The decline, both relative and absolute, of the US steel industry has been precipitous. In the early 1950s it was still the largest producer, accounting for around half of total world output; by 1960, it produced only a quarter, by 1989 just a tenth. By the mid-1980s, output was only slightly higher than thirty years before. A massive steel strike in 1956 made it a net importer for the first time, and it has remained one ever since: by 1979, its net trade balance was 16.8 million tonnes in the red; by 1987 it was 22.2.[4] But while heavily protected since the mid-1970s, state intervention has been slight. And while there is some dispute over the level of subsidies, the US steel industry, to its constant irritation, has almost certainly received less public funding than its European counterparts.[5]

But it *has* been cocooned by a cosy set of import restrictions, and these have provided significant rents from uncompetitive pricing. The first of these were adopted in the form of VRAs in the late 1960s to stem a rising tide of imports from Europe and Japan. Their most important effect was to increase prices for US consumers. These rises, in turn, were used to boost the levels of profit and dividends rather than productivity, thus postponing essential structural change. This was to set the pattern for subsequent episodes. Thus, when the initial VRAs were replaced in 1977 by a new protectionist weapon – the 'trigger price mechanism' (TPM) under which imports below a reference price would attract anti-dumping proceedings – an inflexible and legally enforceable minimum price floor was created which further sheltered US firms from foreign competition.

By 1979, the retarded state of US steel was clear. While US investment was amongst the highest in the world, much of it was spent unproductively on outmoded plant and equipment. Measured against international best practice, much American plant was obsolete. As a result, productivity, at 210 tonnes per employee year, compared poorly with the 300 tonnes achieved in Japan, although more favourably against a 180-tonne EC average.[6] But any productivity advantage over the Europeans was cancelled out by manpower costs: due to the so-called 'steel premium' – sustained by the United Steelworkers of America – salaries in the early 1980s were double the US manufacturing average. And even when they fell in US terms after 1982 (to about 60 per cent above the average), hourly labour costs were still twice those in Japan and West Germany.[7]

By 1982, and despite the TPM, foreign producers held some 20 per cent of a depressed US market. By 1984 this had risen to over a quarter. The industry was operating at below 50 per cent capacity and some 100,000 workers had been placed on indefinite lay off.[8] High interest rates and an overvalued US dollar hardly helped. Calls for greater protection from the steel lobby were growing louder, and a succession of countervailing duty (CVD) and anti-dumping suits were filed against foreign producers. The Congressional steel caucus demanded quotas limiting imports to 10 per cent of domestic consumption, and the Department of Commerce accused EC governments of exporting unfairly subsidised products.

Although a trade war over this dispute was eventually averted at the end of 1982 under further pressure from the steel lobby, the TPM was replaced by a succession of bilaterally negotiated VRAs. These were justified by the industrial support policies of European, Japanese and NIC governments which were accused of heavily subsidising exports and thus engaging in 'unfair trade' – a notion defined, in the absence of a GATT code for the sector, by the United States itself. At the end of 1984, the Reagan administration made a further concession to the lobby, agreeing to cut back steel imports to 18.5 per cent of the US market through VRAs with thirty-one countries. The US steel industry had achieved what it had always wanted – a wall of quantitative import restrictions.[9]

The European Community: the cartelised market

In Western Europe, steel markets have been managed more often than not. In the late nineteenth and early twentieth centuries, regional production and price cartels gradually took national form, giving rise to the German *Stahlwerksverband* (1904) and the French *Comptoir sidérurgique* (1919). The first European-wide cartel emerged as the International Steel Cartel in 1926, involving Belgium, Luxemburg, Germany, the Saar and France. Thus, the European Coal and Steel Community (ECSC), created in 1951 by the Treaty of Paris, had a noble lineage: for while it was inspired primarily by Robert Schuman's ideals of Franco-German reconciliation, European integration, and the liberalisation of internal trade, it was also, in its less prosaic aspects, a form of cartel.

Reflecting the ethos of 1950s French planning, it sought to stabilise the market through a price fixing mechanism known as the 'basing point system' (BPS), the effect of which was 'to create a market "transparency" which encourages explicit or implicit collusion among firms, each firm undertaking to publish its basic factory price as well as its delivery charges throughout the market area in question'.[10] Allowing a geographical division of the market, and helping sustain a long-standing tradition of collusion, the BPS, combined with state support in most ECSC countries, created a 'privileged zone of growth for each national steel industry'.[11] This, in turn, helped produce national oligopolies from the myriad of competing firms which still existed in the early 1950s.

But the Treaty of Paris also contained more explicit cartel provisions in the form of 'imminent' and 'manifest' crisis measures, to be invoked in the event of a market collapse. European producers – who were also being out-competed when demand was weak in the mid-1970s – were initially pushed towards protectionism by US developments: fearing a diversion of exports to Europe from the newly protected US market, the EC negotiated its own VRA with the Japanese. The first major steps towards market management were taken in 1976 when appeals for export restraint were made to suppliers of steel to the Community. But intervention began in earnest after Etienne Davignon became EC Industry Commissioner in 1977; over the next three years, a European cartel was constructed, with Eurofer – the new EC lobby of large, integrated steel producers – playing a central coordinating role.

Until 1980, the cartel was a voluntary one which, based on minimum prices and production quotas, sought to prevent a price war. To minimise the competitive threat from abroad, import licenses and anti-dumping penalties (on products sold at prices below set levels) were introduced, operating along similar lines to the US TPM, and exerting a similar upward influence on prices. Annual VRAs – fixing both quantity and price – were concluded with some fifteen exporters to the EC as of 1 January 1978 and renewed each year. But in 1980, this voluntary cartel collapsed under the weight of the second oil price shock and the threat of US anti-dumping duties on European exports. It was replaced by a mandatory cartel based on the interventionist powers given by the Treaty of Paris by the High Authority of the ECSC. In October 1980, the Treaty's so-called 'manifest crisis' measures were introduced, fixing mandatory minimum prices and production quotas for all EC producers. To diminish surplus capacity, these were linked to a ban on subsidies (unless linked to restructuring) from 1981 and a parallel programme of production cuts. All state aid was to be terminated in 1985, by when the steel firms were expected to 'regain their competitive breath'.[12]

Dismantling the cartel began on schedule. But the process was delayed by disputes. There was still substantial surplus capacity in the European industry, but little agreement on either where, or how, it should be cut. Nor, given the still depressed market in the middle of the decade, was there a consensus on the cartel's termination: while the fitter companies (the British, Germans and Dutch) were bullish about the future, and able to stay afloat unaided, the rest – including the heavily indebted French and Italians – were afraid of sinking in the stormy seas of the steel market. The result was several years of inertia. It was not until mid-1988 that, in the midst of a boom in steel demand, the Commission could finally conclude the cartel. But quotas on imports stayed in place.

Japan: the administered market

In Japan, state intervention and market management in steel have a long and honourable history. This began in the 1920s and 1930s with a successful policy of import substitution and export promotion. The industry benefited from several types of government support including tariffs, tax exemptions for steel producers, subsidies for the production of steel for ship-building, the toleration of cartels and a growth strategy led by the state-owned firm Yawata.[13]

After 1945, this tradition continued as an archetypal case of 'administrative guidance'. Organised around horizontal, intra-industry cartels (of the type forbidden by US anti-trust law), steel was targetted by MITI (the Ministry of International Trade and Industry) as a key sector of growth. It had infant industry protection until the mid-1960s, and in the immediate postwar period, the government Reconstruction Finance Bank provided most of the capital for expansion. Subsequently the government encouraged public sector banks and private financial institutions to assume this role. MITI also designed ways of protecting the industry from the dangers of over-capacity and helped coordinate a system of new capacity allocation based on each companies' demonstrated efficiency: only the most productive were allowed to expand production or build new plant.[14]

When MITI withdrew after the mid-1960s, voluntary self-regulation continued. However, MITI still calculates future demand and communicates generally respected production objectives to the largest firms in the sector. It also coordinates a system of price formation in consultation with producers and the major user companies. Steel distribution control is exercised by trading companies (*Sogo Shosha*), the nine most important of which controlled 57 per cent of the sector's sales in 1980. Since 1971, collaboration between steel producers, MITI and the *Sogo Shosha* has been institutionalised through the Steel Distribution Problem Conference, which monitors comsumption and arranges the distribution of sales among members. This type of domestic market control has been the target of the recent US Structural Impediments Initiative and of attempts to lever open the Japanese market through the new bilateral steel pacts (see below): its success in cementing 'relational contracts' between suppliers and clients is revealed by the fact that in 1986, foreign steel represented only 4.6 per cent of domestic demand, despite the fact that certain foreign products were as much as 25 per cent cheaper than their Japanese counterparts, due to the strength at that stage of the yen.[15]

Combined with high gearing (high debt/equity ratios), low interest rates, collaborative trade unions, and the flexibility of the Japanese labour market,[16] 'administrative guidance' – and its essential corollary, a 'collective' form of entrepreneurialism, linked to inter-firm coordination – have been of critical importance for the Japanese steel groups: creating an extraordinary capacity for scrapping and replacing old plant, it has allowed them to avoid the enormous sunken capital costs incurred by their EC and US counterparts when, from the late 1960s, they became locked into obsolete technology, traditional product markets and poorly located plants. Between 1966 and 1972, the Japanese increased their assets by over 23 per cent a year – compared with only 4 per cent for the US – and funded 91 per cent of this growth from debt, incurring a marginal debt-to-equity ratio of almost 11 to 1.[17] It was in this period that the Japanese overtook both US and EC producers in terms of efficiency and costs, while also importing all raw materials, and spending more on pollution control and work conditions.[18] More recently, the availability of cheap capital in Japan has helped its steel giants invest in, and embark on joint ventures with capital-hungry US companies.[19]

While more discreet in its activities than in the past, MITI has recently been involved in promoting the smaller Japanese mini-mill firms.[20] As in the case of their larger, integrated counterparts, a MITI-orchestrated rationalisation plan over the last decade has trimmed excess capacity and improved efficiency. MITI has also helped set up a system of market management. In the late 1980s, mini-mills were aggressively producing to maintain individual market shares, prompting oversupply and pricefalls. Since 1989, to keep supply tight, the mills have engaged in 'voluntary' production cuts of between 5 and 10 per cent and a loose cartel has stabilised market volatility.[21]

THE RESULTS OF MARKET MANAGEMENT

Japan

Japan provides the benchmark against which other systems of market management must be judged. Of course, the rapid expansion of Japanese steel after the war owed much to the growth characteristics of the Japanese economy, which, throughout the 1950s and 1960s, experienced an increase in demand for steel products above that of national income. The same level of demand, and therefore of profits, could not be guaranteed in the West. Yet the Japanese have recently faced the same problems as their Western counterparts: shifts in the nature of demand, a decline in the growth of consumption, and a challenge from lower-cost producers. But their capacity for adjustment has been greater; and the factors which delivered their earlier success have clearly played a part. In the five years since 1985 (when the high Yen sent relative costs soaring), the Japanese 'big five' – Nippon Steel, Nippon Kokan, Kawasaki Steel, Sumitomo Metal Industries and Kobe Steel – have closed almost a quarter of their blast furnaces, cut their workforce by 47,000, increased automation, and moved quickly into higher-margin products, thereby retaining their competitive edge over Western producers, and fighting back against the home market incursions made by the South Koreans and Brazilians.

One key feature of the Japanese system stands out: the combination of policy goals and collective corporate discipline which, backed by the ready availability of investment funds, have allowed constant adaptation to changing domestic and international markets. State financial support, and bureaucratic guidance played a significant role in the early postwar period, but the state's role has become increasingly subtle and indirect during the last twenty years. The principle virtue of the Japanese system, as also revealed in the postwar emergence of highly competitive machine tool, automobile and computer industries, is *flexibility*, in production, marketing, organisation and finance.

The initial impetus to this process in steel *was* provided by MITI which, in the early postwar period, restricted the right to add new capacity to only the most productive firms. But, even in the 1950s, when MITI officials were at their most interventionist, the process of decision-making in steel was heavily imbued with a market ethos, and great emphasis has always been placed on strength through competition and managerial competence.[22] Patterns of market management in the US and the EC have been very different. On neither side of the Atlantic has the collective, flexible and market-oriented rationality of the Japanese been aspired to or achieved.

The United States

In the United States the absence of an internal rationalisation cartel can be explained by the tradition of business individualism and anti-trust. Collective action has been limited to price maintenance, market sharing and persistent lobbying for protection,[23] while government involvement has been limited to meeting these demands, and to providing certain minimal forms of tax credit and adjustment support. What has been lacking is a *purposive*, market-oriented programme of adjustment. Indeed, until the period after 1984, neither VRAs nor the trigger price mechanism encouraged an upturn in investment or an increase in efficiency: between 1968 and 1982 productivity grew at less than half the manufacturing average.[24] It was not until the 1984 Trade and Tariff Act that the continuation of trade relief in any year became contingent on the investment of cash flows into the modernisation of steel industry facilities. Until then, the profits generated by protection were used to cover closure costs, restore high dividend levels and finance the movement of firms into more profitable, mostly non-steel areas of investment.[25]

Since the mid-1980s, and the restriction of imports to 18.5 per cent of the market, it must be said that US steel has made some major advances. In 1984, the sector was in a sorry state: import penetration had reached 26.4 per cent, losses of $30.5m were recorded, and investment levels since 1979 had been less than half the level required. Unlike in Japan, a high debt/equity ratio could not be sustained: and after the mid-1970s, a combination of low profitability and higher than average debt limited access to new funds.[26] But by 1987, the major companies were back in the black (with a net income of $1bn), $5,800m had been invested in retooling, and the pace of modernisation had quickened.

But the role of protection in the upturn is debatable. The steel boom and the weakness of the dollar during much of this period were probably more important, both in boosting US profits and diverting exports into other markets.[27] And many weaknesses remain: although productivity has increased by 40 per cent since 1984, and pre-tax costs per tonne have been reduced to around the West German level, labour costs remain high, profit margins narrow and the overall recovery susceptible to exchange rate fluctuations. Hence the vigour of the VRA renewal campaign in 1989.

Moreover, the costs inflicted on the rest of the economy have been high. Economists have estimated the annual cost to US consumers of the 18.5 per cent quota at $1.1bn (in 1983 dollars) – $114,000 per annum for every steel job saved.[28] And quotas have done nothing to protect the large producers from the growth of non-unionised, lower capital-cost, US mini-mills. Between 1983 and 1989 – the years of US steel's recovery – mini-mills increased their share of the market from 13 to 20 per cent.[29]

The European Community

Regardless of its competitive merits, or its economic costs, US protectionism has been politically unavoidable. This much it shares with the crisis cartel in the European Community. For although EC policies, like those in the US, have sheltered producers and imposed higher costs on consumers, they have at least prevented price and subsidy wars and the break-up of ECSC arrangements, while easing the social and political costs of adjustment.[30] But, as a much more complete example of collective market management, the EC system has had some additional defects, given the imperative of spreading these costs as widely and evenly as possible. For while subsidies have been tied to restructuring since 1981 (a total of $35bn was dispensed by 1985) allocating market shares through a quantitative quota system propped up prices for uncompetitive firms and punished the most efficient.

Adjustment was therefore distorted: by allowing the weaker firms to modernise, the cost-efficient companies could not achieve their potential.[31] Hence the opposition to quotas and minimum prices of the EC's most efficient firms, the West Germans and the small Italian mini-mill producers, the *Bresciani*. Since these were also the least subsidised – both before and after the creation of the cartel – they were doubly penalised. And while most EC firms were again making profits by 1988–9, as in the US, the cyclical boom in steel demand disguised persistent weaknesses: on some calculations, the EC in 1990 still had some 47m tonnes of excess capacity, and a deal of painful restructuring in store.

Within the EC itself, the only corporate strategies comparable to those of Japan (backed by state support in the form of indirect subsidies and favourable access to credit in the early postwar period) have been in West Germany. There, the strength, diversification and capacity for adjustment of the steel firms can be attributed in part to collaboration: marketing cartels encouraged price discipline, while rationalisation agreements allowed for market organisation, product substitution among plants and surplus capacity management. Co-ordination within the system was assisted by close links between the steel firms, banks and large insurance companies, providing for a steady source of investment capital and financial security during downturns.[32] Overall, the German industry's success has been attributed to similar factors to those existing in Japan – consensus, skilled management and an irreplaceable 'spirit of enterprise'.[33]

STEEL TRADE AND THE URUGUAY ROUND

One of the consequences of longstanding protectionist systems is the creation of a culture of dependency: even when profitability has been restored, companies propped up by quotas and minimum prices are reluctant to abandon their crutches. In the EC, however, the upturn in the steel market after 1987 coincided with the triumph of a deregulatory ethos in the Commission's Single Market programme, and lobbying by the Community's most competitive steel firms – the British, Dutch and West Germans – helped ensure the cartel's termination in July 1988. But in the US, the protectionists still prevail and want to rewrite the rules of international trade. Given the greater dependency of the world on the US market created by the scale of its trade deficit, they certainly have the potential to do so. For this reason, the US has failed to bring steel within the ambit of GATT, despite the opportunity provided by the Uruguay Round. Doing so would have prevented it from using the threat of protection to change its trading partners' policies.

VRA renewal and the steel pacts

Thus, while there were several options available to the US Administration only an extension of the VRA system could win the essential support of the protectionist steel lobby. As it was, the industry was bitterly disappointed by the form of the renewal: an extension of

VRAs until March 1992 only, with provision for an increase of the total quota on exports to the US by 1 per cent each year from its current 18.5 per cent. Steel producers wanted longer to consolidate their strengths, doubting that 'unfair trading practices' could be eliminated so quickly. By way of compensation, the lobby demanded a tough US stance in the trade negotiations.

The trade representatives complied. The renewal of quota shares in the US market was made contingent upon concessions to US demands for a 'level playing field' in trade. True to the spirit of the 1988 US Trade Act and its 'Super 301' provisions, the negotiators used the rather blunt weapon of 'specific reciprocity' to attack both subsidies and forms of market organisation they found inimical. In the EC case, the US wanted all subsidies removed as well as the elimination of certain non-tariff barriers, such as the trigger price monitoring of non-VRA steel imports which enables quick initiation of anti-dumping actions. The US call for a ban on cross-border purchases of steel stockholders by EC producers was especially imperious, and was backed by the specious argument that a dense producer-stockholder network would create a non-tariff barrier to US exporters.

The Japanese initially rejected the bilateral negotiating track, arguing for its replacement by a more formal, GATT-compatible framework. And even when under way, the negotiations stalled over the US proposal to reduce the Japanese quota of its market (from 5.8 to 3.0 per cent), and demands that MITI reform its traditional ties with the steel groups. Japan was also asked to prohibit preferential export treatment, and modify the links between its trading companies and producers. As in the case of the EC, the US eventually withdrew its more extreme demands, but the Japanese, already labelled an 'unfair trader' under US 'Super 301' actions, were anxious to avoid allegations of improbity, and agreed to abolish all tariffs and subsidies. In return, the US agreed to increase its quota offer from 3.0 to 5.0 per cent.

Predictably, the EC was also unwilling to concede any ground on the more radical US demands. While concessions were made, these tended to conform with the Community's own liberalising initiatives. Thus, like the Japanese, it agreed to the removal of subsidies, although government support for pollution controls, R&D, worker retraining and business closure were exempted. But it also accepted what amounts to a ban on future public support by acknowledging US objections to tax concessions, the transfer of public resources to companies – either through capital stakes or subsidies – or any funding incompatible with liberal market conditions.[34]

Steel and US 'minilateralism'

The thrust of US strategy is clear. The old concept of reciprocity – which has long been the basis of GATT negotiations – is steadily being perverted. Demands for equal market access have been replaced by demands for equal market conditions, a 'minilateralist' attempt to turn all foreign markets into US mirror images.[35] This is the logical conclusion of the 'level playing field' strategy in which the most powerful player imposes his own definition of the rules. Hence the recent demands from some countries for a stronger referee – perhaps by turning the GATT into a fully-fledged international trade organisation with greater policy impetus, or by creating a type of security council for trade based on strengthened rules and political authority.

The NICs are particularly vulnerable to US 'minilateralism'. Their development strategies have typically depended on very different market conditions from those in the West. For most, cheap government loans, tax breaks and direct state aid have been essential for developing an indigenous steel industry, although private entrepreneurs have successfully funded mini-mills. These industrial take-off strategies have also provided the basis for export success, which, through a complex chain of causation, has linked NIC development with 'de-industrialisation' across a range of manufacturing sectors in certain advanced economies.[36] This process lies at the root of the present problem. For it is precisely these strategies of 'assertive industrialisation' which are now under attack.

The stronger NICs will be able to accommodate these demands. Their cost advantage, as in textiles and certain other manufactures, should protect them from any competitive threat. South Korea, which has partially privatised its steel giant POSCO, also has the advantage of investments in the US, through a 50–50 joint venture with USX (formerly US Steel) in California. Brazil has had its VRA quota increased in return for a pledge to abolish all domestic subsidies and price controls.[37] Mexico, which is also liberalising its economy, and privatising its steel industry, has had its US market steel quota doubled. When introduced in 1984, the VRAs restricted the NICs to quotas of the US market which were significantly lower than their actual share at the time: thus while the Japanese VRA entitlement of 5.8 per cent compared well with actual US market share, Brazil's entitlement was just half.[38] Now, accepting US demands for reform, the more advanced NICs are being admitted to the club. But it will be harder for newer NICs like Thailand to follow them in, given the limits now imposed on state-supported strategies of 'assertive industrialisation'.

Implications for the Uruguay Round

One risk of the US success in steel was that it would encourage the extension of bilateralism into the Uruguay Round. After all, US steel trade policies are part and parcel of a wider strategy which, based on an amalgam of unilateral, bilateral and multilateral initiatives, seeks to make the domestic structures of other countries more congruent with its own. But the steel sector has some special characteristics; and these make a straightforward generalisation of its new practices – and thus of successful US trade coercion – unlikely. These include the confidence of the NICs in their ability to compete in this, and other manufacturing sectors (whereas they are hopelessly behind in high technology and in services like insurance, banking, and accounting); the benefits derived from VRAs by the EC countries and Japan (apart from protecting market shares they also help stabilise prices); and the fact that, unlike in computing, for example, the production technology of steel is already internationalised and there are few problems with intellectual property rights, except in plant design and administration. But in other areas, more central to the Uruguay Round, both the NICs and the Western industrialised countries are proving much less compliant in the face of US demands.

Thus, more generally, there is little common ground between Europe and the US on the issue of subsidies: while the EC accepted the US position on steel, it is opposing calls for an outright ban on subsidies, including those for exports, in both industry and agriculture. It argues that domestic subsidies are only illegitimate if they have demonstrable negative effects on another country's trade interests. They both seem to agree, however, that GATT-illegal, selective export restraint arrangements (such as VRAs in steel and other sectors) should be legitimised under certain circumstances. This reflects the interest of the US, and more recently the Europeans, in using market access as a means of leverage.

For some years now, the US has tried to use a combination of restraints and concessions in manufactures to lever open NIC markets in services and agriculture.[39] It is now attempting to force the pace of services liberalisation bilaterally, as in steel, *before* agreement has been reached within GATT on a multilateral framework of principles and rules.[40] Once again, the main objective of the US is to impose its market-based philosophy and concept of 'fair trade' upon others. But the NICs are much more hostile to such attempts in services, intellectual property and foreign investment than, for example, in steel; they fear that US transnationals will be given free rein in banking, insurance and computer software where they have a huge competitive advantage and the monopoly power to limit independent technological development and sovereignty.

CONCLUSIONS

The professed objectives of the US steel 'consensus agreements' are to help trade in the sector move towards the liberal conditions which are expected to result more generally from new GATT rules and disciplines after the conclusion of the Uruguay Round. But the danger is that, in using 'selective safeguards' like VRAs to lever open foreign markets, their renewal can always be justified by claims that competitors are still indulging in 'trade distorting practices'. And given that the latter now include a seemingly unlimited range of micro-economic policies, new ones can readily be identified.

But a more serious flaw in current US trade tactics, whether in steel, services, Super 301 'unfair trading' initiatives, or in the 'Structural Impediments' talks with the Japanese, is that they are based on a false premise: that the loss of competitive advantage is due to the failure of US trading partners to play by the rules of the liberal market game. The simple fact is that the America's most effective industrial competitors have developed alternative, and more successful forms of capitalist organisation.[41] As the Japanese have constantly pointed out in recent trade discussions, the US trade deficit is partly the consequence of its own flawed economic policies; and its loss of industrial prowess is to be attributed more to certain domestic conditions – a low savings-investment ratio, poor educational standards, and short-termism in finance – than to perfidy on the part of its trading partners.

Furthermore, many of the problems faced by the US and other first generation industrial countries stem from growing economic interdependence and exchange rate volatility, and only domestic *macro-*

economic policies, allied to changes in international monetary arrangements, can deal with issues such as these. So although supported by dispute settlement mechanisms and arbitration panels, the success or failure of the steel 'consensus' is likely to be determined as much by fluctuating demand and currency rates as by transgressions of its terms by the signatories.

From the broader vantage point of US trade strategy, the steel case suggests a number of conclusions concerning the interplay between industrial policy and international trade regulation. At present, the primacy of the United States in the world economy is both more constrained and more aggressively asserted than in the past. Moreover, those developments provoking a more predatory form of US hegemony are unlikely to dissipate. Under these conditions, several trends in the exercise and adaptation of US global power can be anticipated. First, the US will continue to press for changes in the micro-economic and structural policies of other sovereign states to make them more congruent with its own liberal market philosophy. This strategy will be underpinned by the size and importance of the US market, negotiated access to which will be the most important weapon in its trade policy arsenal. The extent and range of its deployment will depend both on the willingness of other states to concede to US demands, and on the balance of power between protectionists and pragmatists in the American trade policy community.

Second, international trade negotiations will become ever more complex and based on a growing number of bilateral trade-offs which, far from initiating an era of free trade, may well extend domestic forms of market management to the transnational domain, perhaps within regulated trading blocs. These will undermine the formalisation of multilateral GATT rules and hinder their authoritative enforcement. The subjugation of the interests of the weak under these circumstances will lead to louder calls for a new world trade organisation – of the type that the US has always opposed – based on strengthened rules and political authority. Taken together, these developments do not necessarily signal either a decline in American economic hegemony or a collapse of GATT arrangements. But the portents for growing instability – both in US hegemony and the international trading order – are clearly identifiable.

NOTES

1. I am grateful to Stephen Gill for his comments on an earlier version of this paper.
2. See J. N. Bhagwati, 'United States Trade Policy at the Crossroads', *World Economy*, 12, 4 (1989) 440.
3. In its December 1989 review of US trade policy, the GATT secretariat strongly attacked its own protective practices across a range of sectors including textiles, steel, automobiles, machine tools, semiconductors and a number of farm products.
4. OECD, *The Steel Market in 1988 and the Outlook for 1989* (Paris: OECD, 1989) 34.
5. Assessments of US steel subsidies may have been underestimated by calculations which ignore state government support. See A. Anderson and A. Rugman, 'Subsidies in the U.S. Steel Industry: A New Conceptual Framework and Literature Review', *Journal of World Trade*, 23, 6 (1989) 59–83.
6. OECD, *The Iron and Steel Industry in 1980*, (Paris: OECD, 1982), pp. 8–10.
7. See E. Dourille, 'Sidérurgie et aluminium: la crise et son issue', in M. Fouquin (ed.), *Industrie mondiale: la compétitivité à tout prix* (Paris: Economica, 1986) pp. 206–10.
8. For a detailed analysis of this period, see H. Van der Ven and T. Grunert, 'The Politics of Transatlantic Steel Trade', in Y. Mény and V. Wright (eds), *The Politics of Steel: Western Europe and the Steel Industry in the Crisis Years (1974–1984)* (Berlin and New York: De Gruyter, 1987) pp. 137–85.
9. *Ibid.*, 178.
10. For further details see P. Messerlin, 'The European Iron and Steel Industry and the World Crisis', in Mény and Wright (eds.), *op.cit.*, p. 124ff.
11. *Ibid.*, 125.
12. For detailed analyses of the EC's steel 'crisis management' system, see L. Tsoukalis and R. Strauss, 'Community Policies on Steel 1974–1982: A Case of Collective Management', in Mény and Wright, *op.cit.*, 186–221 and D. G. Tarr, 'The Steel Crisis in the United States and the European Community: Causes and Adjustments' in R. E. Baldwin et al. (eds), *Issues in US-EC Trade Relations* (Chicago and London: University of Chicago Press, 1988) pp. 179–187.
13. See I. Yamazawa, 'Industry Growth and Foreign Trade: A Study of Japan's Steel Industry', *Hitotsubashi Journal of Economics*, 2 (1972) 41–59.
14. See T. K. McCraw and P. A. O'Brien, 'Production and Distribution: Competition Policy and Industry Structure', in T. K. McCraw (ed.), *America versus Japan*, (Boston: Harvard Business School Press 1988, p. 84ff and I. C. Magaziner and T. M. Hout, *Japanese Industrial Policy*, (London: Policy Studies Institute, 1980) pp. 45–53.
15. See A. Rémy, 'Les stratégies japonaises et allemandes dans les secteurs en crise: le cas de la sidérurgie', *Problèmes Economiques*, 2095 (1988)

26–32. On 'relational contracts' in Japanese industry, see R. Dore, *Flexible Rigidities: Industrial Policy and Structural Adjustment in the Japanese Economy 1970–1980* (London: The Athlone Press, 1986) pp. 72–85.

16. See R. Dore et al., *Japan at Work: Markets, Management and Flexibility*, (Paris: OECD, 1989).

17. See T. Kono, *Strategy and Structure of Japanese Enterprises* (London: Macmillan, 1985) pp. 310–11.

18. See I. C. Magaziner and R. B. Reich, *Minding America's Business: The Decline and Rise of the American Economy*, (New York: Vintage Books, 1982) pp. 154–68.

19. Japanese companies have stepped up their steel investments in the US in recent years, partly to circumvent US trade barriers and supply steel of the quality required to their US auto plants, but also because US producers find them to be rich in capital and technical expertise. NKK owns 70 per cent of National Steel, Nippon Steel has a 13 per cent stake in Inland Steel, Nisshin Steel owns 10 per cent of Wheeling-Pittsburgh, and Kobe, Kawasaki and Sumitomo are involved in joint ventures with USX, Armco and LTV respectively. These are an example of how protectionism can promote global economic integration through foreign direct investment.

20. Mini-mills, based on direct-reduction, electric arc furnaces have gained growing shares of the world steel market over the last decade. Transforming scrap steel into a range of semi-finished and finished products, they enjoy major cost advantages, especially in fuel consumption, over their larger, integrated counterparts.

21. *Metal Bulletin*, 19 May 1990.

22. See McCraw and O'Brien, *op.cit.*, pp. 79–100. On the success of the Japanese management system, and the superiority of Japanese middle managers and engineers in steel, see T. Kono, *op.cit.*, pp. 306–7.

23. See R. B. Reich, *The Next American Frontier* (New York: Penguin Books, 1984) pp. 174–7 and M. Borrus, 'The Politics of Competitive Erosion in the US Steel Industry', in J. Zysman and L. Tyson (eds), *American Industry in International Competition: Government Policies and Corporate Strategies* (Ithaca, NY, and London: Cornell University Press, 1983) pp. 60–105.

24. Congressional Budget Office, *Has Trade Protection Revitalised Domestic Industries?* (Washington DC.: US Government Printing Office, 1986) pp. 39–58.

25. M. Borrus, *op.cit.*, pp. 103–5.

26. Congressional Budget Office, *op.cit.*, 55.

27. 'VRAs and Market Forces', *Metal Bulletin*, 3 August 1989.

28. Tarr *op.cit.*, pp. 179–87.

29. *Metal Bulletin*, 17 May 1990.

30. See Tsoukalis and Strauss, *op.cit.*, 219.

31. Messerlin, *op.cit.*, pp. 131–4.

32. See K. Stegemann, *Price Competition and Output Adjustment in the European Steel Market* (Tübingen: Mohr 1977) and K. Dyson, 'West Germany: the Search for a Rationalist Consensus' in J. Richardson (ed.)

Policy Styles in Western Europe (London: Allen and Unwin, 1982) pp. 17–46.

33. See J. Esser and W. Fach, 'Crisis Management "Made in Germany": The Steel Industry', in P. J. Katzenstein (ed.), *Industry and Politics in West Germany: Towards the Third Republic* (Ithaca, NY, and London: Cornell University Press, 1989) pp. 228–9.

34. 'EC agrees VRAs, nears 'consensus' with USA', *Metal Bulletin*, 9 November 1989.

35. On the concept of 'minilateralism', see R. Gilpin, *The Political Economy of International Relations* (Princeton, NJ: Princeton University Press, 1987) p. 372.

36. See A. Singh, 'Third World Competition and De-industrialisation in Advanced Countries', *Cambridge Journal of Economics*, 13 (1989) 103–120.

37. For a full survey of the new VRAs, see M. Lovatt, 'VRAs – Up But Not Out', *Metal Bulletin Monthly* 2 (1990) 32–4.

38. See R. Pomfret, 'World Steel Trade at the Crossroads', *Journal of World Trade* 3 (1988) pp. 85–6.

39. For the background to these manoeuvres, see S. Gill and D. Law, *The Global Political Economy: Perspectives, Problems and Policies* (Hemel Hempstead: Harvester-Wheatsheaf, 1988) p. 250ff.

40. See *Financial Times*, 21 June 1990, and F. Lazar, 'Services and the GATT: US Motives and a Blueprint for Negotiations', *Journal of World Trade*, 1 (1990) 135–45.

41. As Ronald Dore has commented, 'Japan has grown to be the second biggest western economy precisely by incorporating [those] features which are deplored elsewhere, as integral functioning elements of its system of 'organised capitalism'. It has seen the shape of the future and made it work'. See R. Dore, *op.cit.*, 250.

Conclusion: The Interdependence of Markets and States

Michael Moran and Maurice Wright

Political science is partly the product of its own political surroundings. Those of British political science have, for over a decade, been dominated by Thatcherism. Political argument in Britain in the 1980s took its cue from Thatcherism, even when that ideology was rejected. The most distinctive feature of Thatcherite ideology was the argument that 'state' and 'market' were two distinct, and contradictory, forms of social organisation. Even the opponents of Thatcherism have commonly accepted this argument – but have opted for the state rather than for the market. It is not surprising, therefore, that the political science produced in these surroundings should likewise instinctively assume that state and market were clearly separable.

But political science is not only the product of its surroundings, and instinctive assumptions do not always survive argument and investigation. That point was hammered home by the contributions to this book, and by the seminar discussions in which those contributions were reshaped. Market and state are not simply opposed forms of social organisation; they are bound by complex ties. We saw in the introduction to this collection that the relationship was already complicated by the language in which the 'market' is discussed. More substantively, the essays and the seminar discussions demonstrated that states and markets are interdependent, not opposed. Our purpose in this conclusion is to sketch the ways in which the contributions identify the main sources of that interdependence.

MARKET PROCESS, POLITICAL PROCESS

There is an established tradition in political theory, discussed in Parry and Moyser's contribution, which contrasts the social processes by which markets work with those operating in arenas conventionally thought of as political, where the institutions of the state dominate. The contrast is argued most emphatically in the writings of Arendt, where a private sphere dominated by the pursuit of economic interests is normatively separated from a public sphere where participating citizens both discover and reveal their true identities.

The normative content of this argument aside, Parry and Moyser's account of modes of political participation shows that there is indeed a very real difference between giving 'signals' in the marketplace and giving 'voice' in the political arena – differences in both the kinds of preferences expressed and the kinds of interests advanced. When an individual has the choice, it matters a great deal whether she opts to influence the way the state behaves by participating as a citizen or decides to signal her preferences as a consumer.

Markets where separate, individual, private consumers are important agents are indeed numerous and significant. But some of the chief markets discussed in this volume are anything but arenas for the exercise of private choice. They are social arenas where the key actors are not individuals but institutions, and large institutions at that. The most characteristic of these institutions is the giant firm: consider the market in steel described by Rhodes, the defence industries in Williams' chapter, or the broadcasting markets with their multinational media giants described by Humphreys. These firms of course commonly have to operate in a world where they are constrained by consumer choice – but the 'consumers', more often than not, are large firms like themselves or are bureaucratically organised state agencies. The institutions are indeed working in something which it is sensible to call a market. In this arena, however, the process by which resources are allocated not only involves signals sent by a price mechanism, but also involves bargaining by complex institutions whose own behaviour is in turn a response to political pressures generated inside the institution itself. The most important market actors are not individual entrepreneurs, nor unitary organisations responding in an automatic way to signals like price and demand. They are large multidivisional and often multinational firms, and their actions are the result of a process of policy formulation, just as the actions of state agencies are the result of a process of policy formulation. In short, politics shapes the behaviour of firms in the market just as certainly as it shapes the behaviour of institutions operating in more conventionally recognisable political arenas.

The special importance of the political resides in a number of features of the giant firm. First, the behaviour of any large firm reflects in part a process of struggle and bargaining between the institutions and interests contained inside the organisation. We have become accustomed to the notion that it is necessary to disaggregate the 'state' as a social entity in order to recognise the different institutional interests and organisational cultures whose competing and conflicting relations produce those outcomes, which for short-hand we call 'public policy'. But exactly the same act of disaggregation is required in the case of firms, the most important of which have a size and economic complexity in some instances rivalling that of many nation states. The different divisions of firms, producing different products and selling those products into different markets often have strikingly different perceptions of interest: they desire different amounts and kinds of capital, different market conditions, different regulatory frameworks, different kinds of labour and different technologies to produce their goods or services. Many multinationals are conglomerates assembled by a process of acquisition in which, notoriously, the traditions and procedures of the previously separate parts of the corporate empire never adapt to membership of a common institution. As Hawley remarks in his study of how multinational banks reconcile the competing interests of their different managerial divisions:

> transnational enterprises are intentionally structured around bureaucratic units with competing (and often cross-cutting) claims, making 'interests' opaque. In ideological terms what are often taken to be the objective interests of business enterprises are in fact bureaucratic interpretations drawn from a broad matrix of often conflicting possibilities. The larger the scope of the business enterprise, the greater the realm of choice.[1]

In short, much of what happens in markets is the result of political struggles *within* organisations like big firms. To this we can add a second consideration: these internal political struggles are accompanied by struggles of a political character *between* firms. Market outcomes are to a substantial degree the results of these struggles – of alliances created and broken between firms, of firms enlarged at the expense of rivals, or of firms that disappear into rivals. The essentially political character of these processes is well expressed in the words of Cawson and his colleagues, in their study of the central role played by firms' strategies in the reshaping of electronics industries in the most important markets of advanced capitalism. They write:

the stereotype of state versus market which is characteristic of much of the literature is based on a false dichotomy between politically determined decision-making and supposedly 'automatic' mechanisms of the market-place . . . . outcomes depend only partially on the competitive strength of firms . . . the key to unlocking the complexities of industrial politics lies in the corporate strategies of the major firms. Other actors – trade unions, trade associations, even governments – are far less significant.[2]

We now have two major reasons for doubting that 'markets' and 'states' truly are social arenas producing outcomes by very different processes: the behaviour of large firms, the key actors in the most important markets, is the result of an internal political process not at all unlike the bargaining and struggles which go on inside states; and the competitive fortunes of firms are not only settled by how well they compete with each other in terms of price and quality but also by how well they struggle politically – measured by their ability to form strategic alliances and to dominate those alliances.

To these considerations we can now add a third. Thus far we have focused on the characteristics of the institution thought to be quintessentially 'market' in character, the firm. But in the social arena called the market, as the preceding chapters make clear, firms are only one category of actors. Even the minimal state – by its command of coercion and control over law – is an ever-present force as the guarantor of the conditions under which market exchanges take place. Beyond this obvious fact, in most cases the institutional population of markets spans a complex range of organisations. The most important allocational outcomes do not happen in separate social boxes labelled 'market' and 'state'. They are the result of the workings of policy networks joining fragments of all sorts of institutions: firms, trade associations, differing agencies of the central government, hybridisations of public and private bodies. Perhaps the most striking instance of this is provided by Young's chapter, where the progress of privatisation in Africa is substantially explained by an international network of policy actors, in which reforming ideologies and policy demands are carried to domestic African political arenas by a mixture of big firms, western governments and international agencies like the International Monetary Fund. Of course such networks are not permanently fixed in composition. On the contrary, moments of significant policy change are characteristically accompanied by alterations in the composition and boundaries of the network – a process well described in Humphreys' chapter. These networks create a complex division of labour between nominally 'state' and 'market' institutions, and the effectiveness with which institutions work has little to do with their 'state' or 'market' designation. In Williams' words: how 'tasks are divided between the state and the market seems on the evidence to matter much less than that they are performed properly by one or the other, or best of all, by the two in flexible symbiosis.' (p. 198)

The point of this argument, it should be emphasised, is not simply that 'the state' is an important actor in market transaction. That it is so is indisputable; and likewise that it can retreat from this role is equally indisputable, as is shown by Waller's graphic account of the dismantling of command economies in Eastern Europe. But this retreat by the state does not leave the process of allocation commanded by the impersonal 'laws' of supply and demand, guided by an invisible hand. It consigns allocation to the realm of the network of institutions, only some of whom conform to the mode of a 'market' actor.

In summary, the idea that we are witnessing a retreat by 'politics' in the face of the 'market' ignores three key features of markets in modern capitalist economies – features emphasised in the contributions to this volume: the extent to which firms have internal political systems of their own; the extent to which firms bargain and struggle with each other, rather than merely competing on price and quality; and the extent to which 'markets' are populated by networks of institutional actors exhibiting many different legal forms and organisational structures.

MARKET POWER, STATE POWER

But there is a more direct reason still for scepticism about the idea that market and state stand in opposition: market exchanges depend on state power. It is widely accepted that most modern states are guarantors of the sanctity of contract and the institutions of private property. But in the course of the Manchester seminars there emerged a stronger version of this proposition: that the creation of an economy in which free exchange and private property are supreme demands an extensive apparatus of state power, and that the 'freer' the economy the more extensive and powerful the state has to be. Thus 'state' and 'market' are not like two ends of a seesaw, rising and falling in opposition to each other; the power of the state is needed to manage the inputs to markets, the terms on which exchanges are made and the outputs and impacts of those exchanges.

There is nothing historically novel about this observation, as is clear from Vogel's account of the response of the political theory of German Romanticism to the challenge of early capitalism. The argument of Romanticism was precisely that, when the bonds of traditional society were loosened, and humans confronted each other primarily as commercial actors, the state would assume the role of regulator and, in this role, would acquire a powerfully coercive character. In the view of Romantic critics, as Vogel puts it, 'a fully commercialised society requires a coercive state. Where the state is understood as but a regulatory, external power and where its purpose is minimised to provide security for private property, its rule will of necessity be one of force since it cannot rely on any bonds of spontaneous trust and loyalty among its citizens'. (p. 138) It is striking to hear Cammack, in the very different setting of Latin America, and on very different grounds, likewise arrive at the conclusion that 'free markets' need effective interventionist states. He writes: 'it is misleading to depict free market and "interventionist" policies as making low and high demands respectively upon the state: a capacity for effective intervention on the part of the state is as much a requirement for the pursuit of liberal economic policies as it is for intervention aimed at resisting the pressure of market forces.' (p. 152).

Why do free markets need strong states? From the essays, and from the seminar discussions when they were first given, we extract four reasons. They arise, in summary, from the state's role in policing competition, in managing the discontent of those who lose by competition, in creating the legitimacy needed for competition to happen peacefully and, in concert with other states, in managing competitive struggles when they transcend national jurisdictions.

Competition in markets will not survive without powerful policing by the state. Evans' chapter in this volume shows that even many of the early 'classical' theorists of the market recognised that competition was anything but a spontaneously produced condition. Competitive markets are endangered by numerous social forces. They are endangered by businessmen – those 'people of trade' who, in Adam Smith's famous words, 'seldom meet together, even for merriment and diversion, but the conversation ends in a conspiracy against the publick, or in some contrivance to raise prices'.[3] They are endangered by intellectuals: as Schumpeter observed a generation ago, the capitalist order is remorselessly and destructively analysed by the critical and sceptical intellectual stratum which is a characteristic product of advanced capitalism.[4] Markets are endangered by the collective action of sellers of labour; and even by violent resistance in the streets and in the countryside. In some places, as Cammack's chapter graphically shows, the failure to establish a hegemonic status for the idea of freely competing markets means that competitive struggles can only take place with support from state coercion. Establishing hegemony itself demands a considerable application of state resources – in the education system, for instance – to impress on populations the legitimacy of competitive economics. The starting-point of Steiner's chapter – that governments find themselves subjected to ever mounting pressure to extend their regulatory arms to the new area of environmental control – shows how much still needs to be done, even in the age of Reaganism and Thatcherism, to establish the hegemonic status of free market competition. It is inconceivable that this hegemony can be created without mobilising state power. Markets will not function if the state confines itself to providing a framework for the exchange of contracts.

To the observation that state power is needed either to create the hegemony of free market ideologies or, in the absence of that hegemony, to suppress those who contest the practice of free market economics, we can add a second important role for state institutions, notably when competitive conditions in markets are fierce. Freely competitive markets are extraordinarily dynamic. It was in part the fear of their dynamism that produced the sort of enforced stagnation whose breakdown is a central theme of Waller's chapter; and it was likewise fear of their dynamism which led to the historical cartelisation of the steel industry described by Rhodes. When firms compete through price, quality of product or quality of service, radical changes follow. There are clear winners and equally clear losers. These gains and losses have the most drastic consequences for the distribution of economic resources and social prestige – between sectors, between nations and between classes. The desirability of this social arrangement is a matter of some dispute among social theorists, as is shown by the rather different attitudes to market competition evident in Steiner's and Geras's chapters.

More pertinently for the defenders of free market competition, the dispute often goes beyond the tranquillity of the university seminar. The redistributive results of competition are commonly challenged, sometimes violently, by the losers. Unless the losers in competitive struggles are suppressed, then competition and redistribution will be obstructed. That, in essence, is why it is common to speak, in Gamble's phrase, of 'the free economy and the strong state'.[5] Attacks on state control of the economy often picture the state as an obstacle to structural change. That particular states have indeed obstructed change – sided, in other words, with potential losers in the battles unleashed by free competition – is undeniable. But this obscures a deeper truth: without the presence of considerable state power to command the acquiescence of the losers in competitive struggles, the structural change associated with competition just could not be enforced.

In summary, two key reasons why competitive markets and state power are often complementary rather than competing are: state power is needed to create legitimacy (hegemony) for ideologies of market competition or, in the absence of hegemony, to coerce those who actively resist competitive practices; and state power is needed either to legitimise, or to enforce by more brutal means, the redistributive consequences of competitive struggles. To this we can add a third reason for stressing the significance of state power to the functioning of competitive markets: states possess an independent capacity to shape market behaviour and market outcomes. It is impossible to read the chapters on very different events by Waller, Cammack, Humphreys and Rhodes without rapidly concluding that state agencies are central to processes not only of regulation, but also to those of deregulation and reregulation. To take only the single instance of Humphreys' study of broadcasting: he establishes not only that state agencies are central actors in regulatory debates, but that the different outcomes of markets in the Federal Republic of Germany and in the United Kingdom are directly connected to the existence of different state structures. The centralised British structure has produced radical reforms, while the comparatively decentralised German system has resulted in more incremental changes. Likewise, the most striking lesson of Rhodes' chapter is the key part played by states in the process of market adjustment. World steel markets are arenas where states, in alliance with particular sectors of the industry, struggle for comparative advantage. The 'deregulation' of the industry is driven by a process of competition between national steel industries in which states are the key organising actors. The rhetoric of deregulation, with its emphasis on the 'level playing field', Rhodes shows, is actually a shorthand for a rather different process: one where the American state is attempting to counter the industries produced by newly industrialising countries.

Thus far we have stressed the complementarity of states and markets by drawing attention to the way competitive markets need state power to legitimise the ideology and practice of competition, and to shape the behaviour of players in the market. But there is a fourth and final consideration: the interdependence we urge in this largely national setting also has a wider dimension. We argue that the 'freer' the market the more assertive and powerful the state has to be. The growing proportion of goods and services traded internationally means that markets are decreasingly local, regional or even national. In many key industries – like computers, chemicals, electronics – a few transnational firms dominate production and sales in markets organised on a world scale. The structures and organisation of such markets, and the players within them, have changed. The concept and role of the national sovereign state has correspondingly altered. The regulation of agricultural markets in the European Community is only the best known example of this simultaneous widening of a market, and its regulation by states, surrendering sovereignty, acting in concert. Supranational institutions such as the EC, GATT or the G7 emphasise both the interdependence of states and markets, and our general contention that free markets need strong states.

The key role assumed by the state in reshaping markets confirms one of the most important recent innovations in state theory – the realisation that states can and do intervene in markets independent of the desires and interests of the most important private actors in the markets. In other words, states represent substantial concentrations of resources and substantial constellations of interest *distinct* from those in private institutions like firms. The resources in question vary from state to state and, within states, from institution to institution. But most modern states command considerable information, expertise, legitimacy, financial resources, symbolic authority and, in the last analysis, an impressive apparatus of coercion. This bank of resources is lodged in state agencies with their own hierarchies, their own internal 'cultures' – and with actors who, making their careers in those hierarchies, develop a conception of what is desirable independently of the desires and interests of private actors. Autonomy is plainly not automatically bestowed on these state actors: it has to be won and, in many cases, it is lost to private interests in the markets. Nor are the 'interests' of state actors either obvious or unvarying. Dunleavy has recently shown, for instance, that simple 'budget' or 'bureau' maximising models of public officials' behaviour fail to capture the complexity of the interests lodged in public institutions.[6] But insofar as there exists a contest between the market and the state it is plain that states are formidable and independent institutions.

CONCLUSION

A collection of essays is, among other things, an opportunity to educate the editors of that collection. As different minds and skills are applied to a common problem the original conception is necessarily altered. We began this collection by assuming that the best way to make sense of the relationship between state and market was to use the language of opposition. The essays assembled here force a more complex view. States are something more than guarantors of contracts, or mere obstacles to the efficient workings of markets. Competitive markets are themselves social arenas where the key institutions – the giant firms – have their own complex political systems. And state power is the essential precondition for the function of markets. States defend the institutions of the market against opponents; they coerce or induce the losers in competitive struggles to accept unpleasant economic outcomes; and they frequently impose their own independently generated interests and desires on markets. The point is not simply that markets need states; it is that the more brutally competitive are market processes, the more vital is the role of state power. Markets have to be defended: against intellectuals, against the losers in competitive struggles, against capitalists and against workers. How far states can or should do that job is the central issue in the analysis of the relationship between the market and state.

NOTES

We thank several colleagues for advice in writing this conclusion: Michael Evans, Paul Cammack, Geraint Parry and Ursula Vogel. The arguments in the chapter are of course only attributable to us.

1. James P. Hawley, 'Protecting capital from itself: US attempts to regulate the Eurocurrency system', *International Organisation*, 38 (1984) 131–65 (p. 135).
2. Alan Cawson, Kevin Morgan, Douglas Webber, Peter Holmes, Anne Stevens, *Hostile Brothers: Competition and Closure in the European Electronics Industry* (Oxford: Clarendon Press, 1990) pp. 375–6.

3. Adam Smith, *The Wealth of Nations*, Book 1 Chapter x.c. (Oxford: Clarendon Press, eds B. H. Campbell, A. S. Skinner and W. B. Todd, 1976) p. 145.
4. Joseph Schumpeter, *Capitalism, Socialism and Democracy* (London: Allen and Unwin, 1976, 5th ed.) pp. 143–55.
5. Andrew Gamble. *The Free Economy and the Strong State: The Politics of Thatcherism* (London: Macmillan, 1988).
6. Patrick Dunleavy, 'The architecture of the British central state', *Public Administration*, 67 (1989) 249–76.

Index